Daily Devotional

by Marilyn Hickey

P.O. Box 17340
Denver, Colorado 80217
(303) 770-0400

Daily Devotional

Copyright © 1985 by
Marilyn Hickey Ministries
P.O. Box 17340
Denver, CO 80217

All Rights Reserved.

ISBN 1-56441-005-6

Unless otherwise indicated, all
scripture quotations are taken from the
King James Version of the Bible.

Dear Friend,

Because the Bible applies to our everyday practical needs and experiences, I took a special delight in writing this book of daily devotionals. Within this book are true-life anecdotes that apply to each day's scripture. Because the incidents are true, each devotional is a living testimony that God's Word will work in your life.

Each devotional ends with a prayer to remind you to combine the communication of God's Word to you with your personal communication to Him. The prayers allow you to express your desire to live each day according to God's Word.

God's Word will never fail to create His purposes and manifest His power for you. Psalm 119:89 says, "For ever, O Lord, thy word is settled in heaven." God's Word is permanently established. All you need to do is use it! As you read these daily scriptures, anecdotes, and prayers, believe God to settle His thoughts in your thoughts. Believe Him to make His Word practical for you.

I pray that these devotional studies will be more than an end in themselves. I pray that the Lord will use them as a beginning—a beginning that provokes you to a further study of the scriptures and a deeper commitment to prayer.

His love and mine,

Marilyn Hickey

Marilyn Hickey

Day 1

"For thou has girded me with strength unto the battle" (Psalm 18:39a).

I can remember getting tired very easily when I was younger. During the first year of our marriage, my husband Wally would come home and say to me, "How are you?" I would always answer, "I'm so tired." It was so physically exhausting for me to take care of an apartment, carry a full-time job, and then attend a prayer meeting or something every night.

One day Wally said to me, "You know, Marilyn, 'being tired' is the story of your life. It's like a record—you always say the same thing." That hurt me; but I also asked myself, "Is there supernatural strength for me that I'm not taking hold of?" I began to claim GOD'S STRENGTH AND SCHEDULE, rather than the strength and timing of myself and my husband.

Today I look back and see the easy schedule I had kept in my early twenties. I compare it with the tremendous schedule that I now have in my early fifties. I produce 10-15 times more work today than in the past, plus I have such an anointing of strength.

Each of us can have an anointing of strength. Samson experienced it. The Word promises it, and I'm going to pray it for you right now.

Dear heavenly Father, we ask that You gird us with physical, spiritual, mental, and emotional strength for the battle of this day. Thank You, heavenly Father, that we always triumph in Christ. Amen.

Day 2

"Speaking the truth in love, [we] may grow up into him,...which is the head, even Christ" (Ephesians 4:15b).

What we speak each day has a great deal to do with our well-being.

Once I discovered a small, painful growth on my body. My first thought was, "Is this cancer?" The Holy Spirit recalled to me Proverbs 4:22, where it says that the Word of God is life and health to our flesh.

One translation says that the Word is "medicine" to our flesh. So I took that promise and read it to my body once every hour for 24 hours—just like taking medicine. The Word literally became health to my flesh, and the little growth disappeared within 24-hours.

Speaking the Word brought spiritual growth to me, eliminated the harmful physical growth on my body, and increased my faith. As I spoke the truth and knew the love of God that was behind it, I grew up into Him in mental, emotional, spiritual, and physical ways. Speaking the Word in love will create well-being in every area of your life too.

Dear heavenly Father, show us more than ever that faith and speaking faith will cause our minds, emotions, and bodies to grow in line with Your Word. Thank You, Father, today that Your Word works. It is more than words written on a piece of paper; it is a "medicine" that will bring us health, life, and spiritual growth, in Jesus' name, amen.

Day 3

"Thy words were found, and I did eat them; and thy word was unto me the joy and rejoicing of mine heart" (Jeremiah 15:16a).

Some years ago Wally and I were on vacation in New Mexico. We had left a horrendous problem in our office, and though my body was in New Mexico, my head was still in Denver. I was in torment, and the Lord told me, "Read your Bible." I thought, "Lord, read my Bible? I read my Bible all the time. What are You saying?"

But the Lord said, "You are not reading enough of the Bible for this problem. Your problem is an elephant, and the Word you have read today, in comparison, is an ant. You need to read enough of the Word until it becomes the elephant and the problem becomes the ant." I literally consumed the Word until it became the elephant.

When we went home, the Word was so strong in my heart that I began to understand our problem clearly. Six months later it was beautifully resolved.

Dear heavenly Father, give us such a hunger for the Word that, instead of thinking "coffee" in the morning, we will think, "Where's my Bible?" Instead of a midnight snack of ice cream, give us the midnight snack of more scriptures. Let us have a consuming hunger for the Word of God. In Jesus' name, amen.

Day 4

"And by works was faith made perfect" (James 2:22b).

We can "talk" faith, but if we don't have any fruit following it, we have not brought forth what God wants—our faith has not been perfected.

Sometimes we are so involved in our own little family that we forget Jesus was sent to feed the whole world. We are a part of not only a spiritual revival, but also a physical renewal. We cannot say to hungry children, "Be fed," and then let them starve to death. Faith must always produce a work.

We cannot merely go around saying, "The Word works." We have to ACT like the Word works; then it will produce fruit. One night I was murmuring over a situation. My son Mike said, "Mother, you say that what things you desire when you pray, believe that you receive them, and you shall have them. Mother, have you really prayed about your need? If so, then don't you really believe that you will have it?"

The Word was like an arrow to my heart. I then repented to the Father and my family for murmuring.

Dear heavenly Father, we come to You in Jesus' name. We thank You that the Word is working in us and that we are not just "talking" the Word, but also acting the Word. We are not "make-believers," we are believers making the Word work. Thank You, Father, that You are perfecting our faith today. In Jesus' name, amen.

Day 5

"Correction is grievous unto him that forsaketh the way: and he that hateth reproof shall die" (Proverbs 15:10).

Do you hate to be corrected? I don't exactly enjoy it, but I really enjoy the fruits of righteousness that come to pass after correction. Some people believe that God sends bad circumstances as a means of chastening. I believe that the Bible, instead, is God's method of correcting us. I want to encourge you today to let God's Word correct you.

Once I was murmuring to the Lord about a certain woman who, I felt, had used my ministry to her advantage and then had said some very evil things against me. So I said, "Lord, I'm tired of being used."

And the Lord said, "Did you ever use anyone?"

"Never," I said. But then He reminded me of several situations: "Outwardly, it didn't appear like you were using people, but inwardly you were."

I had been simply reaping that which I had planted in my own life. I quickly prayed and repented. Then those ugly seeds were "grubbed out" so they would no longer bear any fruit.

Dear heavenly Father, we come to You in Jesus' name. Today we will not receive defeat when we are corrected. You told us not to despair when You correct us, because You will never correct us beyond what we can handle. And we thank You that You love us enough to reprove us, correct us, and direct our feet in a correct way. In Jesus' name, amen.

Day 6

"If thou knowest any men of activity among them, then make them rulers over my cattle" (Genesis 47:6b).

So many of us would like to have active ministries and zealously serve the Lord. But many people refuse to get active in their local church.

If we are not faithful in little things, God will never give us bigger things. If you want to be a ruler in God's harvest, you must be active in your local church. Active men and women are the ones people depend on to be leaders. You will never be a good chief until you have been an excellent Indian.

When God began to call my husband and me into the ministry, He first made us active in a local church. It was like a tender trap. We kept busy ministering seven nights a week. Soon afterwards God called us into the ministry.

God may never call you into the ministry on a full-time basis, but He calls all of us to minister. Some will be rulers, and some will be activators. Today I'm going to pray for you that you will get up and get about our Father's business.

Dear heavenly Father, we pray that You will cause us and our loved ones to be ACTIVE and ABOUT Your business. Let each of us have a turnaround in our lives and in areas where we have been nonproducers. Father, give us new goals and new desires to be achievers in Jesus' name, amen.

Day 7

"With him is an arm of flesh; but with us is the Lord our God to help us, and to fight our battles" (2 Chronicles 32:8a).

People will let us down. Circumstances will let us down. The devil will certainly come against us to bring us down. We can even let ourselves down. But God and His Word will never let us down.

When our son Michael was 19 years old, he decided to leave the Lord and become a part of the drug culture. He left home, and we soon heard that he was sleeping in parks. At night the devil would say to me, "Well, somebody will come and murder Michael in one of those parks." But I asked our heavenly Father to send angels to watch over Michael and keep him in all his ways. I thanked the Father every night for His vigilance, and I slept like a baby. I literally rested on the Word. Today our son is serving the Lord.

God's Word will never let you down. I cannot emphasize enough to you how powerfully His Word can work in your life and in the lives of your loved ones. We cannot be double-minded and harassed with fear; we must rest on His Word. Let me pray for you:

Dear heavenly Father, we rest upon Your Word now and look not to the arm of flesh, which will always let us down, but to You. We thank You for the stability of Your Word. We thank You that we choose to rest on Your Word, the most stable thing we have in this life and eternal life. In the name of Jesus, amen.

Day 8

"For he is on my right hand, that I should not be moved" (Acts 2:25b).

Sometimes the devil would like to move us off our faith and defeat us. Right after my daughter was born, I had a tremendous problem with my back. An x-ray showed that my back could be thrown out of balance whenever I'd lift anything heavy--even 10 pounds, even my nursing baby. I didn't want to live my life as a cripple with a back that wouldn't work correctly. And so I asked my husband to lay hands on me and pray that God would remake my spine.

We prayed, but outwardly there were no positive manifestations that this prayer had been answered. But we praised the Lord, and I believed, according to Mark 11:24, that I had received. Day after day my body was racked with pain. Then one morning I stood up without any pain. From that time on I had a "miracle" back.

I could have been easily moved by what my senses had experienced, but, instead, I remained stable in God's Word and received the results that His Word can bring.

Dear heavenly Father, we ask today that our faith would stand fast and that we would reap in due season, because You are with us. Thank You, Father, that our faith rests upon You. We are unwavering, we are stable in every way, and we continue to speak the Word to our minds, emotions, and circumstances, in Jesus' name, amen.

Day 9

"For he is strong that executeth his word:..."
(Joel 2:11b).

What IS the secret of strength? The world would pay a big price for this secret, but God has freely GIVEN us the secret of strength. When we execute His Word, He will bring strength to us--spiritually, mentally, emotionally, and physically.

When I first began to travel, a retired army nurse and I held a series of meetings in Texas. Each day I would speak two and three times. On the night of the last day, I was just physically exhausted. I thought, "I don't know if I can get up and say anything. My head's tired, tired, tired." Then I remembered the scripture that said, "Let the weak say, I am strong." I began to say, "I'm strong, I'm strong, I'm strong." I stood to speak the Word. I don't know when I've ever had such supernatural strength! God so blessed me. Some of my dearest relatives were there, and God even dealt with their hearts and lives.

Executing the Word IS the secret of strength. It will help you in every area of your life. Let me pray for you.

Dear heavenly Father, when we say, "I am weak," let us say, "I am strong." When we are weak, help us to execute the Word, no matter what the situation may be. Guide us to do what the Word says, so Your uplifting will come into us. Thank You, Father, for the supernatural power of Your Word working in our lives today, in Jesus' name, amen.

Day 10

"And when these things begin to come to pass, then look up, and lift up your heads; for your redemption draweth nigh" (Luke 21:28).

Some people always look down; others always look around. But God didn't call us to look down, around, or even back. He called us to look up.

When God told Noah to build the ark, He instructed Noah to make only one long window—right near the top, because the only place He wanted Noah to look was upward. If Noah had looked outward, he would have only seen the endless rain, the floating debris, and the people screaming for help.

The secret for our strength today is to LOOK UP. Make a decision right now to look up to our heavenly Father, Who is supernaturally supplying all our needs.

One summer our ministry went through a horrendous financial crisis, when thousands of dollars and checks had been stolen at the post office. Over $200,000 was possibly missing, and we could not pay our bills. The circumstances seemed overwhelming. But when I began to look up, my redemption came. For God truly gave us a miracle and supplied all our needs within 30 days.

Dear heavenly Father, we pray that new faith would rise up in our hearts. We will look up, lift up our heads, and see Your plan of deliverance. We thank You, Father, for Your quick answer to prayer, as You hasten to perform Your Word in Jesus' name, amen.

Day 11

"Repent, and turn yourselves from all your transgressions, so iniquity shall not be your ruin" (Ezekiel 18:30b).

*W*hy is iniquity so bad? Because it will be our ruin. We must not be involved in sin, because it absolutely leads to our destruction. Some years ago in our church, we had a young man who had been heavily into drugs. He was married and had three little children. He was born-again, filled with the Spirit, and came to church, but he was back and forth in the drug scene. Our pastors began to counsel with him.

One night the Lord told me that this man was living a double life: he was pretending to be stable, but was actually living in immorality. The Lord showed me that at night this young man was driving around and picking up young women; yet he told his wife he was out witnessing. When I confronted him with my suspicions, I knew that the Lord had shown me the truth. I said, "If you cover your sins, you won't prosper. But if you confess your sins, you will find mercy." But, instead, he covered his sins, and today iniquity has ruined him. Sin is a dangerous thing to play with; it will eat you alive and send you to hell.

Dear heavenly Father, we pray today that we will not take sin lightly. Let us not examine others, but allow, instead, the searchlight of the Holy Spirit to examine us, so we can confess, repent, and find Your mercy, in Jesus' name, amen.

Day 12

"For our God is a consuming fire" (Hebrews 12:29).

When we are baptized in the Holy Spirit, the Bible indicates that the chaff will be burned away. I have noticed that Spirit-filled people are usually dealt with in a strong way by the heavenly Father. God really puts the pressure on us about wrong attitudes, wrong motives, and mental-attitude sins. He just won't allow us to have quirks in our souls.

A well-known evangelist once said to the Lord, "Lord, why are You so hard on me? You don't deal with other people like this. You are always on my back."

And the Lord answered, "Yes, and your mother is always on MY back."

I thought, "Oh God, thank You that You are a consuming fire, that You DO want to consume the chaff in our lives so that we would bring forth more fire. I thank You for the baptism of the Holy Spirit, because it not only gives a zeal, but also it burns up the trash."

Dear heavenly Father, we thank You today for the zeal of God that puts a fire in us. We thank You today that You are working mightily and powerfully in our lives to bring glory and victory to Your name. We thank You today for burning up the chaff, the garbage. Let these areas of our lives be consumed with fire, in Jesus' name, amen.

Day 13

"...and thou holdest fast my name" (Revelation 2:13a).

What brings victory in your life? Holding fast to the name of Jesus! All things in heaven, on earth, and under the earth bow to His name. Do you want your circumstances to get in line? Then let your circumstances bow to Jesus' name. Even sickness and poverty must bow to His name.

The name of Jesus has been freely given to you, and you must freely use it. Hold fast to that wonderful name!

Once I was on a plane going to Albany, New York, for a special church service. The pilot said the plane would be two hours late. My heart dropped. But the Lord spoke sweetly to me, "You know, you have authority, in the name of Jesus." So in Jesus' name I began to bind the enemy from hindering the plane's departure. Within 15 minutes the pilot said, "Well, it was not as big a problem as we thought, and we will be taking off briefly." We arrived in time for the service. The name of Jesus is bigger than a broken plane.

Dear heavenly Father, we pray that we will take fast hold of Your name. We will not give up, but will continue to have faith in Your name and speak the name of Jesus over every circumstance of our lives. Amen.

Day 14

"But your sorrow shall be turned into joy" (John 16:20b).

God has always delighted in turning curses into blessings. Balaam tried to curse God's people; but every time he went up on the mountain to curse them, he ended up blessing them. Finally he said, "I can't curse what God has blessed."

Are you in a time of sorrow or crisis? Remember: the bigger the crisis, the bigger the opportunity that God has for transforming the crisis into a miracle.

I remember one time when I felt very defeated. We had prayed for a young woman with leukemia, but she had died. I felt like I never again wanted to do a healing prayer. But the Lord spoke to me about the three Hebrews who would not bow down to the image of Nebuchadnezzar. God told me, "THAT'S FAITH!"

The Hebrews also said, "If He doesn't deliver us, we still won't bow down." And God said, "THAT'S FAITHFULNESS! Marilyn, I'm growing two things in you, faith and faithfulness. Will you still be faithful to My Word when it appears that your faith has failed?"

God had taught me something very special about the prayer of faith for the sick. My sorrow was turned into joy, and the seeming defeat, into faith.

Dear heavenly Father, we pray that You will take hold of our sorrowful circumstances and turn them into victory. Help us turn each disadvantage into an advantage that will bring glory to Your name. Amen.

Day 15

"Every plant, which my heavenly Father hath not planted, shall be rooted up" (Matthew 15:13).

*Y*ou and I are the plantings of the Lord. We didn't ask to be planted. Our heavenly Father wooed us by His Spirit, drew us close, and planted us so we could not be uprooted. The devil, people, and circumstances may come against us, but our feet are planted in God's Word. Be patient. Stand fast. The last 30 minutes of our faith is often the most important.

A very dear friend had an ugly wart growing on her forehead. She rebuked the wart and prayed over it, but nothing happened. So one day she set her alarm and told the devil that in two hours, when the alarm went off, that growth would have to disappear. Later she answered a salesman's knock at the door. Suddenly the alarm went off. The salesman said to her, "Something just fell off your forehead." She felt her face, and the wart had disappeared. Thank God we can be rooted and grounded in the Word, and it works. So don't pull yourself short. Don't uproot yourself before you get your answers. Keep established in that promise until you see its manifestation.

Dear heavenly Father, help us to be stable in our faith, to believe for the supernatural, and never to give up. NEVER GIVE UP—in Jesus' name, amen.

Day 16

"Order my steps in thy word: and let not any iniquity have dominion over me" (Psalm 119:133).

The devil would like to take dominion over you and every area of your life. Some years ago the devil put the thought into my head that I was going to have a nervous breakdown, just like my father. The devil told me, "You look like your father, act like your father, and you will have a nervous breakdown just like him." I continued to think this until it gained a stronghold in my mind. One day I suddenly had this overwhelming urge to take my life. It was hideous and horrible, and I cried out to the Lord, "Oh God, help me, I'm just like my father. He had a nervous breakdown, and I'm going to have one too!"

And the Lord said, "That's right, you are just like your Father. I am your heavenly Father. I never had a nervous breakdown, and neither will you." Iniquity no longer had dominion over me.

That was many years ago. I will never have a nervous breakdown, and neither will you—because our steps are ordered by His Word.

Dear heavenly Father, we pray that we will order our steps and our thought-life in the Word. Let us renew our minds with the Word. We will not let iniquity have dominion over us in our mental, physical, or emotional lives. Thank You, Father, today that we who the Son has set free are truly free indeed, amen.

Day 17

"Rejoice not against me, O mine enemy: when I fall, I shall arise; when I sit in darkness, the Lord shall be a light unto me" (Micah 7:8).

"When I fall, I shall rise again." All of us have fallen into the traps of the devil. But we do not have to be pushovers for the enemy. We need, instead, to push the enemy over. David did not allow himself to be defeated by his mistakes. In fact, he transformed his mistakes into stepping stones that led toward his loving, heavenly Father.

I once listed all the ways that I had failed in raising our son. Then I repented a thousand times. God spoke so sweetly to my heart, "Yes, you DID fail, and you DID miss it, but you repented and I have forgiven you. But, Marilyn, you have NOT remembered all the things you did RIGHT for your son."

God's words were such encouragement to me. He said, "You've sown good seeds, so you are going to reap a good harvest." I know that God's Word is true. When I fall, I shall rise. And when you fall, you shall rise. If you will take hold of God's Word, He will bring you out of darkness into light.

Dear heavenly Father, when we feel that we have fallen, help us to take hold of the Word. Let us repent and receive Your forgiveness. Then we will forget that which is behind and reach forth for that which is ahead. Thank You, Father, that when we arise, we stand as conquerors, and we stand in Jesus' name, amen.

Day 18

"And make straight paths for your feet, lest that which be lame be turned out of the way; but let it rather be healed" (Hebrews 12:13).

Our personalities can often become lame and bruised because someone has offended us; then we begin to stray from God's path. God doesn't want bitter, wounded Christians walking along the wayside. He wants the lame to be healed and everyone back on the straight and narrow.

Jesus never said, "Blessed are they that are offended." He said, "Blessed are they that are not offended in ME." Years ago a woman in our church offended me by her attitudes. She always had something vindictive to say—just a little barb—but it pierced my heart, and I became bitter. But one day the Lord said that I must forgive her. I tried, but couldn't. So I cried out, "Lord, I can't forgive her."

The Lord said, "You are trying to forgive her with your emotions. Forgive, instead, by faith." Paul said, "Whoever you forgive, I forgive in the person of Jesus Christ." I spoke faith and forgave her in Jesus' name. Then God did a turnaround in our relationship. That woman became a great blessing to our church.

Dear heavenly Father, today we thank You that we are not an offended people. We cast our offenses on Jesus and become free from ugliness, strife, confusion, and division. We are free today, in Jesus' name, amen.

Day 19

"When men are cast down, then thou shalt say, There is lifting up; and he shall save the humble person" (Job 22:29).

God has a sure cure for depression. We need to say, "There is lifting up, and he shall save the humble person." Say it when the devil attacks you with depression. Say it to others.

Once I said to the Lord, "I think it is normal for people to get depressed." And the Lord replied, "Yes, it is normal. But you are not living a normal life, you are living a SUPERNATURAL life." Depression is basically unbelief, and unbelief is a sin. If you were believing, then you would have peace.

You cannot afford depression, because it robs you of your joy and strength. I used to have periods of depression. I just accepted these times. When returning from a vacation, I would always feel depressed and I didn't know why. I began to recognize this as the devil's trash. So I repented for allowing the devil to steal my joy. I just started praising the Lord and believing that, just as God had blessed my "going out," so now He would bless my "going in."

Don't let the devil do a number on you. Do a number on him.

Dear heavenly Father, we pray that we would see that depression is a sin. You didn't call us to sin. You called us to victory. We resist depression, in Jesus' name, amen.

Day 20

"But this I say, He which soweth sparingly shall reap also sparingly; and he which soweth bountifully shall reap also bountifully" (2 Corinthians 9:6).

If we are going to have a big harvest in our lives, we must begin to sow. I receive many, many letters from people with financial problems. Often people with financial problems are the very ones who do not tithe. They are not givers. If you sow nothing, you will reap nothing. If you sow a little, you will reap a little. If you sow a lot, you will reap a lot—that is God's law in every area of our lives.

Do you want love? Then you must sow love. You say, "I want friends." Well, are you sowing friendliness? Are you depressed? Well, make another depressed person joyful, and you will reap joy in your heart.

Once we were in a very serious financial crisis. We needed $10,000, and we needed it quickly. And so our staff sowed $100 as a gift to a well-known ministry and prayed for a one-hundredfold return. Within one month we received our first $10,000 check. It was such a blessing to see the law of sowing and reaping beautifully actualized in our lives.

Dear heavenly Father, if we have sown in a stingy way, let us have the stingy attitude lifted from us, and let us become a bountiful people. We know, Father, that You have called us to have a generous eye so we might reap a generous harvest. God, let generosity flow through us today. Amen.

Day 21

"Whatsoever thy hand findeth to do, do it with thy might" (Ecclesiastes 9:10a).

*Y*ears ago in our church, we had a woman who had the "welfare syndrome." Her husband was in prison; she had three children to raise. She thought she was doomed to be on welfare. Then she became born-again and Spirit-filled. Through the Word she saw that God had better things for her than welfare. She obtained a job, even though she had no skills and hadn't finished high school. She said, "I am going to be the best worker they have." She put her whole heart into that job. She'd do anything—even pick up paper and empty wastebaskets. At the end of the year, they gave her a $5,000 increase in her wages; the next year they doubled her salary.

Today she is a very valuable employee of our government. Why? Because she discovered that God wants everything that our hands touch to prosper. And the only way we can be prosperous is by doing things with ALL OUR MIGHT. Let me pray for you now.

Dear heavenly Father, we pray for an image of ourselves as being achievers. In Jesus' name, strengthen us with might in our inner minds. Let us see ourselves as Your best, whose hands produce prosperity. In Jesus' name, amen.

Day 22

"Fear thou not; for I am with thee: be not dismayed; for I am thy God: I will strengthen thee; yea, I will help thee; yea, I will uphold thee with the right hand of my righteousness" (Isaiah 41:10).

When I first went to Ethiopia, the government confiscated our gifts of food and all our video equipment, called me in for questioning, and accused me of being a spy.

The scripture above was given to me by God; He said it would carry me through. And it did! God gave me a miracle. God turned disfavor into favor. All our food and equipment was returned.

I have now been to Ethiopia several times. I have been on the front page of the major newspaper and on national television, where it was said, "This is the woman who loves us."

Surely in dark times, if we trust God, He will turn disadvantages into advantages. God will shake up nations because Christians won't give up. Let's pray that you won't give up, that your eyes will see the advantage of taking God's Word into every circumstance.

Dear heavenly Father, we pray that we will look upon disadvantages as opportunities from God for miracles. We pray that we take hold of Your Word, instead of our fears, because the Word is our true weapon against the enemy. We thank You that Your Word is a sword and that it will pierce, cut, and divide asunder, in the name of Jesus, amen.

Day 23

"And let us not be weary in well doing: for in due season we shall reap, if we faint not" (Galatians 6:9).

Fainters never reap anything. If we start fainting and our patience grows thin, we may never reap. Just as God has always wanted His people to sow abundantly, so also does He want them to reap. If we faint, God can revive us with His Word.

Sometimes it seems to take so long when you are holding onto a promise. Americans especially have a problem with patience. We believe in INSTANT COFFEE, INSTANT TEA, and INSTANT ANSWERS TO PRAYER. Remember, God's time is very different from our time. God can work His miracles in an instant. And others may take years. Patience is like a Siamese twin to answered prayer. Sometimes the last day or the last 30 minutes before a prayer is answered can be the most difficult. Even in the last hours, we must never faint—or we may reap not. Let's pray:

Dear heavenly Father, we thank You that we are not going to faint. We are going to come through. We are going to pray until we win. We are going to see the victory that You have intended for our lives. In Jesus' name, amen.

Day 24

"Thy words were found, and I did eat them; and thy word was unto me the joy and rejoicing of mine heart: for I am called by thy name, O Lord God of hosts" (Jeremiah 15:16).

God's Word is truly the bread of life, and as we consume the Word, the Word consumes us. It gives us a rejoicing in our hearts.

I was once very upset because we had a financial need that had not been met. We were approximately $150,000 behind on our bills, and we did not know how we were going to get the money. As I began to pray, the Lord gave me a scripture and said, "Thy God, whom thou servest continually, shall deliver thee." I literally ate that scripture. I meditated on it. I spoke it. I thought it. I dreamed it. I consumed it, and soon it began to consume me. Within thirty days our financial crisis had done a turnaround. Eat a lot of the Word. Let the Word "eat" a lot of you, and you will see many situations of despair turn into triumph.

Dear heavenly Father, thank You that we are not a defeated people. We are victorious people because we have been given the means of victory. Help us not to take Your Word lightly, but to know that this book can change and transform every circumstance. It is the most practical thing we possess! Let us practice it daily, in Jesus' name, amen.

Day 25

"And whatsoever we ask, we receive of him because we keep his commandments, and do those things that are pleasing in his sight" (I John 3:22).

If we love the Lord, we will keep His commandments. But sometimes it is very grievous to our flesh to keep His commandments. Once the Lord called upon me to "give" to a certain person whom I felt was unworthy of receiving. I argued with the Lord. (I have since discovered that it is better never to argue, but always to obey.)

I finally obeyed. When I did, God overwhelmingly blessed me and gave me a financial miracle. And the other person received such a peace from God that his own life did a turnaround.

I thank God for what He is doing in the lives of people. I thank God that the two principles of (1) keeping His commandments and (2) asking for blessings go together like Siamese twins. We like to ask, but sometimes we don't like to obey. However, the two must go together. Let us pray:

Dear heavenly Father, don't let us separate the obeying of Your Word from the receiving of Your bountifulness. Today we pray that each of us will make a new commitment to keep the commandments and, thereby, receive Your wonderful blessings. Thank You, Father, that we are a people committed to obedience. In Jesus' name, amen.

Day 26

"For the Lord shall be thy confidence, and shall keep thy foot from being taken" (Proverbs 3:26).

Confidence is an important thing. The Bible says, "Hold fast to your confidence for it has great recompence of reward."

Many years ago the Lord told me to go into the vitamin business. We had just a small church, a small congregation, and a VERY small income. The Lord said He would bless me—and that it would not hurt the ministry on any level. People advised me against it. Some warned, "If you make more money than your husband, you will break up your marriage." But I had confidence in God's Word.

God blessed me so abundantly that I DID make more money than my husband, but it never bothered him at all. He was delighted to write the checks and pay the bills—all because of God's provision! Never base ALL your confidence in people's advice; look to the Word. If God has spoken to you, obey Him; then receive His wonderful rewards. Today I want to pray for your confidence.

Dear heavenly Father, You have said that if our hearts do not condemn us, then we can have confidence that for whatever we pray, thus shall we see the wonderful results. We give You praise and glory for it. In the name of Jesus, amen.

Day 27

"He that is faithful in that which is least is faithful also in much" (Luke 16:10a).

When I read this scripture, I think of a very faithful secretary I had in years past. God led this young woman to our church, and soon she came to work for me as a secretary. Initially, she wasn't the best secretary, but she was willing. Eventually she became so good that sometimes I thought she could climb into my head and think what I thought. She finally became the director of my ministry.

God then began to deal with her husband and called the couple to their own ministry. They became assistant pastors in an Oklahoma church. Then they went to Kansas City, where today my ex-director is a marvelous teacher of the Word. Many people write and tell me how outstanding she is!

This woman had been so faithful in "that which is least," and now she is "faithful also in much." I can see her ministry grow day-by-day. Faithfulness pays. Jesus asked that when He comes, will He find faithfulness on the earth? Let us pray today that God will always give us faith in the smallest of things, so we may reap faith in the greatest!

Dear heavenly Father, You are faithful to us. You live and reign in our hearts; therefore, we are faithful to You and the body of Christ. In Jesus' name, amen.

Day 28

"Keep therefore the words of this covenant, and do them, that ye may prosper in all that ye do" (Deuteronomy 29:9).

People often say that prosperity is a bad word. And certainly the worship of money puts us out of divine order. However, if you will go after the wisdom of God's Word, you won't have to worship money—it will chase YOU down!

In the beginning of our television and radio ministry, we had quite a financial struggle. I was overwhelmed—where would the money come from?

During that time I spoke in a small rural Colorado church. Afterwards an elderly couple invited me to lunch. While we were eating, the woman asked me how much it cost to be on the radio for a year. I gave her a figure. Then she said to her husband, "Honey, write Marilyn out a check for $6,000." I thought to myself, "Honey, do it! We really need it." Our need was supernaturally met. I have found there are lots of "honeys" in God's great harvest—if we keep His Word.

Dear heavenly Father, we pray that You would bless every believer's finances. We pray we would know that the law of sowing and reaping affects our pocketbook. We thank You, Father, that as we go to Your Word today, prosperity will truly follow us. In Jesus' name, amen.

Day 29

"But without faith it is impossible to please him: for he that cometh to God must believe that he is, and that he is a rewarder of them that diligently seek him" (Hebrews 11:6).

Hebrews 11 is one of my favorite chapters—it goes from one leap of faith to another! But this verse is perhaps my favorite: God rewards them who diligently seek Him!

About a year ago my husband initiated morning prayer sessions at our church. My husband selected the 5:00 a.m. session for himself and me. As the alarm rang at 4:30 a.m., I could not imagine how I would ever make it. But I knew that my husband AND God wanted me to go. Often, as I have gone into that prayer meeting with bleary eyes, I claim the scripture that God is a rewarder of them who diligently seek Him—even at 5:00 in the morning.

God has rewarded us! We have seen literally hundreds and hundreds of answers to prayer in the last year. We have seen the lives of many people in our church changed—transformed—because of our diligent seeking of Him. Let's pray:

Dear heavenly Father, we pray today that every person who is seeking the Father in the name of Jesus, who is praying Your promises, who daily commits his life to You, will know that diligence brings rewards. Diligence brings rewards in the natural—and in the supernatural. Thank You for the supernatural at work in our lives. In Jesus' name, amen.

Day 30

"What is man, that thou art mindful of him? and the son of man, that thou visitest him?" (Psalm 8:4).

It is very shocking to me that God's mind is so full of man. Our minds, on the other hand, are often so full of cares, worries, concerns, and everything else—except the Lord. But God is always mindful of man and his needs. JEHOVAH JIRAH not only means "the Lord Who provides," but also "the Lord Who sees ahead and provides." In our worldly walk we buy insurance as a provision for the future. But the Lord is more than INSURANCE; He is ASSURANCE.

One time in the Chicago airport, a young woman saw my Bible and thought maybe I could help her. Her husband had been part of a hijacking and was now in the Joliet prison. Just as I was beginning to minister to her, they called my flight. I thought, "Oh God, I am sure that I am part of Your provision for this woman. Whatever I do, I will have to do quickly." The Lord told me that I was to take her in my arms and He would pour His love and assurance through me to her. I held her hands and began to pray. It was as though liquid love came from heaven through me into her.

Dear heavenly Father, we thank You today that You have seen ahead, gone ahead, and met needs. Help us to lift our eyes and look unto You and not to doubt that we are complete in Jesus. Amen.

Day 31

"But if a man walk in the night, he stumbleth, because there is no light in him" (John 11:10).

have you ever felt like you were walking through dark places? Remember, it is impossible for you to be drowned by your darkness, because, as a born-again believer, you have the Light of the world in your heart. We cannot stumble in the night. We may feel ISOLATED, but we are in fact, INSULATED with the Light of Jesus Christ. Turn to Him. Call upon Him in the day of your need.

Once I was almost involved in a plane crash. It was so extremely dark that few stars were shining. The pilot told us to prepare for a crash landing, but God brought a scripture to my mind: "No weapon formed against you shall prosper."

I declared very boldly in that plane of five people that we would not crash. And indeed, we landed safely. The Light had come from within me!

The Light in you will take you through your darkest night—when you let Jesus be the Light of your heart.

Dear heavenly Father, we pray for every person going through a dark time right now. We pray that each will look for Jesus, Who lives in all hearts, Who will never leave nor forsake His people, Who will give us light to walk in the darkest night and bring us to victory. Amen.

Day 32

"The curse of the Lord is in the house of the wicked: but he blesseth the habitation of the just" (Proverbs 3:33).

*G*od blesses our habitation. Many of you who are reading this may have an unsaved mate, and you will say, "How can God bless my house when one of us is not saved?" But God will sanctify a household because of one believing mate. Your faith sets your household apart for God's blessings. God's light is greater than the darkness that may come from unsaved members in your home.

Trust God, look to Him, and know that He will do a miracle. In our time of pastoring, we have seen many couples get divorced because one was a believer and the other not. However, a good number of these couples were remarried because one mate's faith stood fast. Remember, light is greater than darkness. There is no family situation impossible for God, for "He blesseth the habitation of the just."

Dear heavenly Father, we seek Your blessings for our families. Let the believing speak the Word boldly and not give up—morning, noon, or night. We thank You, Father, that the Word of God works mightily in our homes to bring glory to Your name. Amen.

Day 33

"Let us lay aside every weight, and the sin which doth so easily beset us, and let us run with patience the race that is set before us" (Hebrews 12:1b).

Doctors tell us again and again that excess weight must be shed. This is also true in spiritual ways. We need to lay aside weights that would keep us from following Jesus in the fullness that He has for us. We have to lay aside sins, and we must run our race with patience.

Very early in my spiritual life, God dealt with me about laying aside a certain weight. It wasn't a heavy sin: I was spending many hours weekly reading novels. I read them simply because I enjoyed them. They were not immoral, but they were not glorifying to Jesus. God wanted me to lay aside this weight and spend my time in and around His Word. I HAD to lay aside this weight in order to run the very special race He had called me to run.

I am sure there are personal weights in your life that hinder you in your race. Let the Holy Spirit deal with you today so that you can achieve what He has in store for you.

Dear heavenly Father, we pray that the blinders will be lifted from our eyes and that we will see any hindering weight. We thank You today, dear heavenly Father, that You are at work in our lives in a mighty way. Let any weight that we lay aside give us added achievement and prosperity in Jesus. Amen.

Day 34

"He that hath clean hands, and a pure heart; who hath not lifted up his soul unto vanity, nor sworn deceitfully. He shall receive the blessing from the Lord" (Psalm 24:4-5a).

Everyone likes to be blessed. The word BLESS—INGS is never to be a singular word because God does not know how to give just one! But His blessings DO come with conditions: clean hands, a pure heart, a soul without vanity, no swearing. Only God can search your heart and show you where you are unclean. People may often criticize you and try to tell you what you are doing wrong. But only the Holy Spirit knows your heart.

Recently God told me that I was competitive. I said, "Oh, God, take that from me. I don't want to compete with other Christians."

The Lord said, "Competitiveness is not a bad trait when I am in command of it. But when you are in command of it, you use it carnally." It is good to compete with yourself and to better yourself, but to compete with another Christian is carnality. Today let us pray for any area where perhaps the Holy Spirit is trying to turn the spotlight upon your heart.

Dearest heavenly Father, Your new nature is in my heart because of Jesus. I choose today to make decisions out of my new nature, not my old man. In Jesus' name, amen.

Day 35

"And I sought for a man among them, that should make up the hedge, and stand in the gap before me for the land, that I should not destroy it: but I found none" (Ezekiel 22:30).

This scripture has become a profound part of my life. Years ago the Lord began to show me that I could stand in the gap for other pastors by ministering to their sons and daughters. A well-known evangelist had a daughter who was involved in drugs, alcohol, and immorality. I had never met her, but I began to stand in the gap for her and to take her name daily to the Lord. I told the Lord that she was the seed of the righteous, and the righteous shall be delivered. I told the Lord that in the end-time He would pour out His Holy Spirit upon our seed and that this was the seed of a man who loved God with all his heart.

A year later I met this woman at a meeting in a large city. I said, "What are you doing here?" She told me that she had recently been saved, Spirit-filled, and was going to Bible school. I was so ecstatic. I said, "I have been standing in the gap for you, and I'm going to go home and mark your name off my list!" One of our most beautiful ministries is standing in the gap for others!

Dear heavenly Father, thank You that there is no person, no circumstance too big for You to move or change. Thank You that Your Word will work in every situation, in Jesus' name, amen.

Day 36

"And the earth was without form, and void; and darkness was upon the face of the deep. And the Spirit of God moved upon the face of the waters" (Genesis 1:2).

One of the most beautiful works of the Holy Spirit occurs when He brings COSMOS out of CHAOS. When God's Spirit moved during the Creation, He began to put things in divine order—the natural, as well as the spiritual. God's Spirit can bring divine order to the chaos in your life too.

Some horrendous strife recently erupted at work just as I returned home from an overseas trip. I was extremely tired, but I knew I had to deal with this problem of strife. I awakened early in the morning and began to pray in the Spirit. God told me to wash the feet of the people who were involved in the problem. He said He would lead their feet in peace. I was not to take sides, but merely to wash the feet of those on both sides of the issue. And when I obeyed what the Spirit had called me to do, chaos was transformed into divine order.

God has divine order for your life. Pray in the Spirit. God's Spirit is a moving force that will move circumstances into proper position.

Dear heavenly Father, thank You that one of the Holy Spirit's works is to put our lives in divine order. Thank You for that divine order. In Jesus' name, amen.

Day 37

"And he cometh unto the disciples, and findeth them asleep, and saith unto Peter, What, could ye not watch with me one hour?" (Matthew 26:40).

Jesus had called his disciples to pray with Him for one hour. Why is one hour of such extreme importance? Why did He call them for ONE HOUR? Because if they had prayed for one hour, they would have been kept from temptation. Jesus later told Peter that he would not have denied Christ if he had spent that time in prayer.

An early prayer a day keeps the devil away. Early in the morning I like to name my day—that is, I name it what I believe God wants it to be. Perhaps He wants it to be a day of victory, maybe He wants it to be a day of wisdom, or a day of revelation. I believe that my day will be in line with what I name it.

Adam named the animals, and they came at his call. When he called the dog, the cat didn't come, because Adam had the authority to name each animal. Jesus, our last Adam, has again given us authority in His name to name things. We can name our day, and our day will get in line with what we name it. Take that early hour of prayer. It can keep your whole day in victory.

Dear heavenly Father, help us daily to have an "early prayer that will keep the devil away" and give us a day of victory. In Jesus' name, amen.

Day 38

"Every place whereon the soles of your feet shall tread shall be yours" (Deuteronomy 11:24a).

Please note: it says where YOU tread, not where others tread. It is important for us to walk on areas that we want to claim. Several years ago we desperately needed a new church building. I felt the best new location was a church owned by the Southern Baptists. Practically every car that went north and south in Denver passed that beautiful church. One day we drove around that building and claimed it in Jesus' name. We asked God to bless and prosper the Southern Baptists so much that they would have to move to a bigger church.

Two weeks later the pastor of that church called and asked my husband if he would like to buy the building. We had claimed it, tread upon it, and said, "This is ours!" And we got that church!

What do YOU desire? Go out and walk on it! Claim it in the name of Jesus! Remember, it is YOUR treading, not that of others, that gives it to you.

Dear heavenly Father, we pray today that we will walk into miracle situations and will tread on territory that perhaps has never been taken by God's people. Let us walk forth and walk boldly—in confidence, in the name of Jesus. Amen.

Day 39

"Every kingdom divided against itself is brought to desolation; and every city or house divided against itself shall not stand" (Matthew 12:25).

a divided spirit can ruin a Christian. A divided marriage can ruin a home. A divided business can ruin its prosperity. A divided nation can cause a nation to fall.

Division is the devil's number-one tool. I certainly have seen and experienced his work over the years. But one day the Lord spoke to me, "You can turn the devil's tool back on himself." I then remembered when Paul was called up before the Roman government. There he brought up a point upon which the Sadducees and Pharisees disagreed. The two groups immediately began to fight with each other, and Paul's life was saved. He had brought division among the enemy.

We, too, can bring division in the devil's ranks. I pray that communism will be put to confusion. I pray that they will not be able to agree on goals and that the whole system of communism will eventually fall apart. You, too, can defeat your enemies with division.

Dear heavenly Father, thank You today that we are united with You. Let us be sensitive to areas of strife, but not a part of that strife. We send strife into the devil's kingdom in the name of Jesus, amen.

Day 40

"Ye have not gone up into the gaps, neither made up the hedge for the house of Israel to stand in the battle in the day of the Lord" (Ezekiel 13:5).

God has called us to stand in the gap for Christians when they have a need. Each Christian has a hedge of protection, and wherever a gap occurs in that hedge, then the devil can come in and attack that Christian. When we see the needs of others, we tend to point out their gaps, instead of coming to their aid. Job had three broken hedges. God sent him three friends to stand in each gap of the hedge. But, instead, each simply criticized and pointed out the gaps. Those friends missed a great blessing.

How can we stand in the gap for one another? When the devil is attacking another Christian, go stand in that gap, and speak the Word to the devil. The Bible says that we can overcome the devil by the blood of the Lamb and the Word of our testimony. God says He is looking for men and women who will stand in the gap. Tell Him today to look no further. He has found you, and you will be happy to accept the challenge!

Dear heavenly Father, forgive us today for being gap finders. We commit right now to stand in the gap for the needs of others. We will speak the promises that bring Your miraculous provision, in Jesus' name, amen.

Day 41

"And take heed to yourselves, lest at any time your hearts be overcharged with surfeiting, and drunkenness, and cares of this life, and so that day come upon you unawares" (Luke 21:34).

Many people today are burdened down with cares. Peter tells us to cast all our cares on God because He cares for us. I want to encourage you today to cast your cares on Him. When a situation seems hopeless, we can trust the Lord.

Early in our ministry I had so many cares. I fretted and fussed and worried. One time I thought we had only $15 to our name: $10 for gas to drive to a revival meeting and $5 for lunch. I didn't know that my husband Wally had already put the $10 in an offering, so we couldn't even buy gas to get to our own revival!

I decided that God would just have to take care of our need. Within 30 minutes some people knocked on our door and gave us $10. They said that God had told them to do it.

Learn how to cast cares on the Lord. Your body was not made to carry cares. They will overcharge your heart.

Dear heavenly Father, we pray that we will learn how to cast our cares on Jesus and not to carry them alone. No matter what the need may be, we know that You will do the miraculous for us. In Jesus' name, amen.

Day 42

"From the rising of the sun unto the going down of the same the Lord's name is to be praised" (Psalm 113:3).

Praising the Lord should be a full-time occupation—a way of life.

The Word says, "Bless the Lord, O my soul: and all that is within me, bless His holy name....Who forgiveth all thine iniquities; who healeth all thy diseases" (Psalm 103:1-3). When we praise the Lord, we bring about a healing flow.

When Wally and I were engaged, we attended a service where I began to worship and praise the Lord with great enthusiasm. I did not know anything about healing or redemption rights. I just knew that I wanted to worship God. As we were worshiping, a warm sensation came over my heart. Previously my doctors had told me that I had an enlarged heart and that nothing could change this condition. But that night I knew God had healed my heart.

After that service I became more active than I had ever been in my life. During my latest heart examination, the doctor said, "You have such a good heart." I shared with him that I had a "fixed heart"—Jesus had fixed it in a praise service.

Dear heavenly Father, help us today to enter into worship and to offer the sacrifice of thanksgiving. Teach us to live a life of praise, so that we might live a life of victory, in Jesus' name, amen.

Day 43

"She openeth her mouth with wisdom and in her tongue is the law of kindness" (Proverbs 31:26).

"Out of the abundance of the heart the mouth speaketh" (Matthew 12:34b). If we FILL our hearts with God's Word, we will SPEAK His words. His wisdom will come out of our mouths, and His kindness will flow out of our hearts.

When we read God's Word, it is stored in our hearts. We may not feel as if we are doing anything—but we are!

It's like canning vegetables and fruit. Canning is uncomfortable and hot. It is a very unpleasant job! I know, because my brother and I used to help my mother at canning time every summer. We complained the whole time we were canning, but we never complained in the winter when she unscrewed the lids on the jars of those delicious peaches. It is much the same with God's Word.

If we "can" the Word in our hearts, then during the "wintertime" of our lives, the Holy Spirit will unscrew the lid and out will come the wisdom and kindness that have been "preserved" in our hearts by God's Word. Be a "canner" of the Word.

Dear heavenly Father, we pray that we will have a deep hunger for the Word. We pray that the Holy Spirit will give us revelations out of Your Word. In Jesus' name, amen.

Day 44

"God is faithful, by whom ye were called unto the fellowship of his Son Jesus Christ our Lord" (I Corinthians 1:9).

We are called into fellowship! Can you imagine the Lord calling US to fellowship? We usually feel as though we are calling upon HIM for fellowship. But God loves fellowship with us.

One morning I was lying in prayer on our divan. I was telling the Lord what a privilege it is to live for Him. He spoke to me and said, "You don't live FOR ME, you live WITH ME. We live together, and we are seated together in heavenly places. We meet together in daily fellowship when we join in prayer."

When we pray to the Father, both Jesus and the Holy Spirit pray with us. They intercede for us according to the will of God. Isn't that wonderful! Jesus and the Holy Spirit get in line with what we are praying and pray FOR us as we fellowship together.

We are never alone because He is Jehovah-Shammah—the Lord Who is present. Jesus said, "I will never leave you nor forsake you." Why? Because He has CALLED us into this fellowship.

Dear heavenly Father, help us to live in continual fellowship with You on a day-to-day basis. Thank You that the fellowship of Jesus is sweet. Thank You that we walk daily in newness of life. Thank You that we walk daily in the Spirit and in fellowship with Your Son. Amen.

Day 45

"The fear of the wicked, it shall come upon him: but the desire of the righteous shall be granted" (Proverbs 10:24).

Some years ago I had a desire to have a full-length mink coat. I talked with my husband about it, but he felt it was a foolish expense for the short time that I would be wearing it in the winter. But I was reminded of Psalm 37:4: "Delight thyself also in the Lord; and He shall give thee the desires of thine heart." So I asked God to give me a dark brown, size-six, full-length mink coat.

Several years went by, and I continued to believe that God—not my husband—would be the source of the coat. One day a church member, who was a jeweler, asked to see my husband and me. This man had a dark brown, size-six, full-length mink coat. A widow had come to sell him some diamonds and remarked, "My husband bought a mink coat for me six months ago, but I don't want it." Our jeweler friend remembered my desire, and he brought the coat to us.

I have found that God meets our needs and DESIRES—if we delight in Him.

Dear heavenly Father, we pray that we will grow in seeing You as a God of abundance. You're not stingy; You are a loving heavenly Father, and You want to meet all our needs, and even our desires. In Jesus' name, amen.

Day 46

"Your zeal hath provoked very many"
(2 Corinthians 9:2b).

Zeal has a provoking quality. (PROVOKE means "to stir up or stimulate to action.") I had never thought of it in this way until recently, when a course on evangelism was taught in our church.

I was not able to attend the course because I was traveling in Ethiopia. However, when I came back, I saw one of our pastors absolutely "turned-on" to soul winning. Our people were winning souls right and left by going door to door throughout the city of Denver and personally witnessing of the power and love of the Lord Jesus Christ.

Their zeal provoked me. I thought, "I want to be a soul winner." I have always loved to witness, and so have my husband and daughter, but their zeal stirred me up even more!

ZEAL means to be "white hot" for the Lord. Our zeal not only brings forth good results that are pleasing to the Lord, but it provokes others too.

Dear heavenly Father, give us a tremendous zeal to pray, to witness, to give, to serve—on every level that You would have for us. We don't want to be lukewarm, but rather white-hot. You said You make Your angels fiery ministers. That is what we want to be too. In Jesus' name, amen.

Day 47

"Commit thy works unto the Lord, and thy thoughts shall be established" (Proverbs 16:3).

Do you ever have problems with your thought-life? The devil can put all kinds of junk and trash into our minds. I hate that. Sometimes I think it happens because we have seen a movie that wasn't good or because we have seen something questionable on television. Somehow the enemy has done a number on us.

But I have found a way to establish my thoughts: I need to commit all my works unto the Lord. Many times I have awakened in the night and started to worry. Then I'd catch myself and say, "Lord, I commit my works unto You." Soon my thoughts come back in line, and I can go back to sleep.

The devil would like to harass us through our thought-life. But if we will commit our works unto the Lord, our thought-life will come in line. I know that you want your works and thoughts established in Him.

Dear heavenly Father, in the name of Jesus, we commit our works into Your hand. We thank You that our thoughts are established and our minds are renewed. We have the mind of Christ. Jesus was made unto us wisdom for this day, and we praise and glorify You for it. Amen.

Day 48

"And ye shall be holy unto me: for I the Lord am holy, and have severed you from other people, that ye should be mine" (Leviticus 20:26).

God has called us to be a holy people—that makes us different from the world. The scriptures say that we are a PECULIAR people. I always thought PECULIAR meant someone who looked, acted, and even smelled strange.

But the definition of PECULIAR is "one who is zealous of good works." That's what I want to be! We all know that the world will not accept us because we are different—we are not like others—we've been born anew!

When Sarah, our daughter, went to high school, many of her friends began to drink. They tried to influence her, but she had to make a decision. Would she be different or follow the crowd? I watched her struggle with these decisions, but the Lord helped her boldly establish her identity as a committed Christian. She would be different—peculiar. And in doing so, she has been a light.

Look in the mirror. If you are a born-again believer, you are different—you're the light of the world!

Dear heavenly Father, help us to be a light in every situation—never darkness. When we stand in the Light of God's Words, the Light in us will overcome the darkness around us. In Jesus' name, amen.

Day 49

"He that diligently seeketh good procureth favour: but he that seeketh mischief, it shall come unto him" (Proverbs 11:27).

Please note the phrase "DILIGENTLY seeketh good." Often we seek good only PART OF THE TIME. The rest of the time, we seek our own selfish pursuits and then wonder why we don't receive good all the time.

DILIGENCE means "daily." I am looking for good; so DAILY I am sowing good. Then DAILY I can reap a harvest of good. Sometimes the reaping may come a long time after the sowing. Perhaps this is why we are not always aware of how wonderfully "sowing" can work in our lives.

Years ago I taught a Bible study in a denominational church, and many of the women were saved and Spirit-filled. I thought that surely these women would come to our church, but they did not. They scattered among other churches or stayed in their old churches. Now, after 12 years, we see a lot of those families at Happy Church. One day the Lord reminded me, "You sowed, now you are reaping."

I was reminded of the scripture, "In due season we shall reap, if we faint not" (Galatians 6:9b).

Dear heavenly Father, help us diligently to sow good. If we are sowing mischief, let us repent of it quickly because we do not want to reap mischief back. In Jesus' name, amen.

Day 50

"He hath shewed thee, oh man, what is good; and what doth the Lord require of thee, but to do justly, and to love mercy, and to walk humbly with thy God?" (Micah 6:8).

Sometimes our egos can really get out of line, can't they? I remember one time when I was scheduled for a Christian TV program. There were five or six guests in line before me, and I became worried that they would talk so long that I wouldn't get my time. Oh, how I wanted to be on that TV program! How I wanted people to see me! You would have said, "Marilyn, you are REALLY on an ego trip!"

As you might have guessed, I didn't even get on the air that day. The next day I had the same attitude; and again I didn't get on the program. The third day the Lord really dealt with me on my attitudes, goals, and concerns. And so I said, "Lord, if You want me just to sit and pray in the Spirit for those who are on the program, that is fine with me." At the very end of the program, the Lord miraculously made a way for me to speak. The Holy Spirit really anointed the few words I spoke.

Dear heavenly Father, help us never to look down on others and to exalt ourselves; for while we are looking down, we are not looking up. Help us always to look up to You and see that if we will humble ourselves, You will exalt us, in Jesus' name, amen.

Day 51

"Being born again, not of corruptible seed, but of incorruptible, by the word of God, which liveth and abideth for ever" (I Peter 1:23).

Can you imagine what it will be like to live eternally? God's Word gives us eternal life because it IS eternal. His Word lives and abides forever. Whenever we stand on His Word; trust in His Word; act, think, speak, and meditate upon His Word, we have latched hold of eternity. Our physical bodies may die, but God's Word is incorruptible. It will continue to work and bring forth fruit.

I heard a wonderful testimony from a man whose grandfather spent five minutes a day praying over each grandchild. There were nine grandchildren, so he prayed 45 minutes each day. Today all of those grandchildren are in full-time ministry. Why? Because God's Word lives on, even though our physical bodies do not.

Dear heavenly Father, help us to put our faith in Your Word. Help us not to give up, but to know that when we take hold of the Word, we take hold of eternity. The Word will never let us down because You uphold all things by the Word of Your power. Thank You today that Your promises endure forever. Amen.

Day 52

"All the ways of man are clean in his own eyes; but the Lord weigheth the spirits" (Proverbs 16:2).

We read much in the papers about open-heart surgery. But God has been doing open-heart surgery for years. God opens up your heart and looks at your motives. He sees you as you really are.

God never condemns you, but He convicts you by the Holy Spirit—until your motives get in line with the Word.

There is a difference between condemnation and conviction. THE DEVIL CONDEMNS you; he identifies wrong things in your life and says there is no hope—you will never change. GOD CONVICTS you. He says that you are wrong, but that the power of the Holy Spirit can transform your mind and make you whole.

Let God open up your heart. Allow yourself to receive His divine correction. Don't perform "heart surgery" on yourself. Introspection, without divine intercession, will produce only self-condemnation—and condemnation is from the devil!

Dear heavenly Father, we ask You today to search our hearts for any wicked ways. Let us walk in righteousness, holiness, and newness of life. Forgive us of our sins, in Jesus' name, amen.

Day 53

"And God is able to make all grace abound toward you; that ye, always having all sufficiency in all things, may abound to every good work"
(2 Corinthians 9:8).

What is grace? I believe it is the ability to run on God's ability. Did you ever try to abound in your own ability—on who you are, instead of what He is? I am sure every one of us is guilty of this. It is only when we come to the end of our ability, that His supernatural ability takes over. Some years ago God gave me a word of knowledge during a service. He told me to call out people who had knee problems.

I said, "But, God, what if no one has such a problem? What if I call them out and they are not healed?"

God said, "That's not your problem, that's My problem. Your problem is to obey." I did what He told me to do, but I didn't observe any healings.

A year later my husband and I were on vacation, and a couple who was staying in our motel told us that they had attended that service and saw a former football player receive complete healing from a knee injury.

Dear heavenly Father, help us today to look to Your sufficiency for abundance—not to our lack of it. In Jesus' name, amen.

Day 54

"Here is the patience of the saints: here are they that keep the commandments of God, and the faith of Jesus" (Revelation 14:12).

Do you realize that you are not limited by your own faith? You have the faith of Jesus, and His faith is unlimited.

For years my husband stood on the Word for God to give us a child of our own. Every doctor told me that I had an inherited sterility problem; I could not have a child. At that point, I have to admit, my faith wavered; but my husband's faith did not.

One day I asked him, "How does your faith remain so firm?" He said, "Because I have the faith of Jesus." I had been standing on my faith, instead of Jesus' faith.

Thirteen years after we were married, I gave birth to a baby girl. I went back to one of the doctors who had told me it was impossible for me to have a baby. I told him that I had just had a baby. He replied, "Oh, you just adopted a baby?" I said, "No, I HAD a baby." He said, "That's impossible." I said, "Well, I have one anyway." Aren't you glad you have the faith of Jesus?

Dear heavenly Father, help us not to look at our own LIMITATIONS. Help us to look at Jesus' UNLIMITED faith, which lives and abides in our hearts. Help us to know that Jesus is at work in us, through us, and for us. In Jesus' name, amen.

Day 55

"Therefore all things whatsoever ye would that men should do to you, do ye even so to them: for this is the law and the prophets" (Matthew 7:12).

Here again is the law of sowing and reaping. In the book of Proverbs, God tells us that if we want friends, we ourselves must be friendly—sow friendliness; reap friendliness. Whatsoever we sow is exactly what we are going to reap.

Do you want people to do good things for you? Then do good things for them. Sometimes our harvest won't come directly from those people, but we will reap it in another area. I have found that if I sow in one field, I may reap in 10 other fields. God will always bring a harvest from the seed you sow.

There have been times when God has spoken with me, dealt with me, and has had me pray for the sick, when actually I felt like I WAS the one in need of healing. But as I sowed healing, God would send people to lay hands on me, or He would burden people in the night to pray for me. And I would experience absolutely the healing resurrection power of Jesus Christ. Sowing—what a simple law this is! We need to take advantage of it!

Dear heavenly Father, help us to take advantage of our advantages today. Help us to see that our disadvantages can become advantages if we will apply the law of sowing and reaping. In Jesus' name, amen.

Day 56

"If God be for us, who can be against us?" (Romans 8:31b).

Many times there are terrible circumstances around us. God actually tells us to say to the circumstances, "God is for me, so you cannot be against me."

We had a situation once that just seemed to refuse to crack. Our mail was being stolen, and the postal department didn't even seem to care. It was so frustrating.

I would wake up at night in a cold sweat and wonder, "God, what is going to happen to us? Are You going to let these thieves steal us blind?" God gave me Romans 8:31, "What shall we then say to these things? If God be for us, who can be against us?"

I began to speak to our mail and to the circumstances surrounding the mail theft. I told these circumstances, "God is for us, so you cannot be against us." God took that whole situation and turned it into a blessing. The circumstances became "for" us, instead of "against" us. Tell your circumstances that God is for you. Let's pray together.

Dear heavenly Father, we speak to circumstances in our lives. Father, we know now that these circumstances are coming in line with Your Word. They are not against us; they are for us, and we praise You for it, amen.

Day 57

"Return to thine own house, and shew how great things God hath done unto thee" (Luke 8:39a).

There are many ways to demonstrate Jesus' love in our homes: Loving acts, discipline, and training are just a few. One of the best ways is to apologize when we make mistakes. (We have all made mistakes in handling our children at one time or another.)

One time I badly mishandled my son. He had done something wrong, and my anger erupted way out of bounds. I then felt condemned before God and a failure as a mother.

But God showed me that one of the greatest things I could say to my son was that I was wrong. He was wrong, too, but my reaction had been wrong. I had been out of divine love, out of divine order. I asked him to forgive me. Overwhelmed by my tears and my repentance, he said, "Oh, Mother, of course, I forgive you." It brought our relationship into better focus than it had ever been before.

There are many ways we can witness to our families. Don't be afraid to say, "I'm sorry," "Thank You," or "I'm pleased with you."

Dear heavenly Father, help us to be better parents through the Word and the power of the Holy Spirit. Guide us into the truth about ourselves and our families. Help us to be honest in our relationships. In Jesus' name, amen.

Day 58

"Understanding is a wellspring of life"
(Proverbs 16:22a).

Life gets dull sometimes, and we can feel trapped and bored with situations. But understanding God's Word will be a wellspring of life.

One time a man on our staff had become quite a murmurer. He talked against me, he talked against my husband, he talked against situations and circumstances. I could do one of two things: 1) blast him verbally or, 2) move in the wisdom of God (which I realized I didn't have at that point).

During the night God gave me a scripture: "GODLINESS WITH CONTENTMENT IS GREAT GAIN" (I Timothy 6:6). God showed me that the man on our staff was greatly discontent. But with whom was he discontent—my husband and me? God? Or with himself? I went to him, gave him the scripture, and told him that he would not see a gain in his work as long as he was discontent. If he were discontent with my husband and me, we needed to know where we had failed him. He broke down and wept, we prayed together, and the situation was righted. The man became a gain to himself, us, and the Kingdom. Truly, understanding is a wellspring.

Dear heavenly Father, we pray, more than ever before, that we will go to You for understanding. Your Holy Spirit will lead us to truth, in Jesus' name, amen.

Day 59

"And so were the churches established in the faith, and increased in number daily" (Acts 16:5).

The key to this verse is, very simply, that faith brings increase. Faith has a growing process, just like other things in our lives. When I first began my radio broadcast, it cost me $60 per month. I asked my husband if the church would underwrite that monthly $60 bill. He told me that the church could not, but he would pray with me that God would meet our need. At the time I thought he was very cruel, but later I saw that he was acting in faith. We prayed together, and God met that need of $60 a month. God was beginning to give me the faith for my future needs.

Soon our broadcast budget increased to $500 a month. God met that need too. Now we are growing close to $2 million per year for all media broadcasts. That figure would have caused me to faint in the early days. But as you become established in faith, you begin to increase in your faith vision. Begin believing for the little things. Soon you will believe for medium-sized things, then onto greater things!

Dear heavenly Father, help us to be patient in the Word and know that faith and patience are Siamese twins, which work together to bring increases, in Jesus' name, amen.

Day 60

"And it shall come to pass, that before they call, I will answer; and while they are yet speaking, I will hear" (Isaiah 65:24).

When you read this scripture, do you think it's almost too good to be true? We read in the book of Numbers that Balaam made a decision to curse Israel so that he might receive the honor and finances that his carnal man so desired. Balaam discovered that he could not curse God's people.

Every time he tried to prophesy evil, he prophesied good. Finally he said to the king of Moab, "I don't know what to do. I can only speak what God puts in my mouth; I can't curse what God has blessed."

God is so good to His people. They probably didn't even know that this battle was occurring. Undoubtedly, God told Moses later.

How many times God has protected us! He has sent us angelic protection, and we were not EVEN aware of it. Thank God for His love; thank God for the angels who encamp around about those who fear Him. Let's pray together.

Dear heavenly Father, You say in Your Word that angels move at Your command. We take hold of Your Word, and we ask that angels will help carry it out. We take hold of the promise that You protect us, watch over us, and neither sleep nor slumber. In Jesus' name, amen.

Day 61

"When thou goest, it shall lead thee; when thou sleepest, it shall keep thee; and when thou wakest, it shall talk with thee" (Proverbs 6:22).

God's Word is very practical. This scripture tells us that His Word will talk to us when we wake up, guide us during the day, and keep us while we are asleep.

I claimed this verse while memorizing the book of Proverbs some years ago. I would memorize verses first thing in the morning when my mind was clear. My mind was like a blackboard that had been erased: nothing had been written on it yet, so I could write God's Word on it first.

At lunchtime I would go over those same scriptures and again at night before going to sleep. It was as if those scriptures worked their way in my spirit all night long. It was a powerful time in my life.

It took about 10 months to memorize the entire book of Proverbs, but the truths in that book will stay with me throughout my life. I have "canned" them in my heart, and the Holy Spirit unscrews the lids and brings them to my remembrance.

Dear heavenly Father, we thank You that the Word is not just for inspiration, but it is also wisdom in our lives. We pray that we will have great hunger to read the Word in the morning, at noon, and at night. We pray that Your Word will be the prevailing force of our lives. In Jesus' name, amen.

Day 62

"That your faith should not stand in the wisdom of men, but in the power of God" (I Corinthians 2:5).

If you are putting your faith in people, in yourself, in money, or in your circumstances, your faith won't stand. It can only stand when it is in God's power. Circumstances will change, but God's Word never changes. So if our faith is to stand, it cannot stand in something that is fluctuating. God's Word is constant and faithful.

Once I had a tremendous desire to teach the Bible on local educational stations. We did two pilot programs to test the market. But when the station's president saw the programs, he told me, "No." He said it was a dead issue.

I said, "Good! I'm glad it's dead because I believe in resurrection." I put my faith in God's Word and knew that He would open a door.

Six months later the station aired our program, and it was so popular that we were on the air for two years. The president was shocked to learn that the Word of God was more popular than sex, politics, and violence. God's Word works; His power works.

Dear heavenly Father, may we put our faith in Your Word. We pray that we will absolutely and wholeheartedly lean on Your promises and see them come to pass. In Jesus' name, amen.

Day 63

"And they that be wise shall shine as the brightness of the firmament; and they that turn many to righteousness as the stars for ever and ever" (Daniel 12:3).

It seems that everyone is star-struck today. But being a star in God's kingdom means being a soul winner.

Once two friends were taking me to the airport. At the last minute the couple invited some other friends to go too. I suddenly felt a strong desire to ask if these other people had ever received Christ. The man began to weep. He told me that he had a cocaine habit, which was about to destroy their family.

I told the man that Jesus was his answer—if the man would only invite Jesus into his heart. I then turned to the woman and asked her if she would like to be born again too. She began to weep and cry. She also received Jesus into her heart.

God absolutely performed a miracle in their lives. The man was set free from cocaine, and the couple was kept together.

The greatest privilege we have is to lead someone to Christ.

Dear heavenly Father, give us a tremendous desire to win souls. Let us know that it is not our ABILITY, but simply our AVAILABILITY to express Your love and what You have done for us, in Jesus' name, amen.

Day 64

"And it shall come to pass afterward, that I will pour out my spirit upon all flesh; and your sons and your daughters shall prophesy, your old men shall dream dreams, your young men shall see visions"
(Joel 2:28).

In these scriptures we see that God will move upon us and our seed. I have used Joel 2:28 to claim the baptism of the Holy Spirit for both my son and daughter. God wants to pour out His spirit upon them, too, in these end-times.

When Sarah was just a baby, I claimed this scripture so that she would be born again and baptized in the Holy Spirit. When Sarah was four years old, she said, "Mother, when you put me to bed tonight, I will wake up, and God is going to baptize me in the Holy Spirit, and I am going to pray in tongues." I thought, "Well, she's heard this in Sunday school, and she's saying it because she knows that it will please me." But I did not say that to her. I said, "Sarah, that will be wonderful!"

When I put her to bed, she fell asleep immediately. When I later looked in on her, she was sitting up in her bed and smiling and praying in tongues. Truly, God will pour His Spirit upon all flesh!

Dear heavenly Father, today we pray that our loved ones will be born again, baptized in the Holy Spirit, and "turned on" to Jesus with everything they have. In Jesus' name, amen.

Day 65

"My substance was not hid from thee, when I was made in secret, and curiously wrought in the lowest parts of the earth. Thine eyes did see my substance, yet being unperfect, and in thy book all my members were written" (Psalm 139:15-16a).

abortion is very common in our world today—much too common. Abortion deeply concerns Christians because it is absolute murder. The world tries to say that a fetus is not a real personality as long as it is in the womb. But that is not what the Bible says.

Psalm 139 says that when we were curiously wrought and when we were imperfect, God saw us. He wrote our "members"—parts of our bodies—down in a book. He continues that book about us as our members change. The New Testament tells us that the Father even knows when a hair falls from our heads.

At the moment of our conception, God becomes very concerned about our PHYSICAL BODIES. He keeps minute records on each of us—until we are resurrected and receive our GLORIFIED BODIES.

It overwhelms me to think that God is THAT concerned about my physical body; but He is. He loves our bodies so much that He had Jesus take our infirmities and diseases so that we could be whole.

Dear heavenly Father, You've told us that the body is for the Lord, and the Lord is for the body. Thank You for working in our physical bodies and giving us health and strength. In Jesus' name, amen.

Day 66

"Is any among you afflicted? let him pray. Is any merry? let him sing songs" (James 5:13).

The book of James is often called "The Proverbs of the New Testament." This wonderful book of wisdom has BIG answers to meet you right where you live. Are you afflicted? Prayer will relieve you of your afflictions.

Are you merry? Then sing a song, and rejoice in God. You can sing a psalm out of the book of Psalms. How did David receive psalms? He received them in his time of rejoicing before the Lord.

Some years ago my husband heard a person who ministered in rhymed prophecy. Wally asked God to give him a similar ministry. Immediately after that, whenever Wally prayed and praised the Lord, God would give him a rhymed revelation truth.

Numerous epistles tell us that we are to sing to ourselves and others in psalms and spiritual songs. There are so many depths to the Holy Spirit and what He can do in our lives. We need only to wait upon Him and spend time in His presence.

Dear heavenly Father, we thank You that there is an answer for our needs today. We ask You to give us wisdom and lead us by Your Holy Spirit in this special day. We ask You to make us a blessing to others. Father, we are available and open to sing psalms in Your presence, in Jesus' name, amen.

Day 67

"And wisdom and knowledge shall be the stability of thy times, and strength of salvation: the fear of the Lord is his treasure" (Isaiah 33:6).

Stability is so needed in our day, because everything around us is so unstable. In Genesis 49 Jacob prophesied to Reuben that he was unstable and would not excel. Unstable people never excel.

I started piano lessons when I was about six years old, but I did not practice consistently. I was unstable in my practicing, so now I do not excel. James 1:8 says that a double-minded man is unstable in all his ways. If you believe God's Word one day, but disbelieve it the next, you are unstable. You will not attain the things you desire.

I've seen people tramp from church to church. They stay in a church one year. Suddenly they are offended by something, and they move to another church. These people never bear any fruit. Why? Because they are unstable in their commitment to God AND to man. Today, let God's Word make you stable. Commit yourself to the stability of His Word, and you will excel in your results.

Dear heavenly Father, help us today to see that the most stable thing we have is Your Word. If we are stable in Your Word, we will be stable in OUR circumstances. Thank You, Father, that when we put our feet on Your Word, we cannot be moved. In Jesus' name, amen.

Day 68

"And he said unto them, Unto you it is given to know the mystery of the kingdom of God" (Mark 4:11a).

I have found that God does not want His Word to be a mystery to us; He wants it to be a revealed truth. When I find passages that I don't understand in the Bible, I write a question mark beside them. When I read through those passages again, I ask the Father to reveal them to me. If I'm patient, eventually God will give me a beautiful revelation.

Once I didn't understand why God had not allowed Moses to enter the Promised Land. I knew Moses had hit the rock twice, instead of once. If I had been forced to listen to murmurers for 40 years, I would probably have hit the people, instead of the rock. I put a question mark by that verse!

One day as I was reading the same verse, the Lord said that Moses DID get to enter the Promised Land. God said, "Moses went in on the Mount of Transfiguration with Elijah and Jesus. With whom would you rather enter the Promised Land—murmuring Jews or Jesus?"

We know the mysteries of God through revelation knowledge.

Dear heavenly Father, open our eyes to behold wonders from Your Word today. Give us hearing ears and seeing eyes to receive the revelations that You have for us. In Jesus' name, amen.

Day 69

"Your iniquities have turned away these things, and your sins have withholden good things from you" (Jeremiah 5:25).

Jeremiah 5:25 has a tremendous nugget of truth that can set us free. Our sins hold us back from the good things of God. Sometimes we ask, "Well, God, where are You? What's holding this situation back? Why am I not getting an answer?" If you ask God to search your heart, He will really tell you the truth.

Several years ago a woman on our staff absolutely fell apart when she found out that her husband, a traveling salesman, was involved with another woman.

We began to pray that the blood of Jesus would reconcile this married couple; however, we didn't see any instant results. Finally, she asked God if there was anything she was doing to hinder the reconciliation. She began to change the things that God showed her. Today that marriage is strong and sound because that woman was willing to let the Holy Spirit search her heart and show her where she was wrong.

Dear heavenly Father, as You deal with each one of us individually, we pray that we will be open to change. Show us the truth. We will receive the truth, and it will set us free. We thank You. Amen.

Day 70

"Remembering...your work of faith, and labor of love, and patience of hope in our Lord Jesus Christ, in the sight of God and our Father" (1 Thessalonians 1:3).

There are three things in this verse that stand out to me, and I know that you will love them just as I do:

Faith can work, love can labor, and hope can give you patience. If we feel we have faith, yet do nothing, we don't really have faith. If we say we have love, yet do nothing, we don't really have love. If we say we have hope, then we will be patient until we see the manifestation of what God has for us.

HOPE in the Hebrew means "rope." I believe God lets His rope down from heaven so we can tie a knot in it and hold onto it until we see the manifestation of our faith and our love.

Rahab had hope in God's Word. She even put a red rope in her window. Her wall stood when other walls fell. When other people's walls fall down, their lives fall down too. If you hang onto the rope of God's hope, your wall will stand.

Dear heavenly Father, we know that it is through faith and patience that we inherit Your promises. We make a decision to hold to faith and to have patience until we see the fulfillment of Your promises. In Jesus' name, amen.

Day 71

"That every one of you should know how to possess his vessel in sanctification and honour" (1 Thess. 4:4).

In this scripture VESSEL means "body." Does the devil control your body? Do you control it? Or do you commit your body to God as a living sacrifice to use as He sees fit?

Sometimes we abuse our bodies by doing harmful and hurtful things to them. Why? Because we have not really given God permission to possess our bodies too.

God wants to be in control of our whole life—spirit, soul, and body. When He takes possession of our bodies, He renews them and makes them better.

Today, commit your body to Him. Tell Him to use it according to His will. You may be shocked at some of the things that happen to your physical body.

When Moses was 120 years old, he turned his body over to the Lord. Moses' eye wasn't dimmed, nor was his natural force abated. He didn't die sick; God just took him home. I believe this is God's perfect plan for our bodies too.

Dear heavenly Father, I thank You for giving me a body—a body You now live in. Thank You for giving me a living vessel that is strengthened and renewed daily. Let my strength be as my days are, in Jesus' name, amen.

Day 72

"I will say to the north, Give up; and to the south, Keep not back: bring my sons from afar, and my daughters from the ends of the earth" (Isaiah 43:6).

have your children or other loved ones backslidden? I believe we can use Isaiah 43:6 to bring them back. We can tell the north, the south, the east, and the west to give up our sons and our daughters, so they may come to Jesus.

One night I was very discouraged about my son. I thought, "Where is my own son tonight? Out in some drug culture—away from God." I decided I could either have a "pity party" or take hold of God's Word and receive a promise for my problem. I asked God to send laborers to my son.

Mike was hitchhiking that night, and a man picked him up. He asked Mike his name. "Mike Hickey," he answered. The man asked, "Do you know Marilyn Hickey? I listen to her on the radio." Mike said, in great consternation, "Yes, she's my mother." All the way home the man preached to Mike about Jesus.

How good God is! He wants our children and loved ones to serve Him. Be bold to take God's promises.

Dear heavenly Father, we pray for our loved ones today. We speak to the north, south, east, and west to loosen our loved ones so they may serve Jesus. We call forth laborers to minister to them and lift the blinders from their eyes. In Jesus' name, amen.

Day 73

"And Stephen, full of faith and power, did great wonders and miracles among the people" (Acts 6:8).

*E*very one of us needs miracles and wonders. The two things that precede miracles and wonders are faith and power. POWER means "miracle-working power" or "the fullness of the Holy Spirit."

To be filled with faith, we must be full of God's Word and full of the Holy Spirit. We must pray, live, and walk in the Spirit in order to see wonders and miracles.

Sometimes our faith may seem weak or just neutral. At one service I felt led to pray for people who had foot problems. Afterward a woman came up to me and said, "Please come look at my daughter." The woman's daughter was walking up the steps to the platform with great joy.

I said to the woman, "What happened?" She said, "Several years ago my daughter crushed the bones of her feet, and she could hardly walk. But now she's walking normally." When we go after God's Word, miracles will come after us.

Dear heavenly Father, we pray today that we will be so committed to the Word and to the power of the Holy Spirit that signs and wonders will truly follow us. We give all the glory and praise to Jesus, amen.

Day 74

"He raiseth up the poor out of the dust, and lifteth up the needy out of the dunghill" (Psalms 113:7).

*W*e live in a day when there are many poor and needy people. They literally live on a dunghill.

In San Salvador I visited such a place. The people told me that their homes had been built on the garbage dump of the city. For many years the people of San Salvador had dumped all of their garbage on this hill. Finally the hill had become a mountain and was called "Garbage Mountain."

Very poor people who moved into San Salvador lived on top of that mountain. It became a place of disease, filth, and tragedy. A church was started there, along with a school, to reach the people of this area. Soon both the church and school were flourishing. The school now has many children who are being fed, clothed, and taught the Word of God. Their lives are being changed and transformed. The name of the church is "Miracle Church." God can make a miracle out of a dunghill!

Dear heavenly Father, today we look to You to speak to us to help the poor, especially those of less fortunate countries. We can help these people physically and spiritually. Truly, let us feed both souls and bodies. Help us in this, in Jesus' name, amen.

Day 75

"Let nothing be done through strife or vainglory; but in lowliness of mind let each esteem others better than themselves" (Philippians 2:3).

*E*very now and then you need to check your attitudes and motives. Are you really acting in "lowliness" or humbleness of mind? Do you remember to esteem others higher than yourself?

Once I was flying to a speaking engagement at a large convention in St. Louis. (I was scheduled to speak at the meeting on the evening of my arrival.) In the seat in front of me a woman was having a terrible time eating her meal because her baby was fussy.

The Lord told me to offer to hold the baby so the mother could eat her meal in peace. I had on a beautiful silk dress, and I said, "Oh, Lord, what if that baby burps on my dress?" The Lord reminded me that ministering to this woman could be as important as ministering to a whole convention. He said that He would keep the baby's stomach quiet and my silk dress clean. I thank the Lord that, in His eyes, no ministry is too big or small.

Dear heavenly Father, help us not to esteem ourselves more than we esteem what You would have us do. Thank You, Father, that we can minister to others. In Jesus' name, amen.

Day 76

"For I have learned, in whatsoever state I am, therewith to be content" (Philippians 4:11b).

Sometimes we must learn to be content. I have always thought that contentment came when your circumstances were going well. But you can learn to be content when your circumstances are not going well—or are even horrendous! Contentment does not come from the outside; it comes from the inside. If we have faith in God's Word, we will always be content.

Years ago my husband and I were assistant pastors in an Assembly of God church in Amarillo, Texas. The living quarters given to us were horrendous. I used to say that the cockroaches had a square dance every night. We did everything to clean up that tiny little place, but even at its best, it was still horrible. At first I was so discontent that I murmured and murmured to my poor husband.

But it was there, in Amarillo, that I first began to teach the Bible. I fell in love with teaching the Word. I learned that my contentment was in the Word, not in that little apartment.

I have learned that we carry our own contentment with us. Our contentment should be placed on God's promises, which we have secured in our inner man.

Dear heavenly Father, help us today to find true contentment. Help us to learn that when we are content, we are secure. Help us to insulate ourselves with Your promises, in Jesus' name, amen.

Day 77

"Thy word is a lamp unto my feet, and a light unto my path" (Psalm 119:105).

This scripture has an interesting comment on the subject of "guidance." God only gives you small "lamps" as guidance for your feet in your day-by-day walk. But each lamp is just strong enough to illuminate your way toward the particular goal that He wants you to reach.

When God called me, He told me to cover the earth with the Word. That was my big "searchlight." It was the light at the end of the path, so to speak. "But how do you cover the earth with the Word?" was my question. And God gave me smaller "lamps" for each step of the way. One "lamp" was the teaching of the Bible on radio; another, on television; another was a Bible-reading plan; another was Bible distribution; another was crusades and conventions.

I believe that there will be many, many other "lamps" that God will give me to reach my ultimate calling. Watch for those little lamps that He gives you for your steps. They are very important in reaching the goal He has for you.

Dear heavenly Father, help each of us watch for the glimmers of light that You give us each day. Help us to be sensitive to the direction of the Holy Spirit, for You always lead us to truth, in Jesus' name, amen.

Day 78

"Greater is he that is in you, than he that is in the world" (I John 4:4b).

Before we left for Poland, some Polish pastors warned us that we would have a terrible time bringing video equipment—13 pieces in all—into the country.

We needed this equipment, so I turned my circumstances over to God and knew that He would do exceedingly, abundantly above all that we might ask or think.

Then I claimed the scripture that says, "He who is in me is greater..." and prayed that I would have favor with the customs people. Usually customs officials search video equipment and then confiscate it. But instead, when the customs woman saw all of our luggage, she said, "Pass through." We could hardly believe it!

We said, "What did you say?"

"Pass on through. I don't want to look at any of the equipment. Just get out of here."

We walked through freely, because greater is He Who is in us than he who is in the world.

Dear heavenly Father, we thank You that we're not a people who should hang our heads. We can hold them high and know that You are doing great things in and through us. In Jesus' name, amen.

Day 79

"There is no fear in love; but perfect love casteth out fear: because fear hath torment. He that feareth is not made perfect in love" (I John 4:18).

Fear torments. No one disputes that. But God's love frees us from fear. When we realize the greatness of God's love, then we will not be afraid.

Fear makes us immature, and PERFECT here means "mature." We are not made mature when we allow fear to overwhelm us. The more we read God's Word, the more we realize how much He loves us. We find His provision and His love printed on every page of our Bible. God is absolutely wild about you! He loves you, and the more you bask in His love, the more freedom you will have from fear.

The best thing about God's love is that it is an unconditional love. God loves you no matter who you are or what you do. His love is always there to comfort you. When you go astray, God's love is there to guide you back on the right path. And as God's love fills us, it will overflow from our lips, our hearts and our spirits.

When we speak the truth in love, we begin to grow up in His Son. Speak God's Word today, in love, and watch fear flee from you.

Dear heavenly Father, thank You today that we are set free from fear in the name of Jesus. We are set free from fear because of Jesus' overwhelming love for us. Amen.

Day 80

"And at the end of the days, I...lifted up mine eyes unto heaven, and mine understanding returned unto me, and I blessed the most High, and I praised and honoured him that liveth for ever" (Daniel 4:34a).

*N*ebuchadnezzar was the king of the largest empire in his day. God gave him one sign after another through the dream interpretations of Daniel. Nebuchadnezzar also saw the three Hebrew children, Shadrach, Meshach, and Abed-nego, rescued by the Son of God from a fiery furnace. But although Nebuchadnezzar had heard and seen the miraculous, his heart was stubborn. He refused to recognize God as the real Source of power and authority. Nebuchadnezzar's pride eventually produced a nervous breakdown.

In the above scripture Nebuchadnezzar finally lifted up his eyes to heaven and acknowledged God. His reasoning then returned. Looking up to the Father makes your reasoning return. We lose our reasoning when we look at ourselves and concentrate on hurt feelings and bitterness. The return of godly reasoning brings tremendous results.

Dear heavenly Father, we thank You that we don't need to look down at life's circumstances; instead, we can look up. We thank You for wisdom each day. We praise and honor You because we are entering into a reasonable service that brings reasonable results. In Jesus' name, amen.

Day 81

"But without faith it is impossible to please him: for he that cometh to God must believe that he is, and that he is a rewarder of them that diligently seek him" (Hebrews 11:6).

This is one of my favorite, favorite, favorite, favorite scriptures. In fact, I quote this scripture regularly in prayer. I have certain things I "believe God for." Sometimes the reward seems to take FOREVER, so I remind God and myself that He is a rewarder of them that diligently seek Him. When I set aside a time daily to seek Him, I know that God is going to reward me for that time I spend with Him.

Diligence brings reward; lack of diligence brings no reward. If you are diligent in praying and set aside a special time of day for prayer—genuine prayer that seeks God—then He will reward you for spending time in His presence.

In Proverbs we find that diligence also yields power and prosperity (Proverbs 12:24 and 13:4). Therefore, diligence is desirable and profitable in every area of our lives.

Dear heavenly Father, put a deep desire in each of us to set aside a special time to pray. Let us set aside a special time to be in the Word—on a daily basis. We know that we cannot afford to be without the Word and prayer in our lives, in Jesus' name, amen.

Day 82

"Seeing ye have purified your souls in obeying the truth through the Spirit unto unfeigned love of the brethren, see that ye love one another with a pure heart fervently" (I Peter 1:22).

This scripture calls upon us to love one another. It is important to note that we are not to love because of feeling or emotion or because the other person is sweet and wonderful. We love because the Word tells us to do it.

When people have wronged us, it is difficult to love them. But God says, "I didn't call you to love people because of who they are; I just simply commanded you to love." Sometimes when we are extremely upset with people, the EXPRESSION OF LOVE will bring our feelings into line. Love from the spirit purifies love in our soul, mind, and emotions.

Once I felt led to express love to a woman who had a horrible disposition. My expression of love began to fill my heart. The Holy Spirit began to show me some of her problems and how I could pray for her. This woman has become a marvelous friend to my ministry; she supports me, prays for me, and loves me. I loved by faith—and it purified my soul.

Dear heavenly Father, help us to love by faith, help us to act on Your Word—simply because You have commanded it. So many times we are waiting for a leading and a command. Today we receive Your command to love one another, in Jesus' name, amen.

Day 83

"But be filled with the Spirit; Speaking to yourselves in psalms and hymns and spiritual songs, singing and making melody in your heart to the Lord" (Ephesians 5:18b-19).

*E*veryone of us likes to have spiritual revelation. It is so personal and so warms our hearts about God's deep concern for us and the very circumstances of our lives. Being filled with the Spirit also helps us to receive the personal revelations that we need. God can give us a personal psalm; He can give us a personal hymn. God spoke to David and warmed his heart for all occasions. God ever gave him a "new song."

New songs will take you out of old ruts. New songs give you new revelations that come from being filled with the Holy Spirit.

Once I asked the Lord, "Lord, why is it so necessary to keep being filled and refilled with the Holy Spirit?"

And the Lord answered, "It is because you leak." Circumstances cause us to leak, but praying in the Spirit keeps our cup full of His Spirit.

Dear heavenly Father, thank You for filling the leaks in our souls with the patching of the Holy Spirit. Thank You that You have not left us as orphans, without guidance from the Holy Spirit Who reinforces us in every situation. In Jesus' name, amen.

Day 84

"Keep back thy servant also from presumptuous sins; let them not have dominion over me" (Psalm 19:13a).

Have you ever done something that was presumptuous? You knew that God did not want you to do it. Yet you rebelled and did it anyway. One time I decided to write a letter to a certain minister who I felt had a problem. Deep in my heart I heard the Lord check me. But I just went ahead anyway. My letter came back because the address was wrong. I think that was a second warning from God. But I ignored that check also and re-sent the letter to the minister.

Soon I received his response. He was tremendously offended and felt I was totally out of line. It was one of the most corrective letters I have ever received. I had been very presumptuous. In my own arrogance, in my own rebellion, I had overstepped my proper bounds.

God wants to help us stay within the bounds He has set for us. When we avoid rebellion, then we can live within the bounds of success and triumphant living.

Dear heavenly Father, we thank You that we are not going to be rebellious in our ways, but sensitive to the voice of the Holy Spirit, so we can walk in the way You have called us. We commit our will, not our willfulness to You, in Jesus' name, amen.

Day 85

"He that overcometh shall inherit all things; and I will be his God, and he shall be my son" (Revelation 21:7).

*T*hese promises made to overcomers are absolutely, positively marvelous. Sometimes we want to ride through our lives on a pink cloud and play a harp—with nothing to overcome. But we are not in a kindergarten; we are in a battle. Battles take weapons, endurance, and guts. God wants His people to have spiritual guts. With His Word in us, we can overcome wrong mental attitudes, bad habits, and any defeat.

Years ago God told me to be an overcomer in one area of my life. I thought, "God, I can't do it." This area had been a stumbling block for so long that I was blind to it. But the Lord sweetly said, "I'm not asking YOU alone to overcome, I am asking you to release Jesus to be the Overcomer in you. You have a new nature—an overcoming nature." I then made the decision to allow His nature to take over in my life. Too often we are "undercomers" and will never surmount that which God would set before us.

Dear heavenly Father, we thank You today we're not defeated Christians—we're victorious Christians. We are Christians who overcome in all things. We are more than conquerors, in Jesus' name, amen.

Day 86

"For the Lord shall be thy confidence, and shall keep thy foot from being taken" (Proverbs 3:26).

When I first began our radio and television ministry, I had such a yearning to get the Word out. But I was naive, inexperienced, and, what the world would call, "as green as they come." A Texas public relations agency said that it wanted to help me. I didn't know about agencies—how they would take 15% of all income. I guess I was just kind of flattered that someone would be interested enough to help me.

After signing up, I soon learned that the head of this agency was literally a crook. He was an alcoholic; his life was totally out of line with God, and I was walking in the counsel of the ungodly. In our six-month association with this agency, we fortunately used some of the man's good advice and were never damaged by his bad advice.

Even when we are ignorant to certain situations, if our confidence is in the Lord, He will keep our foot from "being taken."

Dear heavenly Father, we pray that today we will commit our ways unto You so that all thoughts may be established in Your way. There is no question, You will lead us in safety and deliver us from evil. In Jesus' name, amen.

Day 87

"My foot standeth in an even place" (Psalm 26:12a).

Did you ever feel like your foot was slipping? That you were slipping in your faith and commitment? The devil would like for all of us to slip and slide. But God says, "Our feet stand in an even place." When we stand on His Word, we are in an even place.

Once when our ministry went through a financial trial, the devil told me just to close the doors and hang it up. He said that I had never been capable of making good financial decisions—that I had blown it. But God didn't say that to me; in fact, God gave me a promise that if I would trust Him, He would bring me through. While the staff was crying the blues, I stood on an even place. I said, "God will deliver us, God is delivering us," and in one month we had a total turnaround.

When it looks uneven, put your confidence in the Word, and it will keep you even—until the circumstances come in line with the evenness of God's Word. Let me pray for you.

Dear heavenly Father, we pray that if we slip and slide, we will know in our hearts that there is no temptation You cannot lead us through victoriously. We have Your deliverance because we are the righteousness of God in Christ Jesus. Thank You for our deliverance and our strong place of standing on Your Word. In Jesus' name, amen.

Day 88

"But speak the word only, and my servant shall be healed" (Matthew 8:8b).

Sometimes I think we make faith sound so difficult; here the scripture tells us that speaking "the Word ONLY" is great faith. Occasionally the Lord will deal with me about my conversation. He will say, "You are NOT speaking the Word only. You are also speaking your doubt, unbelief, and circumstances."

Years ago a difficult situation arose when a staff member was speaking negatively against my leadership. He had been corrected, but his negativity continued. In return, I was speaking back evil words; I was returning evil for evil. God showed me that this would never change the situation. So I began to speak good things about the man. He did not change immediately. But at the end of six months, we experienced a miracle, and this man is now my friend. The Bible says when a man's ways please the Lord, He makes even one's enemies to be at peace with him.

Dear heavenly Father, help us today to give our tongues to You. Put a guard in our mouths that we would speak from the Word only, so that we can enter into great faith. We give our voices willingly to You, in Jesus' name, amen.

Day 89

"And Jesus said unto him, Go thy way; thy faith hath made thee whole" (Mark 10:52a).

Faith makes us whole. Physically, spiritually, and emotionally. We may think that the Bible is not useful for today's situations, but it really will work in whatever area we need. Sometimes we look to the natural world for wisdom, when God's supernatural wisdom, instead, will absolutely answer our dilemma.

Once I had horrendous battles with my thought-life. A person had wronged me in a certain circumstance. I had great bitterness in my heart.

I said, "God, help me. Give me an answer. Certainly my mind is sick in this area."

And God gave me a beautiful scripture, "Commit thy ways unto the Lord, and thy thoughts shall be established" (Proverbs 16:3). So I began to pray that scripture. I said, "God, I commit my ways to You this day." My thoughts began to get in line. It was so wonderful. My thought-life did a turnaround, and wholeness came into that area of my thinking again. Faith makes you whole, wherever you are.

Dear heavenly Father, we thank You that we have Your promises that will bring provisions and answers to all problems. Give to each of us a special promise that will bring forth a needed provision. In Jesus' name, amen.

Day 90

"Thy way, O God, is in the sanctuary: who is so great a God as our God?" (Psalms 77:13).

Many times I have known people who simply shift from church to church. They make no commitment to a church body; they may call themselves Charismatics, but I think they are "cruisematics"—just cruising from church to church. Like rolling stones, they produce no fruit. Jude calls them "wandering stars"; they don't give off much light.

God says He will bless us in the sanctuary. The Lord wants us committed to a church family. He wants us loyal to the church where He has placed us. In Ephesians 4:10-11, He set forth the five-fold ministry so that we will not be blown about by every wind of doctrine.

As a pastor's wife, I have found that people who become established in a church and are not moved by offenses, but by the Holy Spirit, are the people who become productive in the kingdom. Jesus ordained us to bring forth fruit that would remain. Remaining fruit grows within the protection of a church and a caring pastor.

Dear heavenly Father, we pray that we will have the blinders lifted from our eyes. Let us see how important it is to be part of a local church body. Let us see that You call us by the direction of the Holy Spirit, not by people-pressure. Thank You for blessing us in our obedience to You. In Jesus' name, amen.

Day 91

"Open thy mouth for the dumb in the cause of all such as are appointed to destruction" (Proverbs 31:8).

This is a scripture that God unfolded to me some years ago in regards to abortion. Unborn babies are mute or "dumb"; they cannot speak for themselves. Babies who die by abortion cannot cry out against this abomination. We must open our mouths and cry out for them.

When this scripture was opened to me, I knew that it was not enough for me to be "against" abortion, but I must "open my mouth" against it, because it was literally destroying human lives. Why does the world participate in such things? Because it does not understand what the Word of God says, nor does it respect it. Many times when I have wondered about world issues, God has given me specific scriptures to open up my understanding. Today my prayer is that God will give you revelation truth as you read His Word.

Dear heavenly Father, we pray that today we will have some key verse simply leap off the pages and be transformed into a revealed truth for some specific situation or circumstance. In Jesus' name, amen.

Day 92

"Let every thing that hath breath praise the Lord. Praise ye the Lord" (Psalm 150:6).

*G*od commands us that if we are living, we need to praise Him. In Hebrew one of the words for "praise" is JUDAH. As we follow the tribe of Judah throughout the Bible, we see that where it goes, so goes praise.

Moses prophesied in Deuteronomy that the voice of Judah would be heard throughout the earth. David was of the tribe of Judah and wrote most of the Psalms, which certainly have become worldwide praises for the Lord.

We find that Jesus often praised the Father and gave Him thanks. Jesus also came from the tribe of Judah.

We, who are born-again, also come from a "tribe of praise." We are in the lineage of Jesus Christ; thus, we too are of the tribe of Judah and bring praise.

We need to let the earth hear our voices as we praise the Lord. Do you have breath? Then praise Him today! Praise Him everywhere, not just at a worship service—for praise is a way of life!

Dear heavenly Father, today we praise You and give thanks to You. We major on the good things that You are doing in our lives. We are not unthankful; we are a grateful people. In Jesus' name, amen.

Day 93

"Call unto me, and I will answer thee, and shew thee great and mighty things, which thou knowest not" (Jeremiah 33:3).

Why do some Christians experience great and mighty things in their lives, while others do not? Basically, it's because some Christians do not call unto the Lord. Why don't they call? Because they really don't believe that God is THAT good or that He can do all those mighty things for them. We do have a BIG GOD, Who loves us with a BIG LOVE and wants to give His people BIG THINGS.

It's time for Christians to look beyond their own church and community. It's time to see how we Christians can affect and change the hearts of all people.

It's time for Christians to start calling on God to save the leaders of nations and to pour out His Spirit worldwide. I believe it's time we begin to call for the great outpouring of the Holy Spirit upon all flesh.

I have also recently discovered that God is enlarging my own heart. I now have a heart for the world. God's heart is for the world. Let's call for the great and mighty things He has for the world in our day.

Dear heavenly Father, give each of us a heart for the world. Let us not see just our own small circumstances, but, instead, see Your world plan. Let us be in prayer for the great things that You have for our day, in Jesus' name, amen.

Day 94

"The Lord also will be a refuge for the oppressed, a refuge in times of trouble" (Psalm 9:9).

*Y*ears ago while I was on a plane to a speaking engagement, I began to feel a pain in my left breast. I discovered that I had a lump with red streaks coming out of it. It frightened me greatly. The devil taunted me, "You are going to die if you don't do something about this IMMEDIATELY."

But I rebuked the devil and demanded that the affliction dry up and disappear. When I got off the plane, I went directly to the pulpit to minister. The growth was throbbing all that time, but I continued to speak the Word to it.

I was staying in a convent. The small room had no air conditioning, and it was a rather uncomfortable situation. All night the little growth throbbed and hurt me. The devil really began to speak to my mind. So I decided, "Devil, if you want to wake me up, you are going to be sorry because I'm going to listen to the Word. I'll come out of this stronger than ever before." I put some New Testament scriptures on my tape recorder and went to sleep. The next morning the growth was smaller, the streaks had begun to lessen, and later that evening it had disappeared.

Dear heavenly Father, we thank You today that we can look to You as our refuge. We are sure and secure in our time of trouble because we know that You will be there for us and set us free!

Day 95

"He that hath pity upon the poor lendeth unto the Lord; and that which he hath will he pay him again" (Proverbs 19:17).

*E*arly in my husband Wally's spiritual commitment, he encountered a blind man selling pencils in a restaurant. Wally's income was so tight that he had to count every penny in order to have enough money for his own food. When the blind man came by Wally's table, Wally didn't plan to give the man anything. But the Lord told Wally that he would be blessed if he helped the poor. And so instead of considering his budget and questioning the way of the Lord, Wally gave the last dollar he had to the blind man.

Wally told me that for the next three days it was as though he had walked into a realm of glory. His simple, simple act of obedience was blessed with a sweet presence from the Lord.

Our ministry also has been blessed through our acts of giving. When I was in El Salvador to help the poor, Mrs. Duarte, the wife of the President, requested that I come and pray with her. God gives us favor in unusual places when we have pity on the poor. The Lord's returns are beyond anything we can imagine or expect.

Dear heavenly Father, help us today not to ignore the poor, but, instead, to share our blessings. Everything we do in the name of Jesus will be returned to us many times. In Jesus' name, amen.

Day 96

"Blessed is the man that trusteth in the Lord, and whose hope the Lord is. For he shall be as a tree planted by the waters,...and shall not be careful in the year of drought, nor shall cease from yielding fruit" (Jeremiah 17:7-8).

When I read these scriptures, I find that they closely parallel the words in Psalms 1. Truly when we put our trust in the Lord and meditate on His Word, then we are fruitful and productive, even when the circumstances around us are falling apart.

Jeremiah lived in a day when the people worshiped idols. Even when Jeremiah knew that an enemy kingdom was soon to overwhelm Israel, he kept fresh and alive in God. There may have been a drought AROUND him, but there was no drought IN him.

When at one time I found my circumstances very overwhelming, I said to the Lord, "What's wrong with my life? I just want to run away and change my name." The Lord answered, "This is not the time for 'isolation'; this is the time for 'insulation' with the Word. A right heart can overcome bad circumstances." I insulated my thought-life with His Word, and soon my circumstances became fruitful.

Dear Father, don't let us put our trust in natural things, but let us put our trust in You, our SUPER-natural God. Turn our times of drought into times of fruitfulness. Amen.

Day 97

"Whosoever committeth sin is the servant of sin. And the servant abideth not in the house for ever: but the Son abideth ever. If the Son therefore shall make you free, ye shall be free indeed" (John 8:34b-36).

Some of my best witnessing has occurred on planes. Once on a return trip from Tulsa, I almost missed the plane. To reach my seat, I had to climb over a man who had put his belongings not only under his seat, but under mine too. He refused to move his belongings, so I had to hold my briefcase.

I began to look over my sermon notes while the man ordered one drink after another. I was so "turned off" by him! Finally he said to me, "Are you reading a Bible?"

I replied curtly, "Yes, I am." Then he said, "Could you answer a question? " He told me that he had been born again one week ago. Someone had told him about the baptism of the Holy Spirit. He asked, "Do you know anything about the baptism of the Holy Spirit?" I quickly repented for my earlier anger and ministered the Word to that man.

Sometimes we miss God-given opportunities; but when we repent, the Son sets us free and makes our circumstances free too.

Dear heavenly Father, help us today to repent quickly. Help us to know that we don't have to serve sin; we serve Jesus. In Jesus' name, amen.

Day 98

"Now thanks be unto God, which always causeth us to triumph in Christ, and maketh manifest the savour of his knowledge by us in every place"
(2 Corinthians 2:14).

One day the Lord said to me, "It is NEVER My will for you to lose."

I said, "Lord, I see that Your Word says we will always triumph; but it does not appear that I always do." And the Lord told me that my problem was that I gave up too soon. God said, "The game is never over until you win. It is always My will for you to win." That SO encouraged me never to give up.

When my daughter Sarah first began in basketball, we encouraged her to keep believing for great things. Sometimes she was almost ready to give up, but we would go to the scriptures and speak the Word. In her sophomore year her team lost the state championship by one game. We said, "Well, you have another year." And true enough, the team "took state" in their junior year. The game is not over until we win, because God's will is that we always triumph in Christ.

Dear heavenly Father, help us to see today that we are not a defeated people—that you want us to win. It is Your will for us to win and triumph in Christ, Who is our SAVIOUR and brings the sweet SAVOUR of victory in all things. In Jesus' name, amen.

Day 99

"To whom ye forgive any thing, I forgive also: for if I forgave it in the person of Christ: Lest Satan should get an advantage of us: for we are not ignorant of his devices"(2 Corinthians 2:10-11).

No one wants to play a game and have disadvantages against himself. Every one of us want to get every advantage possible in both spiritual and natural things. Unforgiveness is a DISADVANTAGE. It gives SATAN an advantage over you. The scriptures tell us to FORGET what others have done to us and to "press toward the mark for the prize of the high calling of God in Christ Jesus." This is an ADVANTAGE. In the past I have occasionally felt that I had a right to be unforgiving. But one day the Lord said to me, "Unforgiveness is a luxury you can't afford. It is too expensive; it costs you your spiritual advantages."

You will have already formed your victory for the day if you pray this prayer in the early morning, before your day begins: "Father, I forgive all people their trespasses before they EVEN trespass against me."

Dear heavenly Father, with an act of our wills, we forgive those who trespass against us. We forgive with the forgiveness of Jesus. We forgive in the person of Jesus. We do not walk by feelings of forgiveness. We walk by faith and obedience to Your Word, in Jesus' name, amen.

Day 100

"Ye are cursed with a curse: for ye have robbed me, even this whole nation. Bring ye all the tithes into the storehouse, that there may be meat in mine house, and prove me now herewith, saith the Lord of hosts, if I will not open you the windows of heaven, and pour you out a blessing, that there shall not be room enough to receive it" (Malachi 3:9-10).

God tells us exactly how to handle our tithes. We must bring our tithes into a STOREHOUSE. What is a STOREHOUSE? It is a church where there is seed for the sower and bread for the eater. If your church is both feeding you God's Word and sowing seed by sending forth and supporting missionaries, then it is scripturally a storehouse. Your tithe belongs to that storehouse.

If you will be faithful in your tithing, God says there are five blessings He will give you. He will give you "meat" or revelation knowledge. He will open the windows of heaven and pour out blessings to you. He will rebuke the devourer. Other nations shall call you blessed. Your own nation will be blessed (Malachi 3:11-12). Even when I was an unsaved person, I tithed, and God has continually blessed my finances. It is simply the law of sowing and reaping. You can never reap what you do not sow.

Dear heavenly Father, help us to sow our tithes in our local church. Help us to be a blessing to our local church. Help us to support, with prayer and our finances, our local situation. In Jesus' name, amen.

Day 101

"And I heard a voice from heaven saying unto me, Write, Blessed are the dead which die in the Lord from henceforth: Yes, saith the Spirit, that they may rest from their labours; and their works do follow them" (Revelation 14:13).

Sometimes we forget that our labor in the Lord is never in vain. At times it feels as though we aren't producing anything, even though we may be working very hard and endeavoring to believe and trust God.

When I first began to minister, I taught a little Bible study group that seven women attended. It didn't look like much, but gradually those women became Christians and then Spirit-filled. The Bible study program grew, and new groups came forth, until I taught as many as 22 home Bible studies each month. That was some years ago, but those early seeds of labor produced full-time ministries that are very active in God's end-time harvest.

When you sow seed, you have no idea what it is going to produce. Remember that your labor is never in vain; it will go on and on and on. So be encouraged. Don't look at the temporal. Look at the eternal.

Dear heavenly Father, we turn our eyes upward. We choose to believe that everything to which we put our hand will prosper and that You are at work in every circumstance in our lives. In Jesus' name, amen.

Day 102

"Give, and it shall be given unto you; good measure, pressed down, and shaken together, and running over,...For with the same measure that ye mete withal it shall be measured to you again" (Luke 6:38).

I have a lighthearted anecdote for today's scripture. Once I needed some additional dress shoes, but couldn't afford to buy them. So I confessed Luke 6:38 and then gave one of my nicest pairs of shoes to a woman whose shoe size was exactly the same as mine. (This may sound a little trivial—but God provides in all areas of our lives—even shoes!)

During a meeting in Dallas several months later, a young woman walked up to me and remarked that my shoe size seemed to be the same as hers. I looked down at her feet and commented on her beautiful shoes. The next night she gave me those shoes. I was embarrassed because I certainly had not admired them for any mercenary reasons. But she said, "Don't worry. A shoe salesman gives me all his samples in this size."

A month later she mentioned my name to the salesman, and he sent me 23 new pairs of shoes. I know Luke 6:38 works! The measure of shoes I received back was overwhelming.

Dear heavenly Father, help us to confess the law of giving and receiving. If we are abundant givers, certainly we will be abundant receivers. Let us enter a life of generosity and giving, in Jesus' name, amen.

Day 103

"That ye put off concerning the former conversation the old man, which is corrupt according to the deceitful lusts; And be renewed in the spirit of your mind" (Ephesians 4:22-23).

Lust can happen anywhere. You can have a lust for food, sex, money, power, or approval. Any desire that gets out of bounds is a lust. Some Christians try to cover up their lusts. "Well, at least I'm not a drunkard or an adulterer." Any lust can deceive us, but the Word of God and the Holy Spirit will lead you to the truth. Remember the truth will set you free.

The Lord once showed me that I had a tremendous lust for approval. Compliments indicated to me that someone liked me. So I did everything to win approvals. I worked very hard in school and earned good grades. This carried into my Christian life too. I desperately wanted the approval of everyone—when actually the only approval I truly needed was God's. This truth was finally revealed to me through the reading of His Word. The blinders were lifted, and I knew that I would never want or need the approval of any person—not with Christ as my holy Approver.

Dear heavenly Father, help us today to let the Lord renew us in the spirit of our minds. If we have any area of lust that is deceiving us, lift the blinders from our eyes, in Jesus' name, amen.

Day 104

"Let every one that nameth the name of Christ depart from iniquity" (2 Timothy 2:19b).

Sometimes the act of departing from sin seems like an overwhelming mountain, especially if the sin is a habitual thing or exists in a blinded area of our lives.

Some Christians fall into the trap of "grading themselves on the curve." This can be very deceiving. We should never compare the sin in our lives to what we see in the lives of people around us.

The Lord, instead, has shown me there are three easy ways to overcome iniquity. First, we look ahead to what would happen if we were to continue committing this sin. When we look at the ultimate results of sin, we often realize that they are very dangerous.

Secondly, we must look around. God has been so good to us. Look at all of the many blessings He has given us. Start counting blessings. We are complete in Christ. We don't have to be involved in sin. Finally, we need to look within. He Who is in us is greater than he that is in the world. We are vessels to bring glory to God. By looking ahead, looking around, and looking within, we can depart from iniquity.

Dear heavenly Father, help us today to name sin as sin, help us not to grade ourselves on the curve, but by Your Word. Help us to forsake sin and receive Your mercy, in Jesus' name, amen.

Day 105

"Their heart is divided; now shall they be found faulty" (Hosea 10:2a).

a divided heart is a double mind. James tells us that a double-minded man is unstable in all his ways (James 1:8).

When I first investigated the possibility of having a television program, I was told, "Marilyn, you're not television material. You'll never make it. Stick with radio. Forget TV!" But I truly believed that God was directing me toward television. I would not let people discourage me and divide my heart. I remained stable in my desire to bring our program to TV, and today we broadcast on over 40 stations, plus all the TBN affiliates.

Stability is an important element in all areas of our lives. If we are stable in spiritual things, we will excel in spiritual results. If we are stable in natural things, we will excel in natural results. Years ago God showed me that in some areas of my life I was a "yo-yo Christian"—up today and down tomorrow. But I have repented and God has let me excel in many areas. I want always to excel, and I know that you do too.

Dear heavenly Father, help us today to excel in the areas where we have been divided. Thank You that we see the truth: daily stability is what will bring us through. In Jesus' name, amen.

Day 106

"For in that he himself hath suffered being tempted, he is able to succour them that are tempted" (Hebrews 2:18).

Because He Himself was tempted in that which He had suffered, Christ is able "to succour" or come to the aid of others who are tempted.

Do you remember my story of how the Ethiopians confiscated all my video equipment? That second night, when I was locked in my hotel room, a man who worked in the hotel came to me and said, "If you give me money, I can get your video equipment released because I have friends in customs." It was very tempting to me because I felt that the government, the circumstances, and the devil were against me, and I hated to think of losing all that expensive equipment. But I knew that if I tried to take short cuts in order to get God's blessings, then I would lose. God then gave me a scripture to stand fast on so that He could show me great and mighty things.

I did not succumb to the enemy's temptation. The following day God moved upon the hearts of the government officials, and they released the video equipment. God is faithful, and He will give us assistance in the time of our distress.

Dear heavenly Father, help us today not to look at our circumstances as being impossible, but to know that every circumstance has a supernatural key that will unlock it and turn it into a blessing. Amen.

Day 107

"Sanctify yourselves therefore, and be ye holy: for I am the Lord your God" (Leviticus 20:7).

SANCTIFY basically means "to be set apart." We are set apart for God, not for the devil or the world, nor even for ourselves.

A young Christian man once told me that he couldn't read his Bible. I asked him why. He said, "Because the devil won't let me. When I open my Bible, it is as though an evil spirit comes into the room and harasses me, and I can't read my Bible."

"Don't you know," I said, "that you are set apart under God and have authority over the devil?" I gave him the scriptures of authority in Luke 10:19. "Go back to your room and begin to read your Bible. If the devil tries to harass you, tell him to get out, in Jesus' name, that you have been sanctified and set apart, that you have the authority in the name of Jesus."

At dinner that evening the young man told me that when he began to read his Bible, sure enough, the devil tried to harass him. But the man stood his ground and used his authority in Jesus. The devil fled. The devil is dumb; but he is smart enough to fear the name of Jesus.

Dear heavenly Father, we pray today that we will see that we are set apart to bring glory to You. We are set apart to achieve and do great and mighty exploits in Your name. Amen.

Day 108

"(For the weapons of our warfare are not carnal, but mighty through God to the pulling down of strong holds;) Casting down imaginations, and every high thing that exalteth itself against the knowledge of God, and bringing into captivity every thought to the obedience of Christ" (2 Corinthians 10:4-5).

When worldly thoughts become a strong part of us, they can hurt us. On the other hand, we can take God's Word, begin to imagine it, and let it become a stronghold in our thinking.

I have developed a stronghold in my thinking about healing. I have claimed the scripture that Jesus Himself takes our infirmities and by His stripes we are healed. Whenever I feel the symptoms of sickness, I let that scripture become a stronghold, because I know that Jesus carried my diseases for me.

When we take hold of a scripture, we should think it, imagine it, envision it. Let it become a stronghold. Then you can tell the world, "I cast all my cares on the Lord, for He cares for me." God's Word can positively take THE strongest hold in your mind—above anything else! Let's pray:

Dear heavenly Father, we pray that each of us will take a strong hold upon Your Word. Let us know that Your Word is working mightily and powerfully in us and that You are bringing about renewed, refreshed minds which can take hold of God's promises. In Jesus' name, amen.

Day 109

"The Lord God hath given me the tongue of the learned, that I should know how to speak a word in season to him that is weary: he wakeneth morning by morning, he wakeneth my ear to hear as the learned" (Isaiah 50:4).

One of the most encouraging parts of this scripture is where He awakens us "morning by morning...my ear to hear." God doesn't want to throw us a revelation every now and then. He wants to give us a personal revelation every day. He wants to give us daily a hearing ear for what He has to speak to us. For me, early morning is the best time to hear from the Lord. It's scriptural too.

When our alarm goes off at 4:15 a.m., I may inwardly groan. But I have found that when I begin to pray and seek Him, He speaks precious things to me.

One morning I was very discouraged, and I cried out, "Lord, what about these circumstances? They are terrible!" And the Lord said, "Don't you understand? It's CIRCUMSTANCES that I use." He had awakened my ear to hear a word for that day.

Dear heavenly Father, today we ask that You give us hearing ears and seeing eyes to receive the revelation knowledge that You have for us personally this very day, in Jesus' name, amen.

Day 110

"But as many as received him, to them gave he power to become the sons of God, even to them that believe on his name" (John 1:12).

have you ever wanted to become something that you are not? Have you ever said, "If only I could be strong in faith and free from fear. If only I could do certain things." Jesus has given us all power to do and power to become anything that He is—in all our circumstances.

Once I received some heavy criticism from a pastor in our city. I was so angry that I wanted to tell him off immediately. But the Lord said this: "How should you treat your enemies?" I admitted that the Word says we should pray for them, do good to them, and bless them. And God said, "THAT is the very way I want YOU to treat your enemy."

I replied, "That may be the way YOU treat Your enemies. But I can't." He said, "Yes, you can. You have Jesus. You have the power to become like Me."

I began to bless that pastor with my mouth. He later invited me to be a guest speaker in his church. When a man's ways please the Lord, He makes one's enemies to be at peace with him.

Dear heavenly Father, we pray that TODAY we will enter into what You have for us. We will walk in the power and anointing of Jesus Christ. We will know that in us is Jesus—doing all the work. In His name, amen.

Day 111

"Rejoice not against me, O mine enemy: when I fall, I shall arise; when I sit in darkness, the Lord shall be a light unto me" (Micah 7:8).

Have you fallen? This does not mean that you cannot rise. Have you blown it? Have you missed it? This does not mean that God won't give you a second chance—and more!

Some years ago I met a young man who had long desired to be in full-time ministry. He was raised in a Christian home. He had married a wonderful Christian girl. They had a little boy. But when his wife went to work, she became "involved" with her employer, and eventually it destroyed her marriage. She left her husband and took their young son with her.

The young man became so despondent. He said, "How can I ever be used of God? I have a broken home. I do not even have my own son."

One night God spoke to him, "I am a Creator. I have created you, and I can also create new beginnings for you." When we fall, we can rise again. Why? Because God is a Creator of new beginnings.

God will always have new beginnings for you too. All you need to do is to ASK!

Dear heavenly Father, we pray that today You would create, in the name of Jesus, new beginnings for us. We pray that You would bring to pass supernatural beginnings for all of us. We pray that God's glory would reside in us. In Jesus' name, amen.

Day 112

"That I may know him, and the power of his resurrection, and the fellowship of his sufferings, being made conformable unto his death" (Philippians 3:10).

For years I did not understand the part of this verse that speaks of "the fellowship of His sufferings." What does it mean "to fellowship" in His sufferings? I could better understand the "power of His resurrection" than the "fellowship of His sufferings."

Then I began to ask, "Why DID Jesus suffer?" I realized that He suffered for the lost. Jesus suffered to the point that He was willing to die. When we enter into the fellowship of His suffering, we feel the way Jesus felt toward lost souls, and we become willing to die.

Moses was willing to die so that his people might enter the Promised Land. He said to God, "If You're going to erase their names from the book, then you might as well erase mine too." Paul felt it, too, when he said, "I would be accursed that my brethren might be saved" (Romans 9:3).

What were these men feeling? The fellowship of the Lord's suffering. I believe that the Holy Spirit will let us enter into that fellowship of suffering for the lost.

Dear heavenly Father, help us to remember that Jesus suffered to save the lost. Never let us think that we are too "spiritual" to have a burden for the lost. Thank You for helping us, by Your Spirit, to enter the fellowship of the Lord's suffering. In Jesus' name, amen.

Day 113

"Be careful for nothing; but in every thing by prayer and supplication with thanksgiving let your requests be made known unto God" (Philippians 4:6).

"**B**e careful for nothing" means "be anxious for nothing." Instead of feeling anxious about circumstances and situations in our lives, the Bible advises us to "pray about them."

If you are anxious about something, take it to God in prayer. Make your petition known, and then thank God that He is answering your requests. Giving thanks demonstrates that you have faith that He will give you things in line with His Word. Remember to give God thanks on a daily basis.

Sometimes I thank the Lord for answers; yet the problems begin to look worse than ever. However, I do not give up and become discouraged; I continue to give thanks. It seems as though the thanksgiving is the very thing that causes my prayers to rise—just like the leaven in bread causes rising power in the dough.

When you feel anxious, turn your worries into praise and thanksgiving. Let your prayers and praise rise up to heaven, and watch your heavenly Father soothe your anxiety and resolve your cares.

Dear heavenly Father, today we will not be worried and anxious, but we will use our faith and make our supplications with thanksgiving. We expect our needs to be met in You. In Jesus' name, amen.

Day 114

"And be ye kind one to another, tenderhearted, forgiving one another, even as God for Christ's sake hath forgiven you" (Ephesians 4:32).

It is so important for us to live forgiving lifestyles. Forgiveness is not something we use now and then, or when we are in a difficult situation. Forgiveness is a way of life. It is a part of the new nature we receive when we are born again.

At times we may grow impatient with people, but we must remember that we sin daily, and we need forgiveness daily. Others sin daily, and they, too, need forgiveness daily. When we expect to receive God's grace for OUR sins, we must also extend it to others.

What is "living in grace"? It is receiving God's grace and giving it to others. I make it a habit, every morning, to forgive anyone who might offend me during that day. Before anyone can offend me, they are forgiven. Today let's choose to be tenderhearted and to forgive in the name of Jesus.

Dear heavenly Father, we forgive anyone who may offend us today—even before they do it! In Jesus' name, we extend the same grace to others that we have so freely received. Amen.

Day 115

"Let nothing be done through strife or vainglory; but in lowliness of mind let each esteem each other better than themselves" (Philippians 2:3).

Strife is a serious matter. Strife prevented the Israelites from entering the Promised Land. Sometimes we do not see strife as our enemy. We just think that it is a natural reaction. That's right, it is a "natural" reaction, but it is not a SUPERNATURAL reaction.

The Bible gives us a very simple answer of how to avoid strife: we avoid strife by esteeming others above ourselves. When we esteem others above ourselves, we allow a spirit of humbleness to come upon us. We are putting on God's humbleness of mind.

When I esteem my husband above myself, then I don't want to fight with him. I don't want to live in strife; I want to believe God for miracles in my marriage. When I esteem my ministry above myself, I begin to look toward its directions, needs, and goals—not my own. Then I can avoid both strife AND vainglory.

If you will practice Philippians 2:3, you will not live in strife or vainglory, but you will live in victory, love, and edification.

Dear heavenly Father, search our hearts today to see if there are any pockets of strife. Reveal them to us, by the Holy Spirit, and forgive us for them. Today we esteem others better than ourselves. In Jesus' name, amen.

Day 116

"Put on the whole armour of God, that ye may be able to stand against the wiles of the devil" (Ephesians 6:11).

How can we stand against the wiles of the devil if we haven't first put on the whole armor of God? In Ephesians 6 we read about seven pieces of armor. We need each one of them.

Each piece of armor is offensive, not defensive. There is nothing to cover our backs because we can never turn our backs on the devil. We're always to move forward in God!

Our orders are to "occupy" until Jesus comes (Luke 19:13b). OCCUPY is not a passive verb, nor does it denote a defensive position. Rather, it denotes action—an active stance—an offensive maneuver.

Then Ephesians 6:13 says, "Having done all to withstand, stand." When I looked up the word STAND, I found that it means "to stand as a conqueror." We stand as conquerors—soldiers who have already won the battle.

What are our orders from the Lord? First, put on the whole armor of God—be prepared! Second, take the offensive—move forward with God as your Captain! Third, occupy the land—until Jesus comes! Fourth, stand as a conqueror—the battle is won!

Dear heavenly Father, thank You that we are victorious and that we always triumph in Christ. We are not defeated. We are victorious through Your Word and the power of Your Holy Spirit. In Jesus' name, amen.

Day 117

"Behold, happy is the man whom God correcteth: therefore despise not thou the chastening of the Almighty" (Job 5:17).

This scripture is also found in the book of Hebrews. Many times we read it and think, "I don't like chastening." But I believe that this scripture is a "Double-D" verse—we are neither to DESPISE the Lord's correction nor DESPAIR in it.

How does God correct us? He corrects us with His Word—His cleansing agent. Notice that this passage talks about chastening, or correction, by the Almighty. The word ALMIGHTY in the orginal Hebrew is EL SHADDAI. EL SHADDAI means "The God of all sufficiency; the God Who is more than enough."

As El Shaddai, God came to Abraham in the context of total impossibility. God said to Abraham, "I'll give you seed as the dust of the earth." Abraham was 99 years old; Sarah was 89. However, God has the capability of superceding all natural events—He caused Abraham and Sarah to have a child.

When God corrects you, He does it so that He can give you more than you ever expected. Let's receive His chastening with love and be blessed by it.

Dear heavenly Father, we thank You today for Your chastening. Search our hearts and reveal any wicked ways that are hidden within us. We desire to walk in Your light. In Jesus' name, amen.

Day 118

"For the joy of the Lord is your strength" (Nehemiah 8:10).

From the time Wally and I were first married, he has used simple, but scriptural methods in dealing with me.

Whenever I have been depressed about something, he has said, "We're going to sing choruses and worship the Lord."

That used to make me mad, so I'd argue, "I don't feel like singing! If you want to sing, go ahead, but I don't feel like singing."

He would reply, "Yes, you ARE going to sing," and he would MAKE me sing!

As we began to sing choruses, the depression and despair would leave. The heaviness would leave, and the strength of the Lord would come in. Singing was such a simple thing, but it released the joy that gave me, in turn, the strength that I needed. Truly the joy of the Lord is our strength.

The devil would like to steal your joy. If he steals your joy, he steals your strength. Be smart! Abide in an attitude of worship.

Dear heavenly Father, in the name of Jesus, I offer the sacrifice of praise. I will praise You seven times today and thank You that "the joy of the Lord is MY strength." In Jesus' name, amen.

Day 119

"And I was strengthened as the hand of the Lord my God was upon me..." (Ezra 7:28b).

One of the most difficult things a parent can experience is having a runaway teenager. Two teenagers in our youth group once ran away and hitchhiked all the way to New York City. My heart absolutely ached for the two sets of parents. I also felt extreme fear as to what dangers the children could encounter.

When I asked one of the mothers how she was doing, I rather expected her to say, "I'm worried and concerned, but I am trusting the Lord." But she said, "I'm radiant and happy. God's hand is upon me, so I am strengthened." She had more peace than I had, and she was the mother of the girl! I knew that she had experienced the touch of God's supernatural hand.

In the midst of circumstances that threaten to overwhelm us, we need to look for His hand to undergird us—we need His supernatural strength.

Satan may try to ensnare and defeat us, but we know we are overcomers because the Word says, "Greater is He that is in you, than he that is in the world." Let's find assurance in knowing that God will never give us more that we can bear.

Dear heavenly Father, today I ask that Your hand will strengthen each one of us. I pray that we will know Your supernatural power in our being. In Jesus' name, amen.

Day 120

"For the eyes of the Lord run to and fro throughout the whole earth, to shew himself strong in the behalf of them whose heart is perfect toward him" (2 Chronicles 16:9a).

This is one of my favorite scriptures. I have used it many times and have found such strength and refreshing power in it.

Recently I was invited to preach in a church in Mexico. I had taught beginning Spanish over 30 years ago, but I was never really fluent in the language. I recently have had a great desire to preach in Spanish. When I prayed about it, my mind said, "It's too big a task. It's too difficult for you." But in Mexico the words seemed to come to me when I began to translate my sermon into Spanish. I cried out to the Lord, and He helped me minister in a language that I had not used consistently for over 30 years! Thank God, the people could understand my message. Many were saved and Spirit-filled, and God moved in our midst.

God is looking to do something special for those who will reach forth for His supernatural power. He loves it when we reach for big things. After all, He is a BIG God!

Dear heavenly Father, we thank You today that, because You are big, great, mighty, and all-powerful, we can trust in You to perform big things in our lives. In Jesus' name, amen.

Day 121

"For he clave to the Lord, and departed not from following him" (2 Kings 18:6a).

This verse reminds me of Freda Lindsay, who is president of Christ for the Nations. At a very young age, Freda found the Lord. She was never a "yo-yo" Christian—up one day and down the next. From the time she met the Lord, she literally cleaved to Him and did not depart from following Him. She stuck to His Word. In fact, she once told me that she has read through her Bible 52 times!

When Freda's husband Gordon passed away, she took on the awesome reponsibility of directing the school's ministry, even though she felt incapable of the task. God alone gave her the wisdom to guide successfully this international organization.

As Freda shared this information with me, I thought, "So many times we bring forth the fruit that we are." Christ for the Nations is a school where both young and older men and women come forth in the same power of God's Word and Spirit. Like Freda, these people cleave to Him, follow Him, and love Him with all their hearts.

Dear heavenly Father, help us to see today that we do not have to be wavering Christians. We can be committed and solid in You. In Jesus' name, amen.

Day 122

"Why sleep ye? rise and pray, lest ye enter into temptation" (Luke 22:46b).

One time a young man in our Bible school was having a problem with lust. He had come out of the drug culture, where he had a very active sexual life. Then he came to Christ, was born-again and Spirit-filled, and was really eager to serve God. But he found himself slipping back into a physically decadent life.

One day he came to me so honestly and asked for help. I prayed with him and encouraged him to come every morning to our 5 o'clock prayers.

After several weeks of this, he came to me one morning and said, "Marilyn, I'm no longer involved in that relationship. I've broken it off clean and clear." And he told me how the Lord had even removed the desire to live that kind of a life.

Thank God, He is faithful. Many times we try to deal with temptation without praying first, and then temptation overwhelms us. Let us, instead, overwhelm temptation with prayer.

Dear heavenly Father, help us today to be men and women of prayer. Help us to see how important it is to give ourselves to prayer on a daily basis. You have given us the weapons for overcoming. In Jesus' name, we take them, amen.

Day 123

"Behold, I come quickly: hold that fast which thou hast, that no man take thy crown" (Revelation 3:11).

Sometimes we think it's the devil who takes our crown, our spiritual rewards, but basically God is saying in this scripture that it's men who take our crowns. Why can people take from us our spiritual rewards? Because we overreact—emotionally, soulishly, and carnally—to offenses. When we are offended by other Christians, we often let offenses guide our lives. Thus, we react to those offenses in ways that are not led by the Holy Spirit. Then we lose the crowns and rewards offered to us by God.

I have seen people get offended at evangelists who minister healing. These people leave the services and perhaps miss the greatest miracle of their lives. I have seen people get offended at their church and change their membership. They were not led of the Spirit. They were led by their offenses. In fact, an offense is the devil's trap, deliberately laid to make you stumble. Don't let an offense from some man take the reward that God has for you.

Dear heavenly Father, we pray today that You will lift the blinders from our eyes so that we will not be led astray by people offending us. Let us see that this is the devil's trap to keep us from our victories. Thank You, Father, that we are wise Christians in Jesus' name, amen.

Day 124

"And the spirit entered into me when he spake unto me, and set me upon my feet, that I heard him that spake unto me" (Ezekiel 2:2).

When the Spirit enters into you, God wants the Spirit to quicken the Word so that it will put you on your feet. Years ago we went through a difficult trial with some people who had become very offended at various teachings of our church. It appeared that these people's attitudes could bring a great division. My husband Wally began to cry out to the Lord and ask how He would want us to handle this situation, which was very, very serious. God gave my husband the scripture that says no plague shall come nigh our dwelling (Psalm 91:10). Wally began to speak that scripture again and again. No plague was going to come nigh the dwelling place to which God had led us.

What the devil intended for evil actually changed into good because the very people who were most AGAINST us shortly did a turnaround and became the most FOR us. Sometimes I just want to laugh at the devil. Whenever Satan plays his hand, God will turn it around into a miracle for us. When you hit a difficult situation, ask the Lord to lead you to the scriptural truth for that circumstance—He will do it!

Dear heavenly Father, let us realize today that Your Word will put us on our feet and keep us on our feet. Thank You that the Holy Spirit will lead us to the unique Word for our situation, in Jesus' name, amen.

Day 125

"And if a kingdom be divided against itself, that kingdom cannot stand" (Mark 3:24).

Recently I read an account stating that modern-day China is making a shift from strict communism and socialism to the introduction of some capitalism. This encourages me because this shift is bringing a division between China and Russia. The communism that China is practicing today differs from that of Russia. Communism isn't working in Russia, and it hasn't worked in China. In fact, it will not work any place in the world because it is based in atheism—it is anti-Christ, demonic.

When we see Satan raising up a stronghold of his kingdom, we need to ask that confusion would come about and bring division into the situation. When I have occasionally been interrogated by officials in communist countries, I have asked God to bring confusion into the leadership of those who are standing against what God has called me to do. And I have seen God literally bring about confusion and turn the situation around to my favor. God can give us wisdom on how to wreck the devices of the devil.

Dear heavenly Father, today help us, in the name of Jesus, to wreck the devices of the devil. Satan, you are the defeated one. You are not going to divide us— we are going to divide you, in Jesus' name, amen.

Day 126

"Behold, I am the Lord, the God of all flesh: is there any thing too hard for me?" (Jeremiah 32:27).

This is a scripture that not only should we memorize, but also meditate, speak, dream, write, and feed upon. It should be a foundation stone in our lives. There is nothing too difficult for the Lord to do for us.

When we were buying our present church building, no bank would give us a loan. We went every place. We had so little money, and the building we were buying was so expensive. We were warned that if we did not come up with the money by the 31st of December, the price on the building would increase by $160,000.

In September things were looking hopeless. There were about six of us who kept holding steady in God and confessing that nothing was too difficult for Him—even a huge loan. In November two banks finally agreed to give us the loan. We signed on our building December 30, just one day before the deadline. Thank God, there is nothing too difficult for Him. I said to the Lord, "You are never late, but sometimes You are really LAST MINUTE." Last minute or not, what counts is that we win.

Dear heavenly Father, we thank You today that no matter what we face, there is nothing too difficult for You to change into a miracle. Help us always to look personally to You, in Jesus' name, amen.

Day 127

"In the day when I cried thou answeredst me, and strengthenedst me" (Psalm 138:3a).

We all have a tremendous desire to see our loved ones know Jesus. This is probably one of the strongest desires that a Christian can have.

In a crusade in Cincinnati, Ohio, I had gone back to our book-and-tape table to pick up something. A very attractive woman stopped me and said, "You don't know me, but I am related to you." She certainly didn't look like any of my relatives. But then she shared that she was a second cousin to my husband.

The woman had never seen my husband, but she knew other members of his family. She shared how she had been born again and Spirit-filled. I wrote down her name so that I wouldn't forget. When I returned home and shared this with my husband, his heart was warmed. He had been claiming his family continually and felt that he had seen so little. The incident in Cincinnati was like a signpost to him that God's Word was working. It encouraged my husband to believe for the rest of his family.

Dear heavenly Father, don't let us give up on our families. Let us focus our eyes on You and recognize that You will work mighty things. In Jesus' name, amen.

Day 128

"And even to your old age I am he; and even to hoar hairs will I carry you: I have made, and I will bear; even I will carry, and will deliver you" (Isaiah 46:4).

How good God is to carry us! He said that even when we become white-haired, He will carry us and take us through and deliver us. Many people are afraid of old age, but God promises that when you can't carry yourself, He will carry you.

It is interesting to compare the idol worshipers in Isaiah with the worshipers of the living God. The idol worshipers have to carry their own gods and idols. But we never carry our loving Father. He carries us.

How foolish for people to worship an idol—something they must carry themselves! Instead, they could worship our living God, and He will carry them through every situation.

My mother is now in her late seventies. Since I was 19 years old, I've watched the Word of God and the power of the Holy Spirit carry my mother through one circumstance after another. There have been times when nothing else but the Lord could have carried her through, and He has always been faithful. He will be the same for You.

Dear heavenly Father, thank You for taking us through every change in our life, be it age or circumstance. Thank You, Father, that whatever we face, You face it with us and will give us the spiritual and physical strength to come through, amen.

Day 129

"And they went forth, and preached every where, the Lord working with them, and confirming the word with signs following" (Mark 16:20a).

Sometimes when we begin speaking the Word, it doesn't appear as if anything will come forth from it. But God promises that if we preach the Word, He will confirm it. Signs FOLLOW. They don't come BEFORE, and sometimes they don't even come DURING the time we speak the Word.

Once in Charlotte, North Carolina, I asked people with lower-back problems to stand up. Several stood. I remember one woman, in particular, who had come from Iowa. Her spine had been slowly disintegrating, and she was in a great deal of pain. After we prayed, she seemingly had no change. But two weeks later I received a letter in which she said that on the way home from the meeting, she noticed the pain was no longer there. At the next rest stop, she ran into the women's restroom and examined her spine. It was totally normal.

The Word DOES work. Be patient when the signs don't follow immediately. Keep holding onto the promise: Signs must follow!

Dear heavenly Father, help us to know today that our labor in the Lord is never in vain and that when we speak the Word, You will bring forth evidence to show that the Word works, in Jesus' name, amen.

Day 130

"And they that shall be of thee shall build up the old waste places: thou shalt raise up the foundations of many generations; and thou shalt be called, The repairer of the breach, The restorer of paths to dwell in " (Isaiah 58:12).

Whenever I read this scripture, I think of David Sumrall. Many years ago his great-uncle Lester Sumrall began a church in Manila, The Philippines. The church did very well under his leadership. But when he left, it began to go downhill and was filled with strife, confusion, and division.

David Sumrall did not even know his great-uncle. David's family was not Christian. However, one day late in his teens, David found Christ—in a broom closet, of all places! He then went to Bible school, married a young, beautiful woman from Canada, and later felt led to go to the Philippines to pastor Lester Sumrall's church. The congregation grew from 1,000 to nearly 6,000. They are now preparing a building that will seat 10,000.

It looked as though the "place" (Lester Sumrall's church) was laid waste, and that the foundation had crumbled. But God sent someone to repair the breach and make the work greater than it had ever been.

Dear heavenly Father, help us to trust You and to know that when we put things in Your hands, we put them in supernatural hands. Help us to realize that we are FINITE; You are INFINITE. In Jesus' name, amen.

Day 131

"And he shall go before him in the spirit and power of Elias, to turn the hearts of the fathers to the children, and the disobedient to the wisdom of the just; to make ready a people prepared for the Lord" (Luke 1:17).

This scripture has been a prayer on my heart in reference to Happy Church, our church in Denver: I pray that our church will go out in the Spirit of power to turn the hearts of the fathers to the children—the children who are disobedient to the wisdom of God—and to make ready a people prepared for the Lord.

Every weekday early in the morning, I pray and call in the people that should be at Happy Church—from the north, the south, the east, and the west. I call in the regular, the irregular, the lost, the hurt, the backslidden, the wounded, the defeated, the sick, the depressed, the oppressed—so that they can come to Happy Church and be transformed by the Word of the power of His Spirit. We rarely hold a service where we do not see people saved and filled with the Spirit.

People become healed, changed, and transformed because of the wonderful Word of God. I believe Luke 1:17 is a call upon each of our hearts.

Dear heavenly Father, thank You that the harvest is white, that You have sent us to be laborers into that harvest, and that You will divinely enable us to do all that You have called us to do, in Jesus' name, amen.

Day 132

"Thou shalt love thy neighbor as thyself" (Romans 13:9b).

This little verse is extremely powerful. It contains a message that is very important to you and me. We cannot love our neighbor if we do not love ourselves. We often have such a bad self-image! We hate ourselves, and, therefore, we hate our neighbor.

One time when my husband Wally was reviewing his failures with the Lord, God told him, "Stop talking against My servant!" Wally said, "Lord, I am not talking against someone else. I'm talking against me. I'm just telling You how I am." (Satan LOVES to "put us down" and tell us what failures we are. This is all part of his plan as he goes around TRYING to destroy our lives. The devil "puts down," but God "builds up.")

Then the Lord told Wally, "You are My servant. I have bought you with a price. You don't belong to yourself. You belong to Me, and I love you. You are very special and valuable to Me. Never criticize yourself again." My husband repented and realized that if God placed such great esteem and value upon Wally, then Wally must do the same. Remember, God is wild over you!

Dear heavenly Father, thank You for the love of Jesus that is shed bountifully in our hearts by the Holy Spirit. In Jesus' name, amen.

Day 133

"For with God nothing shall be impossible" (Luke 1:37).

This special phrase appears more than one time in the Bible, and it almost always has to do with the birth of a child. All our married life the doctors said that I could never have a child, that it was utterly impossible. But with God all things are possible. Thirteen years after we were married, we miraculously gave birth to a child of our own.

Can you imagine the excitement of Abraham and Sarah when they were told that Sarah would receive the strength to conceive Isaac! When I looked up this word STRENGTH, I found out that in Hebrew the word was DUNAMIS, which means "miracle-working power."

With God nothing is impossible, and even though Abraham and Sarah were "old and well stricken in age," Sarah received her strength and Isaac was born.

The word for POSSIBLE is also DUNAMIS—"miracle-working power." With God there is miracle working power for every "impossible" situation.

Make a vow never again to think or say the word "impossible." Instead, flood your life with God's positive and possible power!

Dear heavenly Father, today we thank You, in the name of Jesus, that the impossible is possible when we put our trust and confidence in You. In Jesus' name, amen.

Day 134

"Is not this the fast that I have chosen? to loose the bands of wickedness, to undo the heavy burdens, and to let the oppressed go free, and that ye break every yoke?" (Isaiah 58:6).

Fasting and prayer break yokes. Once we knew a woman who was having a horrible time with mental harassment. She felt like she was going to have a tremendous nervous breakdown.

She looked in the telephone directory and asked God to lead her to a minister. She was led by the Holy Spirit to call my husband. So my husband and I went over to pray for her.

Little did we dream that the woman was terribly demonically oppressed! We had never seen anything like this, and there were no books available on the subject at that time.

But God gave some scripture to my husband and said, "Some only go by fasting and prayer." Wally told her that we were going to encourage several people in our church to go on a seven-day fast for her healing. After much prayer we rebuked and bound the devil, in the name of Jesus, and the woman was set free.

Fasting and prayer CAN break yokes!

Dear heavenly Father, help us today to live a life of fasting and prayer, not just during crisis times, but weekly let us set aside times to fast and pray. Then we shall see victory in our lives. Amen.

Day 135

"Is it not to deal thy bread to the hungry, and that thou bring the poor that are cast out to thy house? when thou seest the naked, that thou cover him; and that thou hide not thyself from thine own flesh?" (Isaiah 58:7).

Sometimes Christians feel that they are only called to minister to people's SPIRITUAL needs, not their NATURAL needs. But this scripture tells us very plainly that we are to help the poor. James tells us that if we say to the hungry and naked, "Be fed and be clothed," but offer no help, we have only dead faith.

We live in a time when the physical feeding of people can often open the door for spiritual feeding. When I have taken food to Ethiopia, some people have asked me, "How can you feed communist people?" But the Bible tells us that we are to feed our enemies and when our ways please the Lord, He will make our enemies to be at peace with us.

I have found that feeding my enemies with NATURAL BREAD allows God to open the door for me to give them SPIRITUAL BREAD. Our food shipments to Ethiopia have been accompanied by 40,000 Bibles. Today all Christians must be concerned about the spiritually and physically hungry people of the world.

Dear heavenly Father, let us see that we are called to sow good things for the people of the world. And, as You have said, "Blessed are they that sow beside all waters." In Jesus' name, amen.

Day 136

"For the kingdom of God is not meat and drink; but righteousness, and peace, and joy in the Holy Ghost" (Romans 14:17).

When I graduated from college, I was given a beautiful diamond ring, which was an heirloom in our family. When my daughter graduates from college, she will receive the same ring.

When I first began to travel, I put all my jewelry in a small plastic bag in my purse. Once when I went to get my ticket at the airport, I dropped my purse, the little plastic bag broke open, and all of the jewelry rolled out. I could never find that little diamond ring. Finally my flight was called, and it was too late to look any further. I felt so hurried, rushed, and harassed. But in the Holy Spirit there is righteousness, peace, and joy. I chose to take these qualities into my situation. I asked the Lord to send angels to find that ring and bring it back to me.

Six months passed, and the ring wasn't returned. One day my husband opened his jewelry case and asked, "What is your ring doing in my jewelry case?" I said, "My angels brought it back. They just put it in the wrong case."

Dear heavenly Father, we thank You that Jesus did not leave us as orphans. He sent His Holy Spirit, Who gives us joy, peace, and righteousness to take us through this life. In Jesus' precious name, amen.

Day 137

"Let us therefore follow after the things which make for peace, and things wherewith one may edify another" (Romans 14:19).

Sometimes it is difficult for us to follow after peace—especially when people say things to us that are totally against the Bible and the leading of the Holy Spirit. Yet God has called us to follow peace.

God miraculously opened a secular radio interview to me when I was in Mexico. The host, a woman, was not a Christian and had no desire to talk to me about spiritual things. She just wanted to talk about how women could deal with family problems. She opened the conversation with, "Don't you agree that God helps those who help themselves?" I knew that it was a slam against trusting God's Word, yet I also knew that I had to follow after peace.

Here I had an unusual opportunity to witness to thousands of people in Mexico. The Holy Spirit prompted me to say, "Absolutely. I believe that God DOES help those who help themselves. But I also believe that God helps those who CANNOT help themselves." I could sense the Holy Spirit absolutely knocking on the door of that woman's heart. The anointing in that studio filled the airwaves.

Dear heavenly Father, thank You today that the Holy Spirit leads us to peace and edification. In Jesus' name, amen.

Day 138

"When thou passest through the waters, I will be with thee; and through the rivers, they shall not overflow thee: when thou walkest through the fire, thou shalt not be burned; neither shall the flame kindle upon thee" (Isaiah 43:2).

This must have been the scripture that Shadrach, Meshach, and Abed-nego stood on when they were thrown in the burning, fiery furnace. They certainly were not burned, nor did they even have the scent of smoke upon them when they came out. Only the rope that held their hands was burned.

What will bring us through the deep waters? What will bring us through the hottest fires of persecution? It is the One Who brought Shadrach, Meshach, and Abed-nego through the burning, fiery furnace. It is the fourth Man in the furnace—the Son of God. Our Lord Jesus Christ will go through the waters when we go through the waters. He will go through the fire when we go through the fire. We will emerge without being bitter, rejected, or damaged in our personalities—we can come out free. Today, remember, whatever your crisis may be, the fourth One is with you too!

Dear heavenly Father, I thank You today that whatever trial I go through, You are there to go through it with me and You are there to bring me through victoriously. It is always Your will that I triumph in Christ, amen.

Day 139

"Repent ye therefore, and be converted, that your sins may be blotted out, when the times of refreshing shall come from the presence of the Lord" (Acts 3:19).

Repentance brings refreshing. I was 19 years old when my mother received the baptism of the Holy Spirit. I was very "turned off" with both her experience and her Spirit-filled friends. For four years she prayed for me and witnessed to me about the Holy Spirit baptism. Finally I met my husband-to-be, who was Spirit-filled. God had begun to work on my heart.

I spent one entire night in repentance for rejecting such a wonderful gift of God, and I promised that I would participate in the next all-night prayer meeting that our church held. Within four days I had received the baptism of the Holy Spirit. After my repentance came one of the greatest refreshings I had experienced.

The major things that we need in our lives often come only after we have truly repented. Then God can send a refreshing peace to us that truly "passeth all understanding."

Dear heavenly Father, today let us repent of those areas where we have blocked Your flow of refreshing to our lives. Help us not to examine others, but to examine ourselves. In Jesus' name, amen.

Day 140

"Peace I leave with you, my peace I give unto you" (John 14:27a).

In this scripture PEACE means "the act of living life at its best." Jesus gave us peace, a way to live life at its best—something that the world can never give. This peace passes natural understanding.

I'll never forget the night when my father had a heart attack. The doctors worked on my father for several hours, but he finally passed away.

My mother was simply overwhelmed with grief. But I experienced a wonderful, wonderful peace that flooded my heart. I remember thinking several times in the night, "My father isn't really dead. It was just a bad dream." But when I would finally remember, "He really IS dead," the peace of Jesus would fill my heart. I knew, beyond the shadow of a doubt, that my father was in heaven.

Once I asked the Lord about this unusual experience on the night of father's death. He told me, "I let you enter into a small portion of the glory in which your father is now walking."

What is that special peace that God leaves with us? An extension of the peace that exists in heaven.

Dear heavenly Father, we thank You today that we have the peace of Jesus. It passes our understanding of circumstances and of ourselves. It's a peace that knows You rule and reign in our lives and that we can trust You. In Jesus' name, amen.

Day 141

"Put on therefore, as the elect of God"
(Colossians 3:12a).

In the Living Bible this scripture is translated: "Since you have been chosen by God who has given you this new kind of life." It is a new life and creation that is placed in our hearts. It is a new nature that hates the old ways. It is a new nature that loves a totally different lifestyle.

When I became born again, my mother didn't know what to do with me! It seemed as though I was just overwhelmed with love. It was as though I lived in the presence of God's love day and night. I couldn't get into the Bible enough; I couldn't pray enough; I couldn't go to church enough. A whole new thought-pattern and lifestyle had emerged from within me.

At first my mother may have thought that I was on an emotional jag. But then she realized that something very real had happened in my heart. What was this very real thing? It was the "new kind of life." We all need to live in its freshness and not lose our new and special love. Stay in love—in the warm close walk with Jesus.

Dear heavenly Father, in the name of Jesus we just ask today for a particular sweetness in our relationship with You. Let us realize more and more that You love us and that we can live joyously in Your presence. In Jesus' name, amen.

Day 142

"Thou wilt keep him in perfect peace, whose mind is stayed on thee: because he trusteth in thee" (Isaiah 26:3).

Sometimes it is difficult to keep our minds "stayed" on the Lord. When we look at our circumstances and the difficulties around us, it is easy to pick up those difficulties and really fall apart with them. I have sometimes found that I have had to discipline my mind severely. When my soul wanted to worry and worry and worry, my mind would react with fear.

To combat this, I began to memorize certain chapters of the Bible. One time I memorized the book of James. Another time I memorized the book of Matthew. Even another time I memorized the book of Proverbs. Those are some of the sweetest, richest times in my life because I had my mind so filled with the Word. I would go over the scriptures early in the morning, again at noon, and one more time before I went to sleep. My mind became so saturated with the Word that I maintained tremendous peace. Of course, having the Word of God in your heart gives the Holy Spirit the opportunity to bring it to your mind at other times when you need peace.

Dear heavenly Father, help us to take the scriptures so seriously that we don't PLAY with them; we USE them, literally, in our daily walk. In Jesus' name, amen.

Day 143

"I live by the faith of the Son of God, who loved me, and gave himself for me" (Galatians 2:20).

Did you ever try to have faith for someone who just lived "like the devil"? Everything about that person may have spoken rebellion against the truths of God, yourself, and your relationship to God. But I want you to know that we can have faith for those people because of Jesus' faith in us. If we try to have faith on our own, we will be guided by the outward manifestations of sense knowledge. But, with Jesus, we can have faith for all men.

In our church we once had a young teenager who constantly gave us a hard time. She was into the drug scene and all kinds of immorality and said dreadful things against us and the church. But my husband had a living faith for her. Six years passed, and one night Jeri came to our service when my husband was preaching. When Wally gave the altar call, the Lord spoke to her. Later she told us that God said, "If you don't take Me now, I'll never deal with you again." She couldn't get to the altar fast enough. Today Jeri is married to a wonderful Christian and is in full-time ministry.

Dear heavenly Father, we don't live by our own limited faith. We live by the unlimited faith of Jesus Christ: unlimited faith for unlimited circumstances. In Jesus' name, amen.

Day 144

"Order my steps in thy word: and let not any iniquity have dominion over me" (Psalm 119:133).

If we will walk in the Word, sin cannot have dominion over us. It is THAT simple.

Years ago when I began to date a certain man, my mother had a strange feeling about this new boyfriend; she felt there was "something wrong." It seemed at the time that she always found "something wrong" with every boy I had ever dated. But so many times she was right.

I told her, "I don't believe you are right this time." After I had dated the man five or six times, he told me that he was married, but in the process of getting a divorce. As much as I hated to, I finally ended up telling my mother.

She told me, "You know what you must do." I broke up with him; but then after a while, I began to date him again.

She warned me again. I said, "Mother, pray that God will take this man out of my life and bring me the right one."

I never heard from that boy again. We had been dating consistently, but suddenly he never wrote, called, or visited. It was as though he had dropped off the earth. Within three months I had met Wally, who was to become my wonderful husband.

Dear heavenly Father, help us to walk in Your Word and see the importance of it. In Jesus' name, amen.

Day 145

"Every word of God is pure: he is a shield unto them that put their trust in him" (Proverbs 30:5).

Several years ago a family in our church asked me to conduct a funeral for a 21-year-old man who had been born again in our church. His family was very involved in politics, and the funeral was to be held in a very conservative denominational church. I had exactly 15 minutes to speak. I knew that there would be many well-known political people at the funeral and that God had opened a door for me to be a bold witness. God showed me exactly what to share: 2 Corinthians 2:14—that we always triumph in Christ.

Because of the young man's early death, it may have seemed to the world that he had been defeated; but, spiritually, he had triumphed and won. Now he was seated with Jesus Christ in heavenly places.

That day I asked God to be a shield to me and give me favor with that congregation. I opened by saying that this young man had been a winner all his life and had achieved his final triumph by accepting Jesus Christ. Then I invited everyone to become winners with him. Every person in that funeral, including the priest, accepted Jesus as their Savior.

Put your trust in God's Word. It will be your shield.

Dear heavenly Father, today we put our trust in Your Word. It will never let us down. In Jesus' name, amen.

Day 146

"He that loveth his brother abideth in the light" (I John 2:10a).

Have you ever felt heavy, depressed, and "out of it" in your spirit—like everything was dark around you? When I think of depression, I think of darkness.

When I am depressed, I have been asking the Holy Spirit to examine my heart to see what is really behind that depression. I believe that in every circumstance, behind any depression, is some unconfessed sin.

If you have some unresolved sin in your life, it is as though you are walking inside a dark cloud. When you look at life around you, you need to peer through the darkened mist—and everything looks gloomy and depressing.

But if, instead, you walk in the light, you will not be depressed. Jesus tells us that we are the light of the world and that we are to let our light so shine that men will follow our example and glorify our Father in heaven.

Dear heavenly Father, today help us to see that if we have sin in our lives, it is an area of darkness. It keeps us from the light. And when we are "out of it," it's usually related to some area of darkness. Let the Holy Spirit shine His light in those areas and expose the sin so that we might confess it and be free. In Jesus' name, amen.

Day 147

"Then said Jesus...If ye continue in my word, then are ye my disciples indeed" (John 8:31).

When I began my TV broadcasts, I was very conscious of my appearance. I was born in the panhandle of Texas where the water badly stains the enamel of one's teeth. Every time I smiled, those brown stains showed. One man wrote to ask if I chewed tobacco. It was so embarrassing to me. But I found Psalm 37:4, "If you will delight yourself in the Lord, He will give you the desires of your heart."

I claimed that scripture day and night for my teeth. I went to a dentist who told me that it was impossible to remove the stains, but that he could cover them with liquid enamel. That was not what I was believing for, but I thought, "This could be a temporary solution." For five years I had liquid enamel put on my teeth. Then I visited the dentist to have new enamel applied. The dentist quietly scraped off the old and showed me that my teeth were perfectly white! All the stains were gone! Continue in God's Word and receive the fruits!

Dear heavenly Father, we thank You today for helping us to continue in Your Word, be disciples to the Word, and see the provisions You have for Your children. We delight ourselves in You and know that You, in turn, will give us the desires of our hearts. We receive those promises in Jesus' name, amen.

Day 148

"Foolishness is bound in the heart of a child; but the rod of correction shall drive it far from him" (Proverbs 22:15).

For years the world has taught that we should not physically discipline a child. But physical discipline is very needed. The Bible says that it drives away foolishness.

I remember the first spanking I ever received. I was four years old and had walked over to the neighbors—without permission from my mother. It was near Christmastime, and the neighbors had decorated apples to resemble Santa Clauses. When I visited that day, I was given one of those apples. I was so excited! It was really quite a sensational treat for a four-year-old. When I walked into our backyard, my mother was standing there waiting for me. Her hands were behind her, and I somehow knew what was in her hand: a cottonwood switch.

She switched my legs with that cottonwood branch. It so hurt, and I cried, but I learned a lesson. I don't ever remember running away again. My Santa Claus apple didn't taste very good to me, but the discipline had driven foolishness from my heart.

Dear heavenly Father, help us today to know that correction is so necessary. Help us to see that biblical ways are what bring biblical results. In Jesus' name, amen.

Day 149

"And they were all filled with the Holy Ghost, and they spake the word of God with boldness" (Acts 4:31b).

There is no question that the Holy Spirit gives you boldness! He gives you boldness in heaven with God, on earth with men, and in hell with the devil.

I'll never forget the first time I met Dr. Paul Yonggi Cho. I was so impressed with the boldness of his faith. I knew that he came to the states twice a year to meet with his Board of Directors, so I claimed that God would make a way for me to be on that board. I became bold with God and even called one of Cho's board members to ask if he thought it were possible for me to get on that board. He asked the men on the board, and they said, "No." But boldness doesn't let you give up.

I continued to pray and believe that Dr. Cho would personally ask me to be on his board. About six months later I received a cablegram asking me to pray about becoming a part of his television board. I quickly replied, "I don't need to pray. Of course, I will accept a position on the board." Only the Holy Spirit can give you boldness to receive the things that God wants you to have.

Dear heavenly Father, let us know the boldness that the Holy Spirit has for us today. Help us, by the power of the Spirit, to be bold in heaven, on earth, and against the powers of hell. Amen.

Day 150

"Which doeth great things past finding out; yea, and wonders without number" (Job 9:10).

In my younger years I was a schoolteacher. I had worked my way through college with the help of two scholarships and various part-time jobs. My home was not Christian, nor did I ever have the opportunity to go to Bible school. I never envisioned that I would be in full-time ministry. I also would never have guessed that God's work could make me so happy and fulfilled. I can say, as Job did, "His wonders are without number."

Remember, Job wrote this before he received his double portion. We need to confess our faith before we see the manifestations. After we have seen them, we are no longer in faith, we are in "sense" knowledge. I believe that I have seen only a few wonders compared to the numbers of miracles that God is going to bring to pass in the future. I believe that I will see people raised from the dead, wheelchairs emptied, and nations shaken by the power of the Word of God. Let's pray for wonders "without number."

Dear heavenly Father, we pray that everyone will look to You and believe that You are a supernatural God Who will do beyond what anyone can imagine. We thank You that You answer our prayers, beyond all expectation! Amen.

Day 151

"Let your speech be alway with grace, seasoned with salt, that ye may know how ye ought to answer every man" (Colossians 4:6).

Jesus said we are the salt of the earth—SALT, "a preservative, a seasoning," is the sealer of the covenant in the Old Testament. We are to be God's salt of the earth through His Word.

Once I sat on a plane next to a man who said he was an "intellectual." He didn't believe in the Bible, but in parapsychology. He told me his mother had just died of a malignant breast tumor. God showed me how to shake a little salt on him. I told him my mother had had a malignant breast tumor, but was healed. Her only treatment had been over 20 years ago, and today she is well and healthy. He quickly replied, "Prayer is just mind-over-matter." I said, "You are an intellectual. Do you think I am?"

He said, "Oh no, you only believe in the Bible."

I said, "Isn't it strange then, if healing is mind-over-matter, that your mother is dead. My mother is living, and I am not the intellectual." It was as though God's Word had slapped him and "seasoned" him. Before we landed, he agreed to invite Jesus Christ into his heart.

Dear heavenly Father, as Christians, we need to make our words salty; help us to have our "salt-shakers" full of God's Word so that we can shake out salt to thirsty people wherever we go. In Jesus' name, amen.

Day 152

"And they that are Christ's have crucified the flesh with the affections and lusts" (Galatians 5:24).

I will never forget a statement that Kathryn Kuhlman once made in a Full Gospel Businessmen's dinner in Denver, Colorado. It was the first time that I had ever heard her preach. I'll never forget the dramatic way she greeted the audience. She took a glass, poured out the water, and wiped it clean. She said, "This is what the Lord wants us to be: wiped clean of every hindrance from our old life so that He might fill us anew with Himself."

Kathryn Kuhlman had a past "hindrance" of her own. She had run away with a married man (an evangelist), broken up his home, and married him. Later she had left him and reentered the ministry. There was much local criticism about her, but she faced it in the power of Jesus Christ. She said, "That 'Kathryn Kuhlman' is dead. This is the new Kathryn Kuhlman. The old has been emptied from that glass, and the new has filled it."

We must recognize that our past has been nailed to the cross. We must leave it there, reckon ourselves dead unto past sin, and become alive unto God!

Dear heavenly Father, today we reckon ourselves dead unto sin and alive in You. We forget those things that are behind and reach forth for those things that are ahead. In Jesus' name, amen.

Day 153

"That I may be comforted together with you by the mutual faith both of you and me" (Romans 1:12b).

*G*reat strength abounds in mutual faith. As you know, several doctors told my husband and me that it would be impossible for us to have a baby.

After we had been married for three years, the Holy Spirit began to deal with Wally about his calling to enter full-time ministry. After Wally finally made that commitment, we went to a Voice of Healing convention in Dallas, Texas. While we were there, an evangelist had this word of knowledge for me: "You are not from here; you are from a wooded area of Denver, Colorado. You have a female condition and have been unable to have a child. Go home and receive your baby." We then believed that we would have that baby during that very same year.

But it was to be 10 years later before our daughter Sarah was born. During that time my faith sometimes wavered, but my husband's faith was ever stable. Mutual faith will bring forth the provision of God's Word. Get people to stand with you in faith. It will help you when the devil tries to steal it from you.

Dear Father, help us to see the strength of mutual faith. Help us to see the strength of mutual love, which, as we stand fast in the Word, will bring forth the supernatural. In Jesus' name, amen.

Day 154

"He sent his word, and healed them, and delivered them from their destructions" (Psalm 107:20).

I think I have used this scripture more than anyone else in the world. I have prayed it for literally thousands of people who did not live in my area or could not come to a meeting where I was speaking. God's Word will prosper and accomplish that which it is sent to do. It is the fastest means of transportation and will do the best job.

Years ago a staff member told me about her husband's horrendous back problem. I was unable to go lay hands upon him, and he was unable to come to church. So I prayed Psalm 107:20 and sent the Word to his back.

Early the next morning I had to call his wife concerning another situation, and he answered the phone. He said, "The most unusual thing happened to me yesterday. Something clicked in my back while I was working. It totally went into place; I was healed. And I slept like a baby all night." I asked him at what time he was healed, and it was at the same time I had sent Psalm 107:20 to him. God's Word will go where you cannot.

Dear heavenly Father, we send Your Word into our circumstances and those of others. We claim triumph in our lives today. In Jesus' name, amen.

Day 155

"They soon forget his works; they waited not for his counsel" (Psalm 106:13).

Sometimes it takes time to receive the counsel we need. When we make hasty decisions, we can miss God's counsel for us. Then we may do something very carnal that blows our opportunity for a God-given miracle.

I'm reminded of King Saul. In the early part of his kingship, he had to fight the Philistines. Saul became impatient as he waited for Samuel to arrive and pray for the battle. The people began to pressure Saul, so he took the place of the priest and offered the sacrifice himself. That sin led to other weaknesses in Saul. Finally he lost his entire kingdom. If Saul had only waited a few more hours, Samuel would have arrived and the requirements of the Lord would have been met. And Saul, instead of being a defeated man, could have been a victorious king.

There are times of my life when I have run ahead of the Lord—often because people pressured me—and I did not wait for God's counsel. Sometimes we think that God is so slow; but really, He is always on time—His time! Let's time our timing with His and wait until we get a word from Him before we move. Then we will have the results that we desire.

Dear heavenly Father, help us to know how to wait on Your counsel. Give us hearing ears and seeing eyes today for what You have for us. In Jesus' name, amen.

Day 156

"For sin shall not have dominion over you: for ye are not under the law, but under grace" (Romans 6:14).

The devil will do his best to convince you that sin has dominion over you. But the Bible says that grace has dominion over you.

A dear pastor friend had been an alcoholic in his past. Two years after he was born again, he was tempted by Satan to take a drink. When he did, he became hopelessly drunk and fell into terrible despair. He felt so condemned that he said, "There is no hope for me. Sin has totally taken over." He decided to take his life because the devil told him that there was no hope. The devil told him that the sin of alcoholism would always have dominion over him. But, thank God, another pastor cursed this work of the devil and strengthened our dear friend's heart in the Word of God. Our friend was set free.

This happened many years ago. But even today, when you talk to this man, he will tell you again and again about the power of grace. We need to know Who Jesus is in us—that He Who is in us is greater that he who is in the world.

Dear heavenly Father, we thank You today that sin does not have dominion over us. We choose, instead, for Your grace to have dominion over us. In Jesus' name, amen.

Day 157

"Touch not mine anointed, and do my prophets no harm" (Psalm 105:15b).

If you read this verse in context, you discover that the "anointed," about whom it speaks, is Sarah. I think that's very interesting because many times we, as women, feel that because we are women, the anointing upon us will not be received by others. Because of these feelings we do not allow God's Word to prevail in our lives. We begin to kick down doors to get them open for us, and soon we are fighting big battles of rejection and really causing more harm than blessing.

Many times I am questioned about how difficult it must be to be a woman in the ministry. I have never found it difficult. Never! If God calls you, it's His responsibility to put you over. God doesn't make mistakes in the people WHOM He calls, so He doesn't make mistakes in HOW He puts them over. It's not our business to fight for our position; it's our business to obey His calling. "For the gifts and the calling of God are without repentance" (Romans 11:29).

If a woman is truly anointed by God for the ministry, He will protect her from all dissension and harm and lead her in His paths.

Dear heavenly Father, help us to see today that we don't have to kick down doors. We don't have to slam people around to get our way. You will put us over by Your anointing. In Jesus' name, amen.

Day 158

"For to be carnally minded is death; but to be spiritually minded is life and peace" (Romans 8:6).

What is a carnal mind? Basically, it is being double-minded. A double-minded person says that God's Word is true, then acts as though it weren't. A single-minded person would, instead, say, "The Word says it, so I believe it, and that settles it!"

Years ago I was scheduled to speak at a large convention in New York state. My ministry was experiencing a very difficult financial trial. When I arrived, the pastor asked if I would take the offering that night. I asked him how much he was praying for, so that I could join my faith with his. He told me that his budget was $15,000, but he was believing for $4-5,000. I began to pray, and the Lord said, "I want you to believe for the whole budget of $15,000." I fell apart inside and said, "God, how can you ask this of me?" I had suddenly became double-minded and experienced terrible fear.

The Lord spoke to my heart, "Thy God whom thou servest continually shall deliver thee" (Daniel 6:16). I knew that not only would MY financial need be met, but also the need of the pastor's budget. His offering totaled almost $16,000.

Dear heavenly Father, help us to keep our mind stayed on You. In Jesus' name, amen.

Day 159

"That your faith should not stand in the wisdom of men, but in the power of God" (I Corinthians 2:5a).

In 1983 I felt led of the Holy Spirit to do a live satellite service from Cairo, Egypt. When we got to Cairo, the Egyptian government began to harass us. The American embassy told me, "The Egyptian government would never allow you to air a Christian program because Egypt is a Moslem country."

If God leads us to do something, we must put our faith in His wisdom. I kept speaking my faith, although everything looked doubtful. Finally some leaders of the Egyptian government came to me and said, "We will let you go on, but you have to promise that you will not use the words "Moslem" or "convert." If you do, we will put you in jail for four months." I promised that I would not use these two words; however, I did not promise that I wouldn't use the phrase "born again."

The very day of the satellite program, I was invited to the home of Mrs. Anwar Sadat for an hour-long visit. Additionally, many thousands of Arabic Bibles were placed in Moslem countries. God did more than what I had asked. Man's wisdom will fail, but the power of God will never fail.

Dear heavenly Father, give us Your wisdom and power. We know, in faith, that when You call, You will provide the means. In Jesus' name, amen.

Day 160

"Not forsaking the assembling of ourselves together, as the manner of some is; but exhorting one another: and so much the more, as ye see the day approaching" (Hebrews 10:25).

*T*oday many people have a very loose, undisciplined attitude toward church attendance and commitment. We once had a church member who went to the mountains every summer for three months. He never darkened the door of a church during that time. He would always say to me, " Well, we're going to worship God in nature. We don't need the church. We have the mountains."

Once when he said this, the Lord gave me an answer. I said, "When you go to worship God in nature, remember: when you get in trouble—don't call on the church for help. Be sure you call on the mountains and let THEM help you." His face dropped when I spoke those words, and perhaps they sounded very harsh. But it was as though a veil were lifted from his eyes. That summer his family started to attend a small church in the mountain community.

Keep active in a local church. Without it, you will never receive the maturing that you should have.

Dear heavenly Father, help us to stop being critical of churches and, instead, to become involved. You've called us to assemble together and be part of a local church body. It is Your plan, and it will bless us if we will be faithful and loyal to it. In Jesus' name, amen.

Day 161

"Enter into his gates with thanksgiving, and into his courts with praise: be thankful unto him, and bless his name" (Psalm 100:4).

God has often dealt with me about the act of thanksgiving. There is power in the giving of thanks. In the Old Testament there was a special offering just for thanksgiving. The New Testament says that when we pray, we are to do so with thanksgiving. We are to thank God for our food. Then our blessings will be sanctified and set apart for us.

Thanksgiving is like yeast: Thanksgiving causes your requests to rise with faith into the presence of God, just as yeast causes bread to rise. The Word teaches that if you are not thankful for the things that God does, He will take away what He has given you.

Of the ten lepers, nine never gave thanks to Jesus. Only one returned to thank Him. I believe that because that one leper gave thanks, he received SPIRITUAL wholeness, as well as PHYSICAL wholeness. Thanksgiving also will help you to be whole—physically, emotionally, and spiritually.

Dear heavenly Father, help us to live in an attitude of thanksgiving. When we give You our praise and thanks, we know that You will bless us in body, soul and Spirit. Thank You for all the good things that You do. In Jesus' name, amen.

Day 162

"Upon the first day of the week let every one of you lay by him in store, as God hath prospered him" (I Corinthians 16:2a).

Many people feel that tithing is not for today, but only a principle of the old law. Abraham was the first man to tithe. He was called the "friend of God," and he lived before the law had even been established. We are the seed of Abraham, and we, also, will be blessed as we tithe. It is true that tithing was taught in the law. But Jesus and the book of Hebrews taught tithing too.

I have found that tithing brings God's blessings. When I was 11 years old, I babysat and sold apples at an apple stand. My mother taught me that I should tithe. I was not even a born-again Christian at that time, but I tithed faithfully in our little Methodist church. Tithing has been a part of my life since that time. God has blessed and prospered me throughout the years. When people tell me that I shouldn't tithe, I always tell them, "You have reached me too late. I've tithed for years, and it has blessed and prospered my life."

Dear heavenly Father, help us to see that we prosper when we obey Your Word. When we reason away Your Word, we cause the curse to come upon us. We choose, instead, to be blessed by obeying Your Word and by tithing. In Jesus' name, amen.

Day 163

"For God,...hath shined in our hearts, to give the light of the knowledge of the glory of God in the face of Jesus Christ" (2 Corinthians 4:6).

Sometimes when we are in a dark situation, we forget to look for the light of the knowledge of Jesus Christ. All the wisdom of God is hidden in Jesus. When we move in God's wisdom, we will bring forth His glory.

At times, I have been uncertain as to how to witness to people whose lives seem to be full of darkness. On vacation some years ago in Santa Fe, New Mexico, we went into a restaurant, and a group of Hari Krishas was sitting at a large table. We could feel the darkness of those people's cultish worship. God told me, "Go over and witness at that table."

I said, "Lord, they will overwhelm me."

But the Lord answered, "It is impossible for darkness to overwhelm light. Light is greater than darkness." The light of one believer is greater than ten people's darkness.

Dear heavenly Father, help us to look for light in Jesus. Help us to know that His light is greater than any darkness that is surrounding us. In Jesus' name, amen.

Day 164

"For what is your life? It is even a vapour, that appeareth for a little time, and then vanisheth away" (James 4:14b).

We never think about how brief our lives are until we begin to hit middle age. When I was young, I probably thought that I'd live almost forever. As I became older, I began to realize that life is brief and I needed to achieve what God has set before me.

Several years ago God told me to set aside some time so that He could speak to me about the future. I knew that I could spend the rest of my life doing good things, yet somehow miss His very best. I asked God to reveal what His REAL goal was for my life.

I knew that I had an allotted number of years and that I should plan my time well so that I could accomplish His perfect will. At that time He showed me that His call for me was to cover the earth with His Word. He gave me Isaiah 11:9, which says that God's Word should cover the earth like the waters cover the sea. Little did I dream how that could be done, but He has shown me, piece by piece, just like a puzzle, many wonderful and creative ways to spread His Word.

Dear heavenly Father, today help us realize that life is brief and that there is a divine plan and purpose for our lives. We must know, from You, what that divine plan is. In Jesus' name, amen.

Day 165

"But strong meat belongeth to them that are of full age, even those who by reason of use have their senses exercised to discern both good and evil" (Hebrews 5:14).

We all desire strong meat from God's Word. We want to have a spirit of might. Hebrews 5:14 shows us very clearly that strong meat belongs to those who use their senses to discern between good and evil.

When we first started our church, some very flaky people attended our services. We had people who prophesied falsely and believed in strange doctrines. People from cults attended our services. We were tested in every area. One day I cried out to the Lord, "I'm tired of pastoring. This is so difficult when so many unusual things happen in our church."

The Lord said to me, "Through use, your senses are exercised so that you can discern what is good and what is evil. You are pastoring a church, and you need to know what is good and evil for your people. Your experiences are preparing you for the strong meat of My Word to feed My sheep." It was greatly encouraging, and, of course, God brought us through that testing period.

Dear heavenly Father, help us to know that our experiences can give us the ability to discern between good and evil. Teach us to discern between God's truth and the works of the devil and the flesh. In Jesus' name, amen.

Day 166

"For the Lord God is a sun and shield: the Lord will give grace and glory: no good thing will he withhold from them that walk uprightly" (Psalm 84:11).

It is so easy to be trapped by offenses—those deliberately laid traps designed by Satan to keep us from walking uprightly and receiving miracles. We can choose whether we will accept the offense—or the miracle.

One Sunday a friend of mine entered her church and went to her customary seat. But the usher rudely told her to sit elsewhere because "more important" people needed the seat. My friend found another seat, but inside she was feeling very angry and offended.

The Lord dealt with her, "I have good things—a miracle—waiting for you, but if you choose to be offended, you will miss out." She replied, "God, I'll take Your miracle."

At the end of the service, the pastor invited my friend forward to share information about her program of Bible studies. He had never before done this; it was truly an unexpected miracle—over 5,000 people learned of her ministry!

Dear heavenly Father, today we thank You for loading us with benefits. We know that it is Your desire to pour out miracles upon Your children. We claim those good things, in Jesus' name. Amen.

Day 167

"But the wisdom that is from above is first pure, then peaceable, gentle, and easy to be intreated, full of mercy and good fruits, without partiality, and without hypocrisy" (James 3:17).

James 3 shows the difference between godly wisdom and natural, earthly wisdom. I have used this distinction to determine whether I am hearing from the Lord or from my own personal soul. Is it a decision full of mercy? Will it bring forth good fruit, or will it bring confusion to the body? If it will bring confusion or if it's not merciful, then it must not be God's wisdom. If it's not gentle or open to reason, it must not be God's wisdom.

My number-one daily prayer is that I would be saturated with the wisdom of God because of the many decisions our ministry faces. Nine years ago God dealt with me about doing a Bible reading plan. At that time the ministry was very small, and we didn't have the money for startup costs. Yet I felt a gentle "tugging" of the Holy Spirit. Getting people involved in the Word was certainly God's mercy. Certainly it would bring forth good fruit. I made the decision, and God paid the bills. Cry out for wisdom. He will give it to you.

Dear heavenly Father, we ask to be full of Your wisdom for this day. Let us recognize that which is pure, peaceable, and gentle—that which is full of mercy and good fruits. In Jesus' name, amen.

Day 168

"Go ye therefore, and teach all nations" (Matthew 28:19).

Jesus knew that one of our greatest joys in life would be that of seeing new disciples coming forth from our witnessing, prayers, and ministry. The world has a saying that goes, "There is no success without successors."

Sometimes the disciples who have come forth from our ministries can be very surprising! When our church was very young and small, we had in our Sunday school a young man who caused all kinds of problems. Every teacher dreaded having him. He once drew a knife on one of the teachers. Then at 16 he ran away from home and became involved in the drug scene. He stayed away from home for two years, but finally came home, gave his heart to Jesus, was Spirit-filled, went to Bible school, and is now a missionary.

Every time I think about that young man, I say, "Here is a wonderful disciple for Jesus. Here is true success for our ministry because here is a beautiful successor of Christ and His teachings."

Dear heavenly Father, help us to see people for what they can be, not what they are at the present moment. Help us to see that no person is impossible for You to make Your disciple. In Jesus' name, amen.

Day 169

"Cast me not off in the time of old age; forsake me not when my strength faileth" (Psalm 71:9).

God is not making reTIREment plans for His people. He is making "reFIREment" plans for them. He does not want us going backward because of age; He wants us always to be moving forward.

One of America's faults today is that it has become a "throw-away" culture. Is something a little worn? "THROW IT AWAY!" Unfortunately, we sometimes treat our elderly in a similar fashion. So you've worked 50 years and raised a family? "Well, goodbye. It's time for the old age home." That's not God's way. In the Bible a person was valued for his wisdom and walk with the Lord.

When I see people like Freda Lindsay absolutely supercharging the world with her Christ For The Nations School; Drs. T.L. and Daisy Osborn conducting crusades and institutes in over 70 nations; Charles and Frances Hunter, with a combined age of 134 years, conducting Healing Explosions across America, I realize that age is not important. God's Holy Spirit is in us and the anointing of God is upon the lives of His servants. His Spirit is an eternal Spirit Who keeps us young.

Dear heavenly Father, help us today not to dread old age. Let us not be making retirement plans, but making plans to "refire" in Jesus. Amen.

Day 170

"Let my mouth be filled with thy praise and with thy honour all the day" (Psalm 71:8).

One summer we vacationed in Guanajuato, Mexico, a beautiful colonial city. On the day we arrived, we decided to take a trip to the market where the fruit, vegetables, and all the local culture could be seen.

I felt dirty from our long bus ride, so I told my husband, "I'm going to wash my hair and go down to the market with my hair wet. No one I know will see me."

We were wandering around the marketplace when a teenage girl from our church walked up to us! She had volunteered her summer vacation to work in a small village—and wound up digging latrines!

The girl said she had been extremely homesick and longed for a familiar face from home. Her mother had prayed that we would run into her, and God made the necessary arrangements. It was truly a miracle!

Praise the Lord daily. If He will go to great lengths for one homesick teenager, who knows what a good thing He has in store for you!

Dear heavenly Father, we thank You that today is the best day of our lives. We thank You for loading us with benefits. In Jesus' name, amen.

Day 171

"Walk in the Spirit, and ye shall not fulfil the lust of the flesh" (Galatians 5:16).

Walking in the Spirit is not the only time when we should feel spiritual. Many times we feel spiritual by committing our way to His hands and knowing that He will guide our steps.

One time I was sitting on a plane going from North Dakota to Minneapolis. The man next to me had unusual mannerisms and a strong accent. I realized that he was a Moslem, and I felt very strongly that God wanted me to witness to him. I asked, "Where are you from?" He said that he was from Amman, Jordan. We began to visit.

When I told him that I was a pastor's wife, he began to attack Christianity with everything he had. At first I just wanted to avoid him and even change seats. But God dealt with me to return the attack with the power of the Word and in a spirit of love. We got into a very, very heated conversation about the Word.

I had a small ring in my purse. God told me to give the ring to the man as a gift for his wife. When I did, the man almost broke down and wept. Our time together was very rich. The outcome was very amazing to me, and I'm sure that it was amazing to him also.

Dear heavenly Father, help us today to know that walking in the Spirit is trusting You, walking in Your Word, and letting You direct all that we say and do. In Jesus' name, amen.

Day 172

"My sheep hear my voice, and I know them, and they follow me. And I give unto them eternal life; and they shall never perish, neither shall any man pluck them out of my hand" (John 10:27,28).

God does not play "hide and seek" with us. He wants us to know His voice. Some people make understanding God's Word sound so difficult. They think that it takes years of fasting and prayer to make the smallest Word-directed decision. But Jesus promises us that, as His sheep, we will hear His voice and not follow the voice of a stranger. When we see Jesus calling men by name before they know Him, we realize how well the Good Shepherd knows each one of His sheep. He calls them by name, and they follow.

How can we hear Christ's call? Many of us often hear Him through an inner voice. God's inner voice came to Elijah when he got in trouble and ran from Jezebel. God took Elijah to a cave and let him hear the thunder and the shaking of the earth. Then Elijah heard and heeded—not the outward, tremendous manifestations—but a small, quiet inner voice.

Dear heavenly Father, help us to listen to Your voice, and to learn and know You so intimately and so well that we can recognize Your divine intentions. Help us to live not in the reasoning of our head, but in the perception of our spirit. In Jesus' name, amen.

Day 173

"And they overcame him by the blood of the Lamb, and by the word of their testimony" (Revelation 12:11a).

The book of Revelation makes tremendous promises to those who are overcomers. Revelation 12:11a tells us very simply how to gain the promises: through the blood of Jesus. When we speak God's promises to our circumstances, to ourselves, or about the devil, we literally overcome whatever problems we are experiencing.

The paralyzed man at the pool of Bethesda was a real "overcomer." After waiting 38 years for his healing, the man one day met Jesus, Who told him to "rise." Jesus challenged what seemed impossible. The man rose up, took his bed, and walked.

Many times I have had to speak the Word to overcome fear. I had to tell my mind, "You're not going to be in fear. You are going to trust the Lord."

David spoke to his soul. When the devil attacked David's mind, he told it to get in line with God's Word. Speak God's Word to your mind too.

Dear heavenly Father, today we thank You for the blood of Jesus. We choose to take the Word because it will grow and prevail in any circumstance or situation we face. In Jesus' name, amen.

Day 174

"For I the Lord thy God will hold thy right hand, saying unto thee, Fear not; I will help thee" (Isaiah 41:13).

The right hand has always been the hand that denoted power. When Jesus sat down, He sat down at the right hand of God. Jesus held the seven stars in His right hand. He held the book in Revelation in His right hand. The antichrist said that he would put a mark in the right hand of those who belonged to him. When Jacob put his right hand on Ephraim's head, this indicated that Ephraim would have more power than Manasseh.

Proverbs speaks of wisdom's qualities: "Length of days is in her right hand; and in her left hand are riches and honor" (Proverbs 3:16). If we seek wisdom, we'll have length of days for enjoying the riches and honor.

The Lord promises that He will hold your right hand so you can be empowered for action. At His right hand are pleasures forevermore. We believers shall lay hands on the sick because our hands are to be full of God's healing power. Everything our hands touch will prosper because of His power flowing through us.

Dear heavenly Father, help us today to know Your power, experience Your strength, and receive Your help as it flows through us to others that they might be healed. In Jesus' name, amen.

Day 175

"For therein is the righteousness of God revealed from faith to faith: as it is written, The just shall live by faith" (Romans 1:17).

In 1981 we had the opportunity to visit Turkey. On a brief trip to Istanbul, we stayed with a missionary who had undertaken the translation of the New Testament into the modern-day Turkish language. This task put him in the precarious position where he could have been easily exiled from this Moslem country.

Sometimes we Americans can forget how fortunate we are to live in a country that allows freedom of religious expression. In many parts of the world Bibles are few, and owning one may even be against the law. In some countries Christian gatherings, even as small as two or three people, may be viewed with suspicion or considered illegal.

Yet even in these restricted conditions, there are still people who "live by faith"—through God and His precious Word. Always there will be brave people like this Turkish man who was willing to risk his citizenship in order to bring the Word of God to the people of his country—in their own native tongue!

Dear heavenly Father, we know that we must live by faith. If we lived by our senses during this day, we would feel so defeated. But if we live by Your Word, it will grow and prevail in every situation and circumstance. We choose to live by Your Word today. Amen.

Day 176

"Give us help from trouble: for vain is the help of man. Through God we shall do valiantly: for he IT IS THAT shall tread down our enemies"
(Psalm 60:11,12).

A young woman in our congregation once received a very obscene phone call. As the filthy words and garbled speech came over the line, she was overwhelmed with fear and nauseous with disgust.

The Lord really dealt with her and said, "Give this man light to overcome that evil darkness, and you will give him back his life!"

So she began to tell the man how much Jesus loved him. When the man started to speak more filthy words, she begin to pray in the Spirit. Soon the man broke down and wept.

The woman continued to pray with the man. He promised that he would read the Word, AND he never called her again. This woman had been hit with trouble, but she looked to the Lord. And He did truly tread down her enemy!

Dear heavenly Father, thank You that we can trust You today. People may let us down, and we may let ourselves down, but You will never let us down. Today, through You, we shall do valiantly. You will tread down our enemies; we don't have to tread them down. In Jesus' name, amen.

Day 177

"Having every one of them harps, and golden vials full of odours, which are the prayers of saints" (Revelation 5:8b).

Our prayers are very important to God. But if we really want our prayers to count, we must pray the Word. Why? Because the Word cannot return void.

Prayers of self-pity will never bring supernatural results. It's only when we pray God's Word that we begin to fill up the golden vials of heaven. God keeps those prayers because He keeps His Word. Answers will come. Pity-parties are not the answer. God's Word will bring the supernatural.

When we send our prayers to God, we must also check our hearts to see if there is spiritual "static" that will prevent our prayers from traveling up to heaven. Our messages to God can get lost or waylaid if we have some unconfessed sin. If your prayers are going unanswered, check your heart to see if you are harboring sin. If so, repent, and watch your prayer wing its way to heaven.

Dear heavenly Father, today help us to see that self-pity never does anything. It is unbelief, and it is simply an occasion for the flesh to exalt itself. We trust in Your promises. We put our flesh down and stand fast on Your Word. In Jesus' name, amen.

Day 178

"What time I am afraid, I will trust in thee....in God have I put my trust; I will not fear what flesh can do unto me" (Psalm 56:3,4b).

Fear is a terrible thing, for it is the opposite of faith. Fear caused Adam and Eve to sin. I believe that fear is not only a sin, but it is THE SOURCE of all sin.

The devil loves to confuse people and ensnare them in all sorts of traps. When Satan discovers what our greatest fears are, he immediately uses those fears to trap our minds and prevent us from overcoming frightening situations.

When we fall into Satan's trap, we are tricked into playing his game. And whenever we play games with the devil, we are committing a sin that can lead to even more sin. Therefore, we must repent of it and ask to be delivered from it.

Today let faith be your friend and fear be your enemy. After all, the only part of you that the devil should see is the sole of your shoe.

Tread down fear in Jesus' name.

Dear heavenly Father, today we put our trust in You. We will not be afraid of men. We will have supernatural confidence that You will put us over. In Jesus' name, amen.

Day 179

"To him that overcometh will I grant to sit with me in my throne, even as I also overcame"
(Revelation 3:21a).

Have you ever used the little phrase "under the circumstances"? Once when we were having a tremendous crisis, I said to someone, "Under the circumstances, I think I'm doing quite well."

The Lord spoke back to me, "What are you doing UNDER the circumstances? You're supposed to be ON TOP OF the circumstances." Revelation 3:21a certainly reaffirms that promise! If we want to sit with Jesus in heavenly places, we're going to have to sit in the overcoming position.

Do you have some circumstances that are bowing you under? Do you feel crushed under the weight of situations that seem beyond your control? Take hold of God's promise for "overcomers." Confess God's Word that you will sit on the throne with Jesus, far above the cares of all worldly problems. We can't be under the circumstances; we must be on top of them. Jesus is in us, so He gives us the power to overcome and sit in heavenly places too.

Dear heavenly Father, I thank You today that I am not under my circumstances. I am above them. In fact, I am sitting high above my circumstances and command them to line up with Your Word. In the name of Jesus, amen.

Day 180

"Evening, and morning, and at noon, will I pray, and cry aloud: and he shall hear my voice" (Psalm 55:17).

It is not unusual for a man, who is committed to prayer, to pray morning, noon, and night. Daniel made a commitment to pray morning, noon, and night. In fact, Daniel's enemies could only find one fault with him: his extensive prayer life. That's really something when the only fault that your enemy can find is your prayer life! I wonder how many of our enemies could find that "fault" with us? But such dedication to prayer also brings forth men like Daniel—and David, who wrote Psalm 55:17. They were mighty and powerful in God.

Sometimes Christians will complain, "I just don't have time for a lot of prayer." Only the devil doesn't "have time" for prayer. A dedicated believer will MAKE TIME FOR PRAYER. Jesus always made time for prayer with His heavenly Father—even in the midst of horrendous crises, such as His impending crucifixion and death.

To live in prayer is to live in power. Set aside special times—morning, noon, and night—for your prayer life, and watch your circumstances change!

Dear heavenly Father, today let us emphasize prayer in our own personal lives. We must not look to other people to pray for us. We are committed to a consistent, personal prayer life. We look to You to guide us. In Jesus' name, amen.

Day 181

"Behold, I come quickly: hold that fast which thou hast, that no man take thy crown" (Revelation 3:11).

There is more than one crown in the New Testament. There is a crown for pastoring, and there is a crown for soulwinning. We must hold fast to whatever crown God has given us to wear. Walk worthy of the vocation wherein He has called you.

Sometimes, when pressures come upon us, we want to throw aside our callings. But if we put our hand to the plow, we cannot look back. A woman once asked me if I had ever thought of leaving the ministry. I said, "How many times a day?" The enemy would love to have us throw down the crown that God has given us and reject the vocation into which God has called us. But Jesus is coming quickly. When He comes, I believe that every crown we have received will simply be cast at His feet. He is crowned the One Who is Lord of all.

Remember, Christ is the King of kings. As His children, we have a heritage of royalty. His crown has been passed on to all generations of believers. Recognize and accept the crown of your calling.

Dear heavenly Father, help us today to hold fast to that which You have given us to do in this life. Help us not to look back or around, but look within to the power of Jesus Christ in our hearts. In Jesus' name, amen.

Day 182

"Cast thy burden upon the Lord, and he shall sustain thee: he shall never suffer the righteous to be moved" (Psalm 55:22).

Jesus came to carry our burdens. But so many times we try to carry them alone and, in doing so, we absolutely "crack" ourselves mentally, emotionally, and physically.

When one of my close relatives died, I saw his wife carrying the grief and sorrow. I could see that it was physically robbing her health. She was a born-again believer, so I called her one day and asked her if Jesus had carried her sins. She said, "Yes, He has. You know that He has, because I'm a born-again believer."

I said, "But you are still carrying your griefs and sorrows. Jesus not only carried your sins and sicknesses, He also carried your griefs and sorrows."

When my relative heard and received this message from God's Word, it was as though a great burden had been lifted from her shoulders. The light from the Word had penetrated the darkness of her grief. That very day she cast her grief and sorrow on the Lord and was set free.

Dear heavenly Father, help us today to cast our burdens upon You. Help us to see that You know how to provide for that which is committed into Your hands. In Jesus' name, amen.

Day 183

"To him that overcometh will I give to eat of the manna, and will give him a white stone,..." (Revelation 2:17b).

The white stone was always a winner's prize. Some Christians think that they are supposed to be losers in life. They know about eternal life, but they never expect to win in anything during THIS life. I believe that God has given each of us a "white stone"—a way to win in every situation.

About two miles from our church in Denver is a place called "The Losers' Bar." Whenever I drive past this bar, I think, "Whoever is in there is really a DOUBLE LOSER. Not only do they think that a bar is a place to find happiness, but even worse—they are going through life believing they are losers!" No one has to live the life of a loser—not if they know Jesus Christ.

The scripture says that we ALWAYS triumph in Christ. We don't triumph only one-third of the time or one-half of the time; we triumph ALL the time. In Christ you have received a white stone so that you can be a winner in every situation. Overcome negative thoughts and discouraging words. Take hold of God's Word and win.

Dear heavenly Father, thank You today that You made us to be winners, not losers. You're not sponsoring flops; You're sponsoring winners. We are those winners. In Jesus' name, amen.

Day 184

"Destroy, O Lord, and divide their tongues" (Psalm 55:9a).

God knows how to divide the tongues of evil counselors. He can cause strife to occur between evil people so that He can bring forth a miracle. God will take the wrath of man and cause it to praise Him.

One of the world's most evil counselors was surely the person who invented communism and tried to convince people that God does not exist. But I truly believe that today God is at work to bring division and strife amongst all the communist nations. Each day newspaper articles talk about the arguments between THIS communist leader and THAT communist leader. Communist countries worldwide are always in disagreement about points of doctrine.

When you pray for communist countries, pray that there would be confusion and division among their leadership. Use the devil's own tools against him. We do not have to put up with his evil works. Take your authority in Jesus' name!

Dear heavenly Father, today we pray for Russia. We pray for a great outpouring of the Holy Spirit upon this great country and its people. We ask, in the name of Jesus, that the counsel of communism and atheism will be put to confusion. Divide the tongues of the leadership. In Jesus' name, amen.

Day 185

"Blessed is he that readeth, and they that hear the words of this prophecy, and keep those things which are written therein" (Revelation 1:3a).

There are three verbs that I want you to observe in this scripture. God will bless those who READ His Word, those who HEAR His Word, and those who KEEP His Word. We love God's Word and want it to work in us. But in order for the Word to really work in our lives, it must consume us!

When you read God's Word, ask Him to give you hearing ears. Ask Him to help you remember what you have read so that you might receive the manifestations of His Word in your life.

Ephesians 5:18 warns us not to be drunk with wine, but "filled with the Spirit." In the same way, we should also be filled with the "wine" of the Word so that it can consume our souls, overpower us with its truth, and "keep" us forever in the Word. Remember, blessings come to those who read, hear, and keep the Word.

Dear heavenly Father, we ask You, in Jesus' name, to help us read Your Word today. Open our spiritual eyes so that we can be blessed as we read Your scriptures. Let us receive Your revelations. Help us to keep the Word in our hearts that we might see its manifestations in our daily living. In Jesus' name, amen.

Day 186

"Create in me a clean heart, O God; and renew a right spirit within me" (Psalm 51:10).

CREATE means to "make something out of nothing." When we are born again, God makes us a new creation. He gives us a new seed; we are born again of incorruptible seed, the seed of His new life.

Notice that the Word says "new" life—not second-hand or renovated or revamped—BUT ENTIRELY NEW! God never said to Himself, "Well, here I've got Me a sinner. I think I'll just throw on a new cover, sort of like renovating a mattress!" We're not like a "renovated mattress," but we have, instead, a brand-new life inside!

Because we have that new creation within, we can have a renewed spirit. Our mind, conscience, will, and intellect can be renewed daily with God's Word. We can live in our new nature, rather than our old.

Make this daily decision: "Will I live in the old man, or will I live in the new man?" Today let's crucify the old man and make a decision to live in the newness of Christ's life.

Dear heavenly Father, we thank You that, as born-again Christians, we have a new man inside us. We do not have to live in the old man. We make the choice to live in the newness of life. In Jesus' name, amen.

Day 187

"I can of mine own self do nothing: as I hear, I judge: and my judgment is just; because I seek not mine own will, but the will of the Father which hath sent me" (John 5:30).

Some years ago, when I was first led to teach God's Word, He led me to teach home Bible studies. In those days home Bible studies were rather a novelty—untried territory. Many people would come to a home and—over a cup of coffee and a cookie—get saved.

I thought that, of course, these people who were saved and Spirit-filled in home Bible studies would come to our church. But many of them didn't. They attended other Spirit-filled churches in our city. I was so upset with the Lord. I thought, "Lord, here I am praying with these people and spending time with them, but they don't even come to our church."

God quickened me that I was not to seek my own will, but the will of Him Who sent me. He then dealt with me, "Are you building YOUR church or MY kingdom?" I quickly repented. My business was to be obedient, not to figure out how God could bless our church.

Dear heavenly Father, help us to seek Your will always. When we seek our own will, we begin to walk in darkness. So today we say, "YOUR kingdom come; YOUR will be done this day in me." In Jesus' name, amen.

Day 188

"Offer unto God thanksgiving;...And call upon me in the day of trouble: I will deliver thee, and thou shalt glorify me" (Psalm 50:14,15).

I like the fact that our nation began with Thanksgiving. Thanksgiving day began October, 1621, when our forefathers, the pilgrims, reached Cape Cod and set aside three days to give thanks. In 1680 it was declared that Thanksgiving was to be an annual celebration. In 1777 George Washington began issuing Thanksgiving proclamations. Abraham Lincoln declared, in 1864, that Thanksgiving was an "established holiday."

We see that from the very beginning our nation was established for God—with thanksgiving. I believe that one reason America has been so blessed is because we have thanked, worshiped, and adored Him. We have lifted up the Lord and exalted Him as the Source of our free nation!

Smart people are people who give thanks to the Lord. When you start giving thanks, you will begin to receive a multitude of blessings.

Dear heavenly Father, help us today to notice the things that You do for us and to give You thanks. We do not want to be careless in our attitudes or show a lack of gratitude for Your wonderful blessings. We thank You, in advance, for loading us with Your benefits. In Jesus' name, amen.

Day 189

"Behold, he cometh with clouds; and every eye shall see him" (Revelation 1:7a).

When you know something is eventually going to happen in the future, don't you get prepared? At the first hint of winter, we "winterize" our car. And as we get older, we have wills written up for ourselves so that our families will not be caught "unprepared." But what have you done to prepare yourself for the inevitable and soon-return of our Lord Jesus Christ?

Jesus is coming again, perhaps in our day, perhaps in another day. The important thing for us is to be ready. The Bible doesn't say that only the Christians will behold the Lord. It says that when Jesus comes again, EVERY eye shall see Him.

I have heard people say, "My grandparents said that Jesus would come in their day, but He didn't come. So how can we know?" We cannot KNOW, but we can be READY—and we can encourage others to be ready. The Bible says that this hope keeps us pure.

Dear heavenly Father, we thank You that we have hope in the return of Jesus. We are not hopeless people who despair about the future. We know what is going to happen: Jesus is coming back! Amen.

Day 190

"Thou lovest righteousness, and hatest wickedness: therefore God, thy God, hath anointed thee with the oil of gladness above thy fellows" (Psalm 45:7).

We want to be a joyful people. We want to enter into the joy of the Lord because the joy of the Lord is our strength. If the devil can steal your joy, he will steal your strength.

Have you noticed that evil people—wicked men and women—are not very joyful? It shows on their faces and in their attitudes. They are full of despair and hopelessness. Why? Because they do not love righteousness, and they don't hate wickedness. The way to live in joy is to love righteousness and hate wickedness. Sin puts people in a place of despair and despondency.

Look, instead, at the faces of people who are free from sin. Have you every noticed the face of a person who has just accepted Jesus Christ as Savior? There is such joy and happiness that radiates from someone who has experienced the new birth. Sometimes it looks like 20 years have just been instantaneously wiped away—like a divine face lift. But even better—it's a divine FAITH LIFT!

Dear heavenly Father, we thank You that the joy of the Lord is our strength. We enter this day with the strength of the Lord, and we will worship You and praise You throughout the day. In Jesus' name, amen.

Day 191

"Building up yourselves on your most holy faith, praying in the Holy Ghost" (Jude 20).

I love this scripture. It has become so powerful in my life because I have found that praying in the Holy Spirit—praying in tongues—literally recharges my spirit.

Has your car battery ever "gone dead"? It usually happens when you least expect it—perhaps when you're late for an appointment. Cars will usually recharge themselves. But when we don't take care of the car, sometimes the car doesn't take care of the battery. The same thing can happen to our faith. When we don't recharge it with prayer, it can "go dead" too!

When I feel as though my faith doesn't have the strength to carry me through a situation, I "recharge" it with a time of praying in tongues. I find that it recharges not only my faith, but also my mind, emotions, and physical body. It causes my circumstances to change, and better yet, my attitude changes.

There are many times when we can pray in tongues: when we take a shower, while we're driving, and even on airplanes. Recharge your "battery" daily.

Dear heavenly Father, today we pray that we will be men and women full of the Spirit—overflowing with the Spirit! In Jesus' name, amen.

Day 192

"And Jesus said, I am: and ye shall see the Son of man sitting on the right hand of power, and coming in the clouds of heaven" (Mark 14:62).

*T*his scripture contains a wonderful promise that brings hope to the heart of every believer. Hope is very important because the man without hope becomes involved in sin and despair. He says, "What's the use? I might as well murder, commit adultery, cheat, kill, lie, destroy—because there is no hope anyway."

During the horrible drought in Ethiopia, our ministry sent over many shipments of food, medicine, and Bibles. An Ethiopian told me, "Your gifts have brought a new sense of hope to these children. When they had no hope, they had no will to live." Lack of hope removes the sense of brightness for the future.

This scripture tells us that we have a bright future because we belong to Jesus. When He comes, He will not come to judge us. He will come to take us home. He is coming soon, perhaps in our day.

Dear heavenly Father, we thank You today that You have told us to lift up our eyes in these end-times when we will see the terrors come upon the earth. We must not look down, but up. We look not at ourselves or at our lack. We look up to You and know that soon our redemption draweth nigh. In Jesus' name, amen.

Day 193

"Sing, O heavens; and be joyful, O earth; and break forth into singing, O mountains: for the Lord hath comforted his people, and will have mercy upon his afflicted" (Isaiah 49:13).

This scripture is a promise for the millennium. God doesn't JUST give us promises for our past. (But thank God that He DOES give us promises for our past, and He will heal us of our past sins, if we repent.) Nor does He only give us promises for our present. He also is a God of the future!

What a loving and thoughtful heavenly Father we have! Not only has He made plans to take care of our ugly past and the needs of our present time, but He's also made plans to give us a glorious future! It INDEED gives us a reason for joy and song: God will comfort and protect His children, even through the millennium!

During the millennium there will be 1,000 years of peace, and we will rule and reign with Jesus on this earth. It is very reassuring for us to know that God has promised us future comfort.

Dear heavenly Father, today let us know that we are not people without any security for our future. You have a greater policy for us than any insurance company. You have an "assurance policy" for all eternity. In Jesus' name, amen.

Day 194

"And he that keepeth his commandments dwelleth in him, and he in him. And hereby we know that he abideth in us, by the Spirit which he hath given us" (I John 3:24).

*T*he Spirit bears witness in our hearts that we belong to Jesus Christ. I've never heard the audible voice of God, nor have I seen many visions or outward manifestations. But His Spirit and Word have borne witness to me again and again.

I was 16 years old when I was born again at a Methodist youth camp. At an evening service the Baptist minister just invited people up to receive Jesus. No one told me that I had been born again, saved, or converted. Three years later a Baptist girl witnessed to me about being born again. I told her, "I think I already am."

She asked, "How do you know?" I explained to her my experience from camp. I didn't know the experience by name, but I knew it by the inner witness. Many, many times the witness of the Spirit has been the key focal point of my life. Thank God that He did not leave us as orphans, but He sent His Spirit as our inner guide.

Dear heavenly Father, we thank You today for the Holy Spirit, Who leads us, as born again believers, to truth and Who bears witness to the Father that we belong to Him. In Jesus' name, amen.

Day 195

"The fruit of the Spirit is love, joy, peace, longsuffering, gentleness, goodness, faith, meekness, temperance: against such there is no law" (Galatians 5:22b,23).

The fruit of the Spirit is to be very evident in our lives. When we are born again, we receive the fruits of LOVE, JOY, and PEACE. These are for our personal enjoyment. We experience love, joy, and peace.

In addition to these three fruits, there are three more that relate to others: We need LONGSUFFERING in dealing with other people. We also need GENTLENESS and GOODNESS. Thus, not only do we enjoy personal fruit for ourselves, but we can extend His fruit to others.

Lastly, three final fruits deal with our relationship with our heavenly Father. We give FAITH back to Him, along with MEEKNESS and TEMPERANCE.

Here is a beautiful picture of FRUIT THAT WE OURSELVES CAN ENJOY, FRUIT THAT WE GIVE TO OTHERS, and FRUIT THAT WE MANIFEST TO THE FATHER. How complete God has made us in Jesus! If you have Jesus, you have the seed of all nine of these fruits. Partake of them all.

Dear heavenly Father, no law can win against love, joy, peace, longsuffering, gentleness, goodness, faith, meekness, and temperance—the supernatural traits of Jesus Christ. Thank You, Father, that these abide in us in our new birth. In Jesus' name, amen.

Day 196

"I sought the Lord, and he heard me, and delivered me from all my fears" (Psalm 34:4).

God's will is to deliver us from fear. When I was pregnant with Sarah, my son caught the measles. The doctor and everyone else was frightened. They thought that I would catch them and that, through this disease, my unborn baby would be deformed.

I sought the Lord about it. I knew that God had given me this baby supernaturally. He had caused me to be pregnant even though the doctors had said that it could never happen. I knew that if God could give me a baby, He could also keep my baby healthy. I did not get the measles. Sarah was not harmed, and she leads a very normal, healthy life. It was only as I sought God that I was set free from fear.

Fear can be just like a pit of quicksand. The more you struggle in it, the deeper you sink. But once we realize that fear can be avoided and bypassed, then God is free to work His supernatural wonders in our lives. When you find yourself caught in the "quicksand" of fear, stretch out your hand to God and let Him pull you free!

Dear heavenly Father, help us today to seek You and recognize that fear comes from the devil. We will resist fear, in Jesus' name, and be set free. Amen.

Day 197

"And this is the confidence that we have in him, that, if we ask any thing according to his will, he heareth us" (I John 5:14).

Confidence is important. The Bible says that if our hearts do not condemn us, then we have confidence. When we condemn ourselves, it robs us of our confidence.

In New Mexico there is a religious group called the "Penitentes." They believe that in order to become closer to God, people should beat themselves repeatedly. The walls of their churches are covered with splattered blood; and each Easter they nail a selected male to a huge wooden cross.

As Christians, we would never consciously think of doing this. We would never beat ourselves on the outside—however, we often beat ourselves on the inside by condemning ourselves for past sins. Once we have repented and God has forgiven us, we are to forget past sins. Condemnation causes us to lose confidence and faith in what God has for us. Let's repent of our past, forget it, and reach forth for the future with CONFIDENCE. God will perform great and mighty things for us.

Dear heavenly Father, today I thank You and express my confidence in You. I will not cast away my confidence because it has great recompense of reward. I expect my reward in the name of Jesus. Amen.

Day 198

"The angel of the Lord encampeth round about them that fear him, and delivereth them" (Psalm 34:7).

I was staying at a hotel in Detroit one night several years ago. Before I went to sleep, I asked the Lord to post angels at my door and to take care of me.

At about two o'clock in the morning, I was awakened by an inner voice saying, "Go to your door." I got out of my bed, turned on the light, and went to the door. The chain was still fastened, but the door had been unlocked, and somone had tried to push the door open. I closed the door quickly and locked it. Then I called the front desk.

Someone had broken into several rooms on that floor during the night and robbed them. But the thief never broke into my room. I believe that my angels had protected me.

No matter where we are—in a strange city, in a lonely hotel room, stranded on a deserted country road—God always knows where we are. He will send His angels to camp around us, protect us, and deliver us. He has made us this promise in His Word. Stand on this promise and you will never fear!

Dear heavenly Father, we thank You today that angels encamp around us to protect us and guard our possessions. In Jesus' name, amen.

Day 199

"For whatsoever is born of God overcometh the world: and this is the victory that overcometh the world, even our faith" (I John 5:4).

In 1985, right after Mexico was rocked by a massive earthquake, I traveled to Mexico City to see what aid our ministry might provide. There in a hospital I met a victorious overcomer. For four days this man and his wife had been buried under a collapsed apartment building. When the rescue workers finally reached the couple, they were rushed to a hospital where the man's arm was amputated. This courageous man would not be defeated! His life had been miraculously spared, and he was ready to begin again!

Each of us desires to be victorious and overcome the world. God has given us a simple way to do this: through our faith.

Faith in God's Word is the greatest overcoming agent that Christians possess. When I place my faith in Him, I will never be disappointed. Many times I have experienced physical healing, financial healing, and other miracles in every area of my life. Do you want to be an overcomer? It is not difficult. Keep your faith in God's Word.

Dear heavenly Father, today we thank You that Your Word will make us overcomers. Your Word will paralyze all the weapons and devices that the enemy may use against us. In Jesus' name, amen.

Day 200

"Blessed is the nation whose God is the Lord" (Psalm 33:12a).

Did you know that the United States began its life as a Christian nation? Our forefathers fled to this country so that they could worship God in the manner they wished. Our constitution, our Declaration of Independence, and our Bill of Rights all mention God. We were birthed as a nation of God, and we are blessed for it!

God has used America to bless the world. Our confidence is in God—it is even printed on our money! There are certainly tremendous needs in our nation today, but there are also tremendous Christians who are taking God's Word to intercede for this country. We are the salt that preserves this nation—let's not lose our saltiness. We are the light that overcomes the darkness of this nation—let's not hide our lights under a bushel.

Let's stand boldly in God, speak against evil, pray, and believe God for the miraculous outpouring of His Spirit upon all flesh in the United States.

Dear heavenly Father, We thank You today that our nation is blessed because of the Christians who are praying and believing You. Thank You for doing great and mighty things in our midst and raising up laborers and intercessors. In Jesus' name, amen.

Day 201

"Be not wise in thine own eyes: fear the Lord, and depart from evil" (Proverbs 3:7).

Many years ago we witnessed to a woman about the power of the Holy Spirit baptism and about the anointing it could bring to her marriage. She prayed and was beautifully Spirit-filled. Her husband began to go to church with her, but he did not become a Christian. In addition, he was always murmuring about something. We encouraged her to stand fast.

One day she called and told us that the Word had told her to leave him. We said, "What scripture do you have?" She said, "Well, in I Corinthians 7:13 it says, 'If the unbelieving mate is pleased to dwell with them...' " We answered her, "Yes, he is pleased to dwell with you."

She said, "He is not pleased with my housekeeping, so I am going to leave." We said, "Your housekeeping isn't the sum-total of dwelling with you." She insisted on twisting the scripture to be the way she wanted it to be. She left her husband and three daughters. The marriage was totally destroyed.

We must not twist God's Word our way. We need to go His way with His Word.

Dear heavenly Father, don't let us be wise in our own eyes. But let us respect and honor You and know that in due season we will reap, if we faint not. So help us today to abide by that law and receive the benefits of sowing good things. In Jesus' name, amen.

Day 202

"Many sorrows shall be to the wicked: but he that trusteth in the Lord, mercy shall compass him about" (Psalm 32:10).

Have you ever been to the grocery store to buy some sale item—only to find that the store had "run out" of it? You had two choices: go somewhere else or go home empty-handed.

When it comes to God's mercy, He'll never send you somewhere else and you'll never go home empty-handed—because His mercy will never "run out"! The Word promises that His mercy will endure forever.

There have been times when I know that I failed God and missed the leading of His Spirit. I have been openly rebellious to His Word, and yet I have claimed His mercy and found that it always surrounded me. I was fenced in with His mercy, which never runs out.

Sometimes we say that our PATIENCE runs out. But I want to assure you that God's MERCY never runs out. I'm not giving you an excuse for sin because God does not have "greasy grace." But when we repent and turn from our sin, He has mercy. Remember, God's mercy is all around you and never runs out. Call upon God's mercy today; it is always available to you.

Dear heavenly Father, we thank You today for Your mercy—the mercy that never runs out. Your mercy endures forever. Thank You that it is available to us during our times of need. In Jesus' name, amen.

Day 203

"Whosoever shall confess that Jesus is the Son of God, God dwelleth in him, and he in God" (I John 4:15).

When we confess that Jesus Christ is the Lord of our lives, we enter into a new realm of living. Wally and I went on vacation to Mexico. We changed planes in the Dallas airport. A man came rushing over, and we could see that he was very disturbed. He was a young Christian who had only been saved for six months. He explained that he had come from a bar where he had taken several drinks. He said, "I am on my way to Mexico City for business, and I am afraid that I will become involved in sin."

I proclaimed boldly to him, "He that is in you is greater than he that is in the world." I said that he was not going to sin while he was in Mexico City. I reminded the young man that because he had Jesus in his life, the devil could not have control.

God is so good. Upon our return we met the same young man again at the airport in Mexico. He told us that he had read his Bible and prayed every day. Instead of falling under the dominion of sin, he had led his Mexican business partner to the Lord. Hallelujah! Jesus is Lord.

Dear heavenly Father, thank You that Satan cannot control us, because Jesus will be the Lord of our lives today and every day, if we will just ask Him. In Jesus' name, amen.

Day 204

"Let the words of my mouth, and the meditation of my heart, be acceptable in thy sight, O Lord, my strength, and my redeemer" (Psalm 19:14).

As a man thinketh in his heart, so is he. Whatever we think about is going to come out of our mouths. Out of the abundance of our hearts will our mouths speak.

It is very important that our minds meditate upon the good things of God, upon His Word. MEDITATE means "to go over and over." I find that when my mind wants to dwell on ugly, negative things, the best remedy is to memorize certain scriptures or chapters of the Bible. Then I begin to speak those scriptures aloud, and my mind lines up with the Word. God's Word becomes the abundance of my heart from which my mouth speaks.

Another special blessing that comes from meditation on the Word is that the scriptures will become stored in your mind—like data in a computer. Then when you need the Word in a hurry, you just push a spiritual button and out it comes—ready to be ministered to any situation or circumstance!

Dear heavenly Father, let us take hold of Your Word today. Let us memorize it, think it, speak it, act it, eat it, dream it, and live it. We know that when we are grounded in Your Word, then every word that comes from our mouths will be acceptable to You. Our words come from Your strength. In Jesus' name, amen.

Day 205

"Beloved, if God so loved us, we ought also to love one another" (I John 4:11).

The best way to love one another is to love God and experience His love in our hearts. When we try to love people with our own supply of love, it runs out quickly. Sometimes people are hard to love. Sometimes we are hard to love. But if we go back to His love, we find an endless supply.

I've learned that when we begin to act in love—just because God has asked it—our emotions will get in line, and soon we will feel it.

Sometimes it is very difficult to extend love to others—particularly when they have offended or hurt us. We know in our hearts that we should radiate that AGAPE kind of love. But deep in our souls and bodies lies a strong resistance. That's when it's so important to lean on God and borrow some of His love.

Say something good about a person who has said evil things about you. Begin to speak God's Word about that person, and your feelings and emotions will change into the love of God.

Dear heavenly Father, today we see that it's very important to love our enemies. We should do good to our enemies and pray for them. In doing so, You can change our enemies and make them to be at peace with us. In Jesus' name, amen.

Day 206

"If ye then, being evil, know how to give good gifts unto your children: how much more shall your heavenly Father give the Holy Spirit to them that ask him?" (Luke 11:13).

Once I was caught in an airline strike in Cleveland, Ohio. Instead of the normal one-hour layover, it extended into six hours. I knew of no one to call, so there I was for six hours. I had my Bible and some study material, yet the time seemed to drag. Suddenly a man with a television camera appeared and asked me if he could interview me about the airline strike. I said, "Yes," although I knew very little about the strike. I just said that I was tired of waiting for six hours. After he finished interviewing me, I asked if I could interview HIM.

I asked him, "Do you know Jesus as your personal Savior? Have you ever read the Bible or felt the drawing of the Holy Spirit?" I think that he almost fainted because his parents were born-again, Spirit-filled believers who had been praying for him. He was not yet a Christian, and he didn't accept Christ that day. But I'm sure that our experience was the watering of planted seed and his harvest was on the way.

The Holy Spirit leads us in unique ways, doesn't He?

Dear heavenly Father, we ask today that Your Holy Spirit will lead us to truth in situations where You want us to minister. In Jesus' name, amen.

Day 207

"And when ye stand praying, forgive, if ye have ought against any: that your Father also which is in heaven may forgive you your trespasses" (Mark 11:25).

When we pray the Lord's prayer, it says that we will be forgiven our trespasses IF we forgive others. One morning the Lord spoke to me about a certain situation and asked me to forgive someone. I said, "Lord, I have forgiven that person at least 500 times. My forgiveness is just about worn out."

God answered, "No, your forgiveness never wears out because MY forgiveness never wears out. When I forgave you, it was by My grace. You received My grace. Now the grace that forgave you also lives in you, and you can forgive with the same grace."

His words were such a blessing. I immediately began to forgive this person—not with my own forgiveness—but with the forgiveness that comes from God's mercy. In faith I forgave. And in faith I was forgiven. Now when I pray early in the morning, I just say, "Lord, I forgive anyone who has ever hurt me—even before they do it!"

Dear heavenly Father, show us the victory of being a forgiving people. Show us the victory and Your power of forgiveness in our lives, in Jesus' name, amen.

Day 208

"I take pleasure in infirmities, in reproaches, in necessities, in persecutions, in distresses for Christ's sake: for when I am weak, then am I strong" (II Corinthians 12:10b).

Have you ever made a checklist of all the persecutions that Paul endured? If you have, you know that it's a long list. How could he take it? How could he stand it? The secret is in today's verse: when Paul was at his weakest, he then relied the most on Christ in order to receive strength.

I remember one time when I was scheduled to be in Houston, but I was extemely sick. I had prayed, taken medicine, and done EVERYTHING—but nothing seemed to help.

With great difficulty I dressed myself and boarded the plane. Something happened to me while I was on that plane to Houston. By the time we landed, I walked off feeling strong. In fact, I felt like a million. The secret was that I continued to say, "When I am weak, I have His strength. When I am weak, I have His strength." I experienced His supernatural strength, and it was wonderful.

Dear heavenly Father, help us do what the Word says. You said in the book of Joel, "Let the weak say, 'I am strong.'" Today we say that we are strong in the name of Jesus. Amen.

Day 209

"My little children, let us not love in word, neither in tongue; but in deed and in truth" (I John 3:18).

*Y*ears ago when I first became active in the ministry, I went through a very discouraging situation. My husband arrived home while I was cooking dinner, and he asked, "How are you?"

I groaned and said, "I just want to change my name and run away." The next night when he came home, I was fixing dinner again. He had a beautiful gift-wrapped box that he gave to me. I asked him, "What is this for?"

"It's for your birthday," he answered.

I protested, "This is May. My birthday is not until July."

He replied, "I know, but I thought that if you were going to run away, you'd need your birthday gift early."

His words and gesture warmed my heart! But it shamed me, at the same time, for not trusting the Lord. God's love was demonstrated, and it brought me the truth.

Dear heavenly Father, teach us to love not only with our mouths or in our thoughts, but also through our actions. Help us to act in love. In Jesus' name, amen.

Day 210

"But he that glorieth, let him glory in the Lord. For not he that commendeth himself is approved, but whom the Lord commendeth"
(II Corinthians 10:17,18).

It is good to glory in the Lord because it keeps you from getting into an area of pride. Pride is always the way down, and glorying in the Lord is always the way up.

One thing that often happens to pastors, on their "way up" in the ministry, is that they begin to exalt themselves. The mistake that each of us makes—at least once—is to look at "our" successes and to believe that these things have happened because of our own abilities. Sometimes we forget that God DID these things and we are only the vehicles for His work. When we begin to walk in pride, we then stumble and fall.

I have found that the Lord really DOES want to exalt us—but He doesn't want us to exalt ourselves. Sometimes we count all of the wonderful things that WE have done, but they are actually all the wonderful things HE has done. Be a blessing-counter!

Dear heavenly Father, today we count our blessings. We thank You for each of them. Every advantage, every benefit that we have, truly comes from You, and we praise You for it. In Jesus' name, amen.

Day 211

"And whatsoever we ask, we receive of him, because we keep his commandments, and do those things that are pleasing in his sight" (I John 3:22).

One time I became very provoked at the Lord. While I was praying, I accused the Lord of having favorites. I said, "I know that you have certain pets because some Christians are so much more blessed than others." Then I accused a certain Christian of being one of God's favorites.

The Lord really spoke to me about some of the blessings that this Christian had received. He said, "This man has believed for these things for years. He's claimed them, thanked Me for them, and now he has them. You never claimed them, so you never got them. I don't have pets. I just have bigger believers."

If you are afraid to believe for big things, then check your heart to see if your faith level has taken a nose dive. When your faith has gone downhill, it becomes increasingly difficult to believe for BIG results.

Remember to think BIG, claim BIG, and ask BIG! If you will believe and ask BIG, you will receive in abundance!

Dear heavenly Father, we thank You that we can be BIG believers and BIG askers so that we can see BIG answers. In Jesus' name, amen.

Day 212

"For the weapons of our warfare are not carnal, but mighty through God to the pulling down of strong holds" (II Corinthians 10:4).

When day after day we find it necessary to wage the same spiritual battle, we must realize that we are facing a stronghold. So many times when we face strongholds, we instinctively try to fight the stronghold itself or people associated with the stronghold. But a demonic force can often be the cause of the stronghold.

I have seen the demonic forces of strife, poverty, and physical illness actually fall away when Christians boldly begin to take the name of Jesus and use scripture against those forces. Look closely at the battles you are fighting.

Any of these scriptures will fight demonic strongholds: Exodus 15:6, Psalm 17:4, Psalm 34:19, Joel 2:32, among others. Find one or two that fit your particular stronghold; then commit them to memory so that they will be on the tip of your tongue when crises strike again. Come against strongholds in Jesus' name.

Dear heavenly Father, today we are fighting spiritual battles. Help us use the name of Jesus and His Word to come against strongholds. In Jesus' name, amen.

Day 213

"But whoso hath this world's good, and seeth his brother have need, and shutteth up his bowels of compassion from him, how dwelleth the love of God in him?" (I John 3:17).

We live in a day when most of the world goes to bed hungry. I don't believe that Christians can sit still any longer and say, "Be fed, be clothed, pray for the heathen," yet claim no responsibility.

James tells us that when we speak these things, but don't do them, our faith is dead (James 2:20). God has not called us to dead faith. He has called us to dynamic faith! This is one of the reasons why we feed hungry children all over the world. If you have ever seen starving people by the hundreds, you may never again sit down to a meal without seeing them in your mind's eye. Let's have compassion on the world's hungry—spiritually AND physically.

There are so many ways you can help. Perhaps your church has a special program to aid the hungry in your community. Get involved and give of yourself—your time, your money. If no such program exists, perhaps YOU could start one. Whatever you choose, make a commitment to it today.

Dear heavenly Father, we pray that You will open up opportunities and avenues for us to feed the world with the Word and with physical food. We thank You that we live in a nation where food is plentiful. Help us remember to share our plenty with others. Amen.

Day 214

"Grace and peace be multiplied unto you through the knowledge of God, and of Jesus our Lord" (II Peter 1:2).

When I was 21 years old, my father had a nervous breakdown. His personality changed tremendously. He would drink heavily and say cruel, terrible things. My brother and I were miserable; but my Spirit-filled mother experienced a tremendous peace. No one could understand it.

When my father turned himself in at a psychiatric center, the doctors tried to blame his sickness on my mother's religion. But she said, "No, my 'religion' didn't bring him here; but my 'religion' will take him out." And it was true—her peace and faith in Jesus Christ finally rescued my father.

We live in a day when everyone wants peace. They want it so desperately, yet very few have real peace. The reason there is so little peace is because there is so little knowledge of God and so few people who have really made Jesus the Lord of their lives.

The more we make Jesus the Lord of our circumstances, desires, emotions, and decisions—the more we will find peace that is absolutely multiplied back to us. Saturate yourself with the peace of God's Word.

Dear heavenly Father, we thank You today for grace and peace multiplied to us. As we study Your Word, may we have ears to "hear" and eyes to "see." In Jesus' name, amen.

Day 215

"Love not the world, neither the things that are in the world. If any man love the world, the love of the Father is not in him" (I John 2:15).

Sometimes we find ourselves with one foot in the world and one foot with the Lord. We try to straddle the fence, but it will never work.

One day I was very critical of a certain Christian who I thought was doing some things that were unbecoming for a Christian to do. I began to compare myself with that person. I thought, "I would never do that. I would never think or act that way, or say those things."

But then the Lord brought something to my mind: the very things that I had been thinking and saying were acts that He considered extremely worldly. God spoke to me, "You're grading yourself on a curve, instead of by My Word." I repented quickly.

Remember, if you love the world, you are God's enemy. Whenever you begin to criticize other Christians for doing "un-Christian" things, you are falling into the devil's trap. You have let yourself become critical and condemning—you have stepped from God's path and have started to walk with the world.

Dear heavenly Father, help us today to cast off worldly thoughts and to realize that the world will damage and destroy us. In the name of Jesus, amen.

Day 216

"Submit yourselves therefore to God. Resist the devil, and he will flee from you" (James 4:7).

How many times have you quoted the verse, "Resist the devil, and he will flee from you"? But we cannot resist the devil if we don't submit to God first. When we find ourselves in difficult situations, we must look first at ourselves and ask, "Have I submitted to God in this area of my life, this situation, or this circumstance?" Once we have truly submitted to God, we then have the power to resist the devil. Resist the devil and watch him run!

Sometimes when we are caught in the middle of a difficult situation, our worldly instincts tell us that we must rely on worldly understanding and worldly solutions. We try to analyze the problem, instead of immediately turning it over to God.

Always check your circumstances. Do it in this order: submit to God, resist the devil, and watch him flee.

Dear heavenly Father, we thank You today that we are not ignorant of the devil's devices. We see him for who he is and what he is doing. We submit ourselves to You for this day in every circumstance. And we resist the devil with God's power that is within us. In Jesus' name, amen.

Day 217

"And he did evil, because he prepared not his heart to seek the Lord" (II Chronicles 12:14).

It takes daily preparation to achieve an established heart. We must pray daily and renew our minds in God's Word so we will be spiritually in tune with our Father's will, Jesus' will, and the Holy Spirit's leading.

Many times we become involved in sin because we have not spiritually prepared ourselves to meet the day. It is good to seek God early. Sometimes people find it very difficult to "seek God early." Morning is often a time when our minds are fuzzy. It seems easier to flip on the TV, turn on the radio, flip through the paper—anything except spending some concentrated time with the Lord. But when we make an effort to "meet the Lord," He will, in turn, help us "meet the day."

When God helps us to go out to "meet the day," we're prepared for good, not evil. We, thereby, have brought the supernatural into our day long before we have encountered anything else. Learn to seek the Lord early.

Dear heavenly Father, truly it is good to seek You early in the day; thank You that we have a way to prepare our hearts. In preparing our hearts, we are kept free from evil. In Jesus' name, amen.

Day 218

"Casting all your care upon him; for he careth for you" (1 Peter 5:7).

Have you ever looked at photographs of our Presidents BEFORE their term of office began and then AFTER it had ended? Some of the men had, during that time, visibly aged YEARS beyond their actual stay in office. Each man had carried the cares of an entire nation on his back. The extreme MENTAL worry had caused a very PHYSICAL deterioration.

When you worry, you are carrying your cares. Worry is very dangerous. Your body, mind, and emotions were not designed to carry worry. In some cases worry causes mental breakdown and physical collapse.

Today let's cast our cares on the Lord. I want you literally to do this: lift your hands up as though you were holding all of the cares and worries that have plagued you. Say, "Lord, I cast all of my cares upon You." Literally take your hands and CAST those cares upon the Lord.

Now wave at those cares and say, "Good-bye, cares. You are not mine. You belong to my heavenly Father." He will take care of YOUR cares and turn them into a blessing.

Dear heavenly Father, today we are not going to worry. We thank You for making provision for every area of our lives. We believe that You will take care of the things that concern us. In Jesus' name, amen.

Day 219

"Whereby are given unto us exceeding great and precious promises: that by these ye might be partakers of the divine nature" (II Peter 1:4a).

Sometimes we forget that we have the divine nature of Jesus Christ within us when we are born again. God's promises show us what we already have through our new birth.

Years ago my husband Wally traveled to the Holy Land. During a stop over in Athens, Greece, he was to deliver some special products to a missionary couple. He tried, but he couldn't reach them. It seemed as though everything had gone wrong on that trip—from the very beginning. He said that he just wanted to murmur and murmur.

But God began to deal with him, "I can take a curse and turn it into a blessing. Murmuring is not a part of your new nature, but a part of your old."

While he pondered the situation, my husband overheard the conversation of a middle-aged woman who turned out to be a relative of Wally's! She was also Spirit-filled! Can you imagine meeting a Spirit-filled relative in the Athens airport on a Holy Land tour—very unexpectedly? Wally said, "I quit murmuring; my steps were ordered of the Lord."

Dear heavenly Father, we pray today that we would know with assurance that You are guiding and directing our steps. Increase our desire to read Your Word and live by our new nature. In Jesus' name, amen.

Day 220

"Every man according as he purposeth in his heart, so let him give; not grudgingly, or of necessity: for God loveth a cheerful giver" (II Corinthians 9:7).

God loves cheerful givers. The Greek word for "cheerful" is "hilarious"! God loves hilarious givers—but hilarious givers are also hilarious receivers.

My daughter taught me a beautiful lesson about being a hilarious giver. She once admitted to me that whenever she wanted her father to raise her allowance, she would begin to tithe on the amount that she believed God should give her. She would just give hilariously and cheerfully, and she would tell the Lord that, in giving, she would receive. She said, "Sometimes it would take six months to a year, Mother, but if I gave hilariously and cheerfully, Dad always came through."

When I shared this with my husband, he laughed and said, "Well, she's just practicing the Word. What can I say?"

Learn to be hilarious in your giving, but also learn how to be hilarious in your receiving.

Dear heavenly Father, we thank You today that we are givers. We are givers of love, time, patience, and and joy. We are also givers of money, peace, and healing. In Jesus' name, amen.

Day 221

"Who is a God like unto thee, that pardoneth iniquity, and passeth by the transgression of the remnant of his heritage? he retaineth not his anger for ever, because he delighteth in mercy" (Micah 7:18).

We have a very dear pastor friend who is a living example of God's mercy and grace. He was an alcoholic at age 16. He married five times. His life was just one big crisis after another. He finally became the manager of a grocery store in a large city.

One day a Baptist minister came in the store and said, "If you don't give your heart to God, someone is going to shoot you in the head." The store manager became furious with the minister and replied, "How dare you come in and tell me something like that!"

The following day a man came into the store and literally shot this manager in the head. He was rushed to the hospital, where he was later visited by the minister. The minister told our friend how much Jesus loved him. "And," the minister said, "you're still living." Right there he led that man to Christ.

Today our friend is a mighty soul winner who loves God with all his heart.

Dear heavenly Father, we thank You that Your mercy endures forever and never runs out. We know that we can always run to You for help during our time of need. We thank You, Father, that mercy is our way back to You. In Jesus' name, amen.

Day 222

"And the prayer of faith shall save the sick, and the Lord shall raise him up" (James 5:15a).

*E*very born-again believer has the authority to pray the prayer of faith over the sick and believe the Lord to raise them up.

Years ago my mother found a breast tumor, and the doctor told her that he thought she should have it removed quickly because of its rapid growth. The doctor believed that the tumor was malignant.

At this point, my mother could have given up hope and said, "There's nothing I can do. Operate. Give me radiation. Give me chemicals. I don't want to die." But, instead, my mother turned this problem over to God.

Believers gathered around my mother and prayed the prayer of faith. When she went back to be checked by the doctor, he said, "There is no evidence that you have ever had a tumor." She was given a clean bill of health. Isn't it wonderful that God has made provisions for us to minister one to another and receive His supernatural healing!

Dear heavenly Father, send us today to someone for whom we can pray the prayer of faith. We believe that, in Jesus' name, You will raise up that person from physical affliction. Use our hands to heal the sick. In Jesus' name, amen.

Day 22

"Thou hast enlarged my steps under me; so that my feet did not slip" (II Samuel 22:37).

When we walk as the Lord leads us, we will not stumble because He leads in a very clear direction. Although we may feel that we lack the natural ability to walk where He leads, He will endow us with the spiritual ability to do it.

One time I was a guest speaker at a large convention. One of the other guests was an outstanding preacher whom I had admired for years. When he said that he could hardly wait to hear me, fear struck!

I thought, "Dear Lord, if he stays to hear me, I'll faint on the spot. Let him receive an emergency call from New York City! Get him out of here!"

I was overwhelmed by insecurity. The Lord encouraged me. He reminded me that my presentation alone wouldn't impress anyone, but that the power and anointing of the Holy Spirit would inspire the people.

In my fear I had seen a lack of ability in myself, rather than God's sufficiency. I repented quickly, dismissed the fear, and asked for God's anointing on my message. God's anointing was especially sweet that morning, and I gave Him all praise for it.

Dear heavenly Father, help us today to be led by Your Spirit and not by our flesh. Help us to know that wherever You guide us, You will also enable us. In Jesus' name, amen.

Day 224

"Confess your faults one to another, and pray one for another, that ye may be healed" (James 5:16a).

There is a small and unusual "hook" in this scripture. Not only are we to confess our faults "one to another," but we are to pray "one for another"—that WE might be healed. God is saying that, by praying for someone else, YOU can be healed!

Here again we see the law of sowing and reaping. Do you need healing? Then pray for someone else who needs healing, and watch God heal you. As you sow healing, you reap healing.

The idea that we should confess our faults to one another is not aimed at squeezing confessions out of people, but rather God wants our faith to be released. If we have unconfessed sin, our faith is hindered. God does not want our faith hindered in any area of our lives.

Here is God's beautiful formula: if you need healing, confess your faults one to another. Then pray for someone who needs healing, and expect to be healed yourself. It will work for whatever need you have.

Dear heavenly Father, we thank You today for the power and wisdom of Your Word that works in our bodies and minds. In Jesus' name, amen.

Day 225

"God is my strength and power: and he maketh my way perfect" (II Samuel 22:33).

I never cease to be amazed at God's timing. He is our strength and power, and He will make our way perfect. One time I was enroute to Poland. Our flight was late so I missed my connection. When I finally arrived, I found no one who spoke English. The thought of traveling alone to my destination—over 100 miles away—somewhat frightened me. But I knew that the Lord would make my way perfect—He would put the pieces together.

I got off the plane, and someone paged me in very broken English. I found the message desk and received a letter written in English. It was from the pastor who was my Polish host. The letter told me exactly what I was to do for the extra 100 miles before reaching my destination. Every connection meshed perfectly.

Trust Him. He knows how to guide your steps. Are you in a strange land? The Lord will send someone or something to ease your discomfort. Have unexpected circumstances disrupted your plans? Look to the Lord and He will provide a solution. Trust the Lord and He will always lead you through!

Dear heavenly Father, we trust You to guide our steps today in the direction that You would have us to go. In Jesus' name, amen.

Day 226

"And the barrel of meal wasted not, neither did the cruse of oil fail, according to the word of the Lord" (I Kings 17:16a).

God's Word always brings sufficiency and abundance. When the prophets spoke God's Word, sufficiency came. When we speak God's Word, we bring sufficiency into our natural, as well as our spiritual, circumstances.

One time I truly needed a wristwatch. The Lord said, "Look to Me, and let Me be your sufficiency." So, I said, "Dear heavenly Father, I need a wristwatch."

I knew that my husband was aware of my need, and I thought, "Maybe just a little encouragement would cause him to buy me one." But the Lord said, "Look to Me."

Several months later a deacon in our church came to me and said, "Marilyn, I want you to see the beautiful watch that I purchased for my wife while I was overseas." It WAS a beautiful watch. Then he said, "Marilyn, I felt led to buy you the same kind of watch. Do you need a watch?" My heart was overwhelmed with the sweetness of the Lord, and I thanked the man profusely. Isn't God good? When we look to His Word, we always receive His sufficiency.

Dear heavenly Father, help us to see that You are the true source of sufficiency. Let us partake of Your goodness today. In Jesus' name, amen.

Day 227

"The lips of the wise shall preserve them" (Proverbs 14:3b).

Your lips can preserve you, and they can preserve others too. One time I told my son that I thought he was lazy. I should never have said that, but I did—on several occasions. One day when he hadn't completed his chores, I asked, "Why isn't the lawn finished?"

He replied, "Because I'm lazy."

I said, "Don't say that about yourself!"

He promptly answered, "Well, you say it about me."

I realized that my words were giving him a false self-image that was certainly not from God. I quickly repented and told him that I would never say that about him again. I told him that he was a wise, productive son and that he could do all things. The lips of wisdom will preserve you and others.

The scriptures are filled with warnings about the power that we hold in our words. Our words can uplift—or they can destroy. Our words can be a positive belief for good things—or they can give expectations for negative and unproductive things. Let God control your lips—so that your lips don't control you!

Dear heavenly Father, help us today to speak words of wisdom. Help us to speak anointed words to ourselves and others. In Jesus' name, amen.

Day 230

"As every man hath received the gift, even so minister the same one to another, as good stewards of the manifold grace of God" (I Peter 4:10).

*M*ANIFOLD means "many folds." If we fold a piece of fabric and then unfold it, section by section, we would see, in each section, a different part of the pattern—until the whole piece of fabric was unfolded and the complete pattern revealed.

Peter spoke of "manifold temptations" in I Peter 1:6, while I Peter 4:10 speaks of "manifold grace." Grace will take care of temptation. There are different portions of grace for various sizes of temptation. If you hold up your hand, you will see that your little finger is smaller than your middle finger. Likewise, there are different sizes of temptations. Your little finger could represent small temptations, and your middle finger could be tall temptations.

Now look at your other hand, and see it as God's manifold grace. He has a little amount of grace to go with a little temptation, and so on. God has provided just the right amount of grace to match the size of any temptation that we face. I'm so glad that God has made a way for us to come through every temptation victoriously.

Dear heavenly Father, help us today to look for the grace to match our temptation. Thank You that You have given us a way to have victory in every situation. In Jesus' name, amen.

Day 231

"That ye put off concerning the former conversation the old man, which is corrupt according to the deceitful lusts" (Ephesians 4:22).

When we are born again, we are each given a new nature that is born of an incorruptible seed. I understand that if you take cells from the seed of an apple or an orange, prepare them in the proper way, and place them under a special microscope, you will see the same genetic structure as the mature plant and its fruit.

When we are born again, an incorruptible seed is placed in our hearts. I believe that within the seed is the basic structure of what we can be: Jesus Christ!

Jesus' nature does not sin. When we sin, we are relying on the old, evil nature. The Bible tells us that we are to crucify that nature and reckon our old selves dead unto sin. We're not to let sin rule or reign over us. Our new nature is greater than the old, but we must decide which nature will reign in our lives. He that is in us is greater than he that is in the world. Choose to live in your new mature nature: the love of Jesus, the fruit of the Spirit, and the power of God's Word.

Dear heavenly Father, in the name of Jesus, we cast off our old natures to put on the new nature of Jesus Christ. We reckon ourselves dead to sin, and we walk in newness of life. Amen.

Day 232

"But my God shall supply all your need according to his riches in glory by Christ Jesus" (Philippians 4:19).

God knows how to supply our needs in abundance. Isn't that encouraging? Many years ago when I was a child, my father had a nervous breakdown. We had no income because my father could not hold down a job. My mother faced very serious financial straits. She prayed and believed that God would meet our needs.

One day she walked into her closet and delved far back into the back corner for a summer handbag. When she opened the summer purse, she found over $180—exactly what she needed at that particular time!

We still don't know how that money was placed in her purse. Perhaps an angel placed it there. But we do know that God will supply our needs. He is our Source; people are not our source of supply.

Remember, in God's Word it says,"Not that we are sufficient of ourselves to think of any thing as of ourselves; but our sufficiency is of God" (II Corinthians 3:5). No one—not ourselves or others—can adequately supply ALL our needs. Look UP, instead, to God.

Dear heavenly Father, today we look to You, our Source. We trust You to meet any need that we may have. In Jesus' name, amen.

Day 233

"Whatsoever a man soweth, that shall he also reap" (Galatians 6:7b).

This scripture applies to every area of our lives. The Lord once spoke in an unusual way to me about sowing and reaping. Years ago I was feeling that my husband was overly critical about my teaching. Whenever he heard me teach, he would tell me, on the way home, what I had done wrong. His opinion was important to me, and his criticism was devastating.

Finally I cried out to the Lord, "Why does he do that? Why doesn't he stop? That hurts me."

God said, "What do you tell him about his preaching?"

"I tell him when it's too long or short, when he uses wrong words, or when it doesn't hang together."

The Lord said, "You are reaping what you sowed."

From that time on, I began to point out the good things in my husband's preaching. I began to encourage him about the things that the Holy Spirit gave to him. I didn't flatter him. I just told him the truth. Soon I began to reap positive comments from him about my teaching.

What are you sowing in your mate? That's exactly what you'll reap.

Dear heavenly Father, we choose to sow good things in the lives of others so that we might reap the same. In Jesus' name, amen.

Day 234

"I can do all things through Christ which strengtheneth me" (Philippians 4:13).

I will always remember a speaking engagement in Little Rock, Arkansas. When I stood up to speak, my stomach suddenly seemed to do flip-flops! Halfway through the message I felt that unless I left the stage quickly, I would be sick in front of the entire congregation.

I called for singers to come and minister while I took a break. I began to confess Philippians 4:13 so that my stomach would settle down, so that I could finish the service, and so that God would bring victory in it. As I spoke, I could literally feel strength return to my body. When the singers finished, I went out and finished the service. Many people were saved and Spirit-filled that night. When I returned to my room, my stomach tried to be upset, but I continued to speak to it through the night. Eventually my stomach settled down, and I was fine.

There are so many wonderful scriptures that we can confess whenever we need healing—physically, emotionally, or spiritually. Cry unto the Lord and He will heal you (Psalm 30:2).

Dear heavenly Father, we thank You that we can do ALL things, not through ourselves or others, but through Christ Who strengthens us. In Jesus' name, amen.

Day 235

"For He knoweth our frame" (Psalm 103:14a).

When I travel overseas, the flights are often long and tedious. For example, when you go to the Far East, you may spend as many as 19 hours on a plane before arriving at your destination.

Sometimes I try to catch a little sleep. In the past my body would get twisted into uncomfortable positions in the seat, and there would be little room to move my legs. There always seemed to be one place where the enemy attacked—my back.

When I got off the plane, I often felt like hobbling, but I knew that the Lord had called me to those faraway places and needed to use me there.

I needed physical help, so I cried out to the Lord, "You know my frame, and You know the seats of this airplane." He answered my needs and showed me how I could sleep in any kind of a situation or position. He knows how to keep my frame straight and in proper order.

When I am about the Lord's business, He is about mine.

Dear heavenly Father, thank You that You know our frames. You know our weaknesses, our frailties, and our strengths. You can pour in Your strength, for we are weak. In Jesus' name, amen.

Day 236

"He which soweth sparingly shall reap also sparingly; and he which soweth bountifully shall reap also bountifully" (II Corinthians 9:6).

This law works in the natural, as well as in the spiritual. I have found that if I sow joy in another person's life, I will experience joy in my own life. If I forgive, I will be forgiven.

My husband Wally once sowed a $1,000 gift into someone else's ministry. At that time our church was very small; in fact, we had just started it. Our old car needed replacing, and Wally had given away the very money that we had saved to buy a car. It almost overwhelmed me, but my husband held steady in his faith.

Within six months our old car had been wrecked; so then we didn't even have a car. Of course, we couldn't buy another one because Wally had given our money away. But within a two-week period, God brought a miracle into our midst: We were given a beautiful new station wagon.

You cannot sow without reaping in return. Your labor in the Lord is never in vain.

Dear heavenly Father, help us to see today that sowing and reaping is Your supernatural law. If we want to experience the supernatural, we have to do the works of the law. In Jesus' name, amen.

Day 237

"But now being made free from sin, and become servants to God, ye have your fruit unto holiness, and the end everlasting life" (Romans 6:22).

God wants us to be fruitful. He will provide many ways to be fruitful in His kingdom. Several years ago the United States began to have open doors to trade into China. In one of our services, a woman, who was unquestionably an intercessor, stood up and called our church to pray for China. There was a prophecy in tongues, followed by interpretation: In our midst was an angel who would mark those willing to sigh and cry over the abominations in China and over its losses.

My husband called for people who would give a certain amount of time each day to pray for the nation of China. Our church began to intercede for China, and from that time on, we began to see a breakthrough in that communist country.

Who knows what works God will do through us so that we can bring forth fruits for His glory! Daily we should keep our ears and eyes open to hear God's voice and to see what fruits we can nurture in His kingdom.

Dear heavenly Father, today we make ourselves available to You for prayer. Call upon us. We will pray for those whom You lay upon our hearts. In Jesus' name, amen.

Day 238

"For he that soweth to his flesh shall of the flesh reap corruption; but he that soweth to the Spirit shall of the Spirit reap life everlasting" (Galatians 6:8).

I am deeply concerned about the current emphasis on kinky sex and finding sexual satisfaction in ways that the Bible would never condone. In magazines and on TV, we are told that if we do kinky things in our sex lives, our mates will be better satisfied. I see it creeping even into Christian marriages! But I have noticed that more and more Christians are getting divorced!

Kinky sex (sowing to the flesh) is not going to reap spiritual results in your marriage. Kinky sex is not what's needed to bring satisfaction to our marriages. Kinky sex will not restore a bad marriage, nor will it energize a boring one.

What is the best ingredient to improve a mediocre marriage? The love of Jesus Christ! Ask God to show you how to add the love of Jesus to all aspects of your marriage—physical, emotional, and spiritual—and you will see your marriage grow in leaps and bounds! If you will sow the things of the spirit in your marriage, God will give you a good sexual relationship, a good spiritual relationship, and good communication.

We can't do kinky things and expect spiritual results—it doesn't work that way!

Dear heavenly Father, help us to see that the world is trying to sow demonic ideas in our marriages. Help us to resist these forces. In Jesus' name, amen.

Day 239

"He will fulfil the desire of them that fear him: he also will hear their cry, and will save them" (Psalm 145:19).

When our ministry staff recently visited a Honduran refugee camp, we saw many situations of poverty. But we also saw men and women who declared their faith boldly and lived in great joy and peace through their faith in Jesus Christ.

The people lived in small cabins overlooking a river that was the source of their water. They drank it, bathed in it, and cooked with it. During our visit the people offered us fruit drinks called "refrescos." The drinks looked strange and resembled dishwater. But I knew in my heart that I must accept the drink gratefully, regardless of the poor sanitation.

I asked the Lord to protect me and guard my strength and health. I believed that no plague would come nigh my body. I drank the "refresco," thanked the people for it, and it even tasted good to me.

Later a missionary confided that the people would have been insulted had I refused their offer. They had offered a gift of generosity from the depths of their poverty—it was truly a sacrifice.

God will hear our cries and protect us in all kinds of situations during times of need.

Dear heavenly Father, thank You that You are protecting us from the devil's devices. His plots and plans will be undone. In Jesus' name, amen.

Day 240

"Likewise reckon ye also yourselves to be dead indeed unto sin, but alive unto God through Jesus Christ our Lord" (Romans 6:11).

We must reckon ourselves dead to fear and sin. But we must also remember that the life of Jesus flows through us!

Years ago we traveled to Cyprus because I thought that my radio program was being broadcast there. I talked to the local station manager, but he said that they knew nothing about me! They had never received any tapes, and I was not on his station. He added that it was doubtful my program would ever be aired because it would be too controversial in a Moslem country. I could hardly believe that I had traveled halfway across the world, only to find that I wasn't even on the station.

I asked God to give me favor and to redeem my time. We drove to the airport, and I spoke God's Word against my anguish. When I boarded the plane, a steward called me to the front and said that the Cyprus broadcasting network had received my tapes from the United States. Because they liked me so well after meeting me, they decided to begin airing my programs, starting on the following Monday.

Dear heavenly Father, lead us by the Spirit that we might walk in Your divine timing today. In Jesus' name, amen.

Day 241

"For he hath strengthened the bars of thy gates; he hath blessed thy children within thee" (Psalm 147:13).

God does not give us children as a curse. He gives us children as a blessing. They are to be arrows that will go straight to the mark that God has planned for their lives.

For years my son was backslidden and did not serve the Lord. One morning while I prayed, I felt overwhelmed by the bad circumstances in his life. They were worse than I had ever seen. I cried out to God, "The circumstances are so bad!"

The Lord spoke assuringly, "That's what I use: circumstances."

Not long afterward my son called my husband and said, "Dad, I am in terrible trouble," and he confided the problems that he was experiencing. He said, "I want to rededicate my life to Christ."

Within one week my son and his fiancee had rededicated their lives to Christ, got married, and joined the church. Now my son is serving the Lord. God, in His great mercy, takes overwhelmingly cursed circumstances and transforms them into a blessing.

Dear heavenly Father, we pray today for joy. We pray that You will strengthen the bars of our gates so that the enemy cannot reach under the gate and grab our children. In Jesus' name, amen.

Day 242

"The just shall live by faith" (Romans 1:17b).

In 1981 we had the opportunity to visit Turkey. On a brief trip to Istanbul, we stayed with a missionary who had undertaken the translation of the New Testament into the modern-day Turkish language. This task put him in a precarious position where he could have easily been exiled from this Moslem country.

One evening this missionary took us to a secret prayer meeting. We climbed six flights of stairs to a small room that was jammed, wall-to-wall, with missionaries of all denominations. Baptists, Lutherans, and Pentecostals all worshiped and praised the Lord and encouraged each other with God's Word. They together were trusting God for a great revival in Turkey.

I later discovered that our lives could have been endangered if our prayer meeting had been discovered. But the service was one of the sweetest that I'd ever attended. The Spirit of faith that was present could turn the entire country to Jesus. Thank God for the seed He has sown around the world!

Dear heavenly Father, we know that we must live by faith. If we lived by our senses during this day, we would absolutely fail. But if we live by Your Word, it will grow and prevail in every situation and circumtance. We choose to live by Your Word today. Amen.

Day 243

"Praise him with the timbrel and dance"
(Psalm 150:4a).

When dancing in church was first introduced, many people believed that it was unscriptural. Several young women in our church had been ballet dancers, and they used their talents to minister to the Lord. But some of our people were very offended by the dance.

One day I did a study in Greek and Hebrew on dance in the Old and New Testaments. My research revealed that praise and adoration of God through dance was scriptural. The congregation had various reactions to the study. But one man offered heavy criticism and said that I was teaching people to dance. I told him that I wasn't taking dance myself, nor was I teaching people to dance. I was teaching them that they COULD dance because of God's Word.

That man then became very sweet to me. He said, "Marilyn, I have confidence in you. I have always known that you were walking by the counsel of God's Word."

Sometimes we may be unsure of our actions, but must remain confident that God is controlling our circumstances, as long as we walk in His Word.

Dear heavenly Father, we thank You that we do not need to fight our own battles. You said, "Stand still, and you will see the salvation of the Lord." We choose to stand fast in You today and see Your salvation in our circumstances. In Jesus' name, amen.

Day 244

"Though the Lord be high, yet hath he respect unto the lowly" (Psalm 138:6a).

After the Lord had opened up to me the beautiful opportunity to be on Dr. Yonggi Cho's Board of Directors, I then had a desire to speak at his church. I remember the first time when I asked the Lord to fulfill this desire. The devil said, "Cho can get good speakers. Why should he invite you?" But I believed that God would open the door.

Almost one year later I attended one of the annual board meetings. When I arrived, Dr. Cho said, "Marilyn, will you come to speak in my church in November?" I tried to be so calm. But if you had known what was happening on the inside of me, you probably would have laughed. I said, "First, I will have to check my calendar." But inside I was thinking, "I'll cancel anything on my calendar!"

I very calmly opened my purse, retrieved my calendar, and said, "There is nothing on that date," which there wasn't. When I left the room, I jumped and shouted for joy over this wonderful opportunity to minister in the largest church in the world. How good God is! He will open doors for us.

Dear heavenly Father, we pray that You will open a very special, supernatural door for us today. In Jesus' name, amen.

Day 245

"The Lord is gracious, and full of compassion; slow to anger, and of great mercy" (Psalm 145:8).

Did you ever feel like you were wearing out the Lord with your continual petitions?

Some years ago a woman with a supernatural gift of prophecy was ministering her gift to many well-known evangelists. My heart absolutely yearned for God to use that woman's gift of prophecy in my life.

When I was invited to speak at her home church, I begged the Lord for her to give me a word of wisdom. But nothing happened.

The next year I went again. I begged the Lord again. Nothing happened.

The next year I spoke at a convention in Mississippi. I opened the brochure to discover that this woman was also speaking at the convention. I thought, "God, You have another opportunity to give her a special word for me."

That night I spoke, and nothing happened. The next morning, which was my last time to speak, I didn't even see her in the service. My heart sank, but I kept my faith intact. At the end of the service, she finally arrived, and God gave her a marvelous word of wisdom that was uniquely sustaining for that time in my life.

Dear heavenly Father, we aren't quitters. Extend Your mercy to us, teach us, and train us to never give up, but to stand in faith. In Jesus' name, amen.

Day 246

"I will therefore that men pray every where, lifting up holy hands, without wrath and doubting" (I Timothy 2:8).

My overseas trips can sometimes be filled with feelings of loneliness and darkness—especially in areas where no Christian influence can be found.

We visited such a place in Asia. My husband and I were sitting in a beautiful restaurant of a large city. We felt very alone in this Moslem country. We ordered our meals, and suddenly we heard a beautiful song being played on the bar piano: "Majesty, Worship His Majesty." We sing this song in our church—it absolutely lifts you into the presence of Jesus Christ!

I poked my husband and said, "Honey, that woman is playing a chorus that we sing back home."

He listened very carefully and affirmed, "Yes, she is." We could hardly wait to finish our meal and rush over to the pianist. Sure enough, she was a brand-new born-again believer, who loved Jesus. The restaurant had hired her to play piano, and she would occasionally play a hymn that she had learned. She was expressing her faith with her talent.

Who knows where you'll meet another Christian!

Dear heavenly Father, we can praise You in all kinds of situations! You will be exalted in the most unusual circumstances, and we thank You that You are present everywhere! In Jesus' name, amen.

Day 247

"Behold, how good and how pleasant it is for brethren to dwell together in unity!" (Psalm 133:1).

Before my husband and I entered full-time ministry, we were very active in our church. If a teacher or choir member was needed, we volunteered. If prayer helpers were needed, we would pray for people. We dwelt in unity with our pastor in accordance with the direction of the Holy Spirit.

One night during an altar call for the Holy Spirit baptism, there came forward a certain family whom we deeply desired to see Spirit-filled. The parents and two children went forward, so my husband and I raced up to pray with them. We prayed with the children, and they became Spirit-filled. But when we started to pray with the mother, she said, "I cannot be Spirit-filled until my husband is. Otherwise we will fight."

We rushed over and prayed with the husband, and he received the Holy Spirit. Then we rushed back and said, "He's Spirit-filled." We prayed with her, and she became Spirit-filled too.

That woman wanted unity in her family. This may seem unusual; but however we see it, let's strive for unity in Jesus, even if we aren't in total agreement.

Dear heavenly Father, we thank You that it is good and pleasant when we are in unity. Help us to walk in peace with the Body. We desire harmony and love, not strife and dissension. In Jesus' name, amen.

Day 248

"Commit thy way unto the Lord; trust also in him; and he shall bring it to pass" (Psalm 37:5).

In our church we once had a beautiful, young, and dedicated woman who felt that she was becoming an "old maid." When she hit her 30th birthday, she decided to go into the world and find a mate.

The woman turned away from church and her spiritual responsibility. My husband and I were grieved in heart. But we stood fast in prayer, faith, and love. We prayed that God would work in her heart.

Her time in the world was very brief—perhaps 30 days or less. When she returned, she opened her heart to us, "It doesn't matter if I never marry. Jesus is my sufficiency. If He wants me to have a mate, He will bring me the best. If not, I will serve Him alone."

She committed her life totally to God. She did typing for me, taught Sunday school, and even cleaned my house. Three years passed. Then at a church picnic, she met a very handsome man about 40 years old. When he saw this lovely young woman, it was love at first sight. They were married and have a lovely little girl.

When this woman committed her way unto the Lord, He brought her desires to fulfillment.

Dear heavenly Father, we commit our ways unto You. We can trust You to do the supernatural, and we praise You for it. Amen.

Day 249

"The Lord hath done great things for us; whereof we are glad" (Psalm 126:3).

When I was teaching junior high school, my husband and I started a home Bible study for interested students. One of the first young women who had received the Lord in our home was extremely open and tender toward the Holy Spirit and soon became Spirit-filled. When she shared her new experience with her mother, however, the mother was so upset that her daughter could never again return to our home. The girl's mother did not want her daughter involved in "some kind of fanaticism"!

When this teenage girl told me what happened, my heart dropped. But she was in no way defeated. She said, "If you don't mind, perhaps the students who attend your class can share the Bible study with me on the next day." Carol received the word each week, not through our Bible study itself, but through the help of others who had attended. It was exciting to see her grow in Christ!

God can perform great miracles, even when it appears that the devil has closed doors.

Dear heavenly Father, help us not to accept closed doors. We know that You are a door-opener. You can open doors before us that no man can close! In Jesus' name, amen.

Day 250

"I am Jesus...I have appeared unto thee for this purpose...to open their eyes, and to turn them from darkness to light" (Acts 26:15b,16b,18a).

When my husband and I bought our first home, we committed it to the Lord. We prayed that it would not only be a lovely home for us to enjoy, but also a center of evangelism.

My husband once told me that he was bringing home a young man who was open to receive the Lord as Savior. My husband asked me to prepare a delicious meal, and he suggested red snapper as the main course. I found a recipe in my cookbook, and my husband brought home the fish. When he brought it home, I asked, "What do I do to it?"

"Nothing," he replied. "It's all ready. Just cut off the head." I prepared the sauce, poured it over the fish, and baked it according to the recipe's instructions.

When our guest arrived, I served the fish on my best platter. But when I cut into the fish, we heard a strange crunchy sound. To my dismay I found that the fish had not been scaled. We could in no way eat it. But we certainly caught a fish for Jesus that night because the young man received Christ into his heart and was baptized in the Holy Spirit. Hallelujah!

Dear heavenly Father, our circumstances may not always be as we desire them. But Your Word is supernatural. Your Holy Spirit will use every circumstance to bring You glory. In Jesus' name, amen.

Day 251

"Trust in him at all times; ye people, pour out your heart before him: God is a refuge for us" (Psalm 62:8a).

a missionary once told us about a supernatural experience she had in South America. God spoke to her early one morning before a pastors' breakfast. He said, "I want you to stay home and to pray."

"Oh Lord, this is SUCH an inconvenient time," she protested.

But the Lord dealt with her, "I want you to pray now." During prayer God assured her that when "the crisis" happened, He would produce a miracle.

She had no idea what "the crisis" might be, but she anchored her trust in God. That night when the song leader stood up and touched the microphone, electricity flowed through his body, and he was struck to the ground. Several men attempted to pull him away from the microphone, but it was useless. At that moment the Lord said to the woman, "Remember? I told you that I would give you a miracle in the midst of crisis."

She cried out to God. The voltage was broken, and the man was set free. By all standards he should have died. But he arose to lead the worship.

Dear heavenly Father, we thank You today that the devil will be defeated. If we will fall upon our knees in sensitivity to the Holy Spirit, we can gain the victory before the problem ever arises! In Jesus' name, amen.

Day 252

"It is more blessed to give than to receive" (Acts 20:35b).

When God opened the door for me to teach in Honduras, my great desire was to teach in the camps where the refugee Nicaraguans were sheltered. We drove and hiked many miles into the refugee camp. We were hot and tired upon our arrival.

A young pastor from Tegucigalpa aided us in interpretation. He was such a blessing!

When we returned to the city, we learned that this young pastor had a church of over 500 people, but he didn't even have a car! He rode a motorcycle to the camps so that he could preach to the refugees; he even carried in provisions. One missionary said of this pastor, "He is a mighty preacher."

I knew that God was stirring our hearts to help. I asked the young pastor, "What is your number-one priority that you are asking from God?" He said that he wanted a red pickup truck to drive into the refugee camps and deliver food, clothing, supplies, and prayer. We were happy to purchase that pastor's new truck.

We learned that on the first night he drove into a distant refugee camp, 1,000 people welcomed Jesus into their hearts.

Dear heavenly Father, we thank You for our opportunities to give. You so loved us that You gave us Jesus. We have His nature that loves to give. In Jesus' name, amen.

Day 253

"O Lord of hosts, blessed is the man that trusteth in thee" (Psalm 84:12).

*Y*ears ago we took a group to Beirut on a Holy Land tour. At that time the war had not yet begun.

Beirut is an exceptionally beautiful city. From there we went to visit the ancient ruins of Baa'lbek. One of the men from our group climbed up on a huge boulder in the ruins, fell, and broke his arm. Our tour group immediately gathered around him and prayed.

The woman who guided our tour was deeply touched to see us in prayer. After we had prayed for the man, she asked, "Will you pray for my 19-year-old daughter? She is dying of a rare, incurable disease. She has lost all will to live and is physically deteriorating."

We agreed in prayer with her. Then we invited her to a Christian service we were attending that evening. She AND her daughter agreed to attend.

Later we received a letter saying that the woman and her daughter had received Jesus as their Savior. The daughter had received healing and was walking with Jesus. Praise God for His goodness.

Dear heavenly Father, we thank You for bringing good out of evil. You turn curses to blessings when we turn to You and Your supernatural power. In Jesus' name, amen.

Day 254

"He that goeth forth and weepeth, bearing precious seed, shall doubtless come again with rejoicing, bringing his sheaves with him" (Psalm 126:6).

Sarah and I went to a neighborhood pizza restaurant that we agree has the "best pizza in the world!" As we ordered, a smiling woman approached us and was very friendly. She didn't look familiar to me at all. But she said, "Don't you remember me?" Then she told me her name.

I hadn't seen this woman for 22 years! She had been my student when I taught Spanish in a public junior high. Years ago at our home she had accepted Christ as her Savior. But when we entered full-time ministry, I lost track of the many students whom we had led to Christ.

She told me that she knew her ministry was, in her words, "serving the Lord." It's exciting to see seed become a productive sheaf, isn't it?

Remember, your labor in the Lord is NEVER in vain! Each seed you plant—no matter how small—can bring forth fruit for God's Kingdom!

Dear heavenly Father, we thank You that the good seed of Your Word, which we have sown through faith, will produce fruit. The fruit may not appear immediately, but it WILL appear. In Jesus' name, amen.

Day 255

"In God is my salvation and my glory: the rock of my strength, and my refuge, is in God" (Psalm 62:7).

When my children were young, we took a vacation in California. We visited one of California's beautiful beaches, where the children played on the swings and we enjoyed a half day in the sun. My husband and I joined Mike and Sarah on the swings, which they especially enjoyed.

When we were ready to leave, my husband discovered he couldn't find the car keys. We almost panicked! Where were the keys? What could have happened to them? But we decided to pray, rather than panic. We agreed that God would help us locate the keys.

While we stood there, a woman with a little girl stopped to talk to us. She was very friendly, so my husband took advantage of the situation and witnessed to her. She shared, in return, that she was Christian. She also mentioned that while she and her daughter had been swinging, they had found a set of keys and wondered to whom they belonged.

Isn't God special? He is our refuge, and we can trust Him.

Today, dear heavenly Father, we thank You that not only can You return lost keys, but You have also given us that special Key that unlocks any bad circumstances and gives us miracles. In Jesus' name, amen.

Day 256

"I will go in the strength of the Lord God" (Psalm 71:16a).

This scripture has been the spiritual theme of my life. Many times I have felt weak before speaking at a crusade or convention. But God tells us that when we are weak, we should confess His strength.

I have experienced tremendous anointings when I confess the Lord's strength. Samson received the same anointing of strength. God's anointing would break in upon Samson, and he would experience strength beyond that of any man! He then could perform supernatural feats of might.

God not only can strengthen our inner man, but He can impart strength to our physical being.

The Bible shows us many instances of supernatural strength and endurance being given to a mortal man when he was at work for God's Kingdom. Even Jesus had a man's body—but God's supernatural strength. Let's claim our physical heritage in Jesus.

When we are weak, let's say, "I am strong." We will receive our supply of supernatural strength. It works...I know it!

Dear heavenly Father, today we grasp the physical strength that You have for our day. As our day is mighty in You, so is our strength. In Jesus' name, amen.

Day 257

"For in him we live, and move, and have our being" (Acts 17:28a).

Several summers ago God opened a door for me to preach in Benin City, Nigeria. I knew that men and women would travel many miles from other countries to that convention. So I cried out to God for the greatest anointing that I had ever experienced.

Sometimes we may think that God anoints us only in teaching and preaching. But God's anointing is available in every situation we encounter.

On the conclusion of our first service, a young woman passed by me. I knew immediately that she needed ministry. I confronted her, and she briefly revealed her difficult home situation. We agreed in prayer for a miracle in her life.

Days later she presented me with a beautifully beaded bracelet. It was as though the Lord said to me, "Your ministry to this woman will bear fruit in Africa. When you look at this bracelet, it will remind you of My work in her life."

Sometimes our greatest ministry takes place on the sidelines. Remember, Jesus reigns in us at ALL times. We live, move, and have our being in Him.

Dear heavenly Father, we thank You that we live, move, and have our being in Jesus. He is guiding and directing every aspect of our lives. In Jesus' name, amen.

Day 258

"For thou, Lord, art good, and ready to forgive; and plenteous in mercy unto all them that call upon thee" (Psalm 86:5).

I remember when a beautiful door opened for me to minister the Word in an Episcopalian cathedral. Many women from my daytime home Bible studies brought their husbands to that evening service.

I remember one husband, in particular, who would sit quietly in each Bible study and stare at me as though to say, "I don't believe what you are saying." But God can do great things. Although a person's outward appearance may imply that they are unreceptive to God, His Word never returns void.

One year later the man's wife called me. "My husband is ready to receive the Lord," she said, "and he wants to be baptized in the Holy Spirit. But you are the only person with whom he will pray. I hate to pressure you, but will you come over to our house?"

I love that kind of pressure! I drove to the man's house. His heart was warm and open. He prayed, received Jesus as his Savior, and was baptized in the Holy Spirit.

God always beckons us to focus on the inward work, not the outward appearance.

Dear heavenly Father, we thank You today that we walk by the Spirit and not by sight. When we pray, You are at work in people's hearts. In Jesus' name, amen.

Day 259

"And immediately the angel of the Lord smote him, because he gave not God the glory: and he was eaten of worms, and gave up the ghost" (Acts 12:23).

God dealt with a pastor friend of ours to enlarge his church. But the pastor's board was very opposed to enlargement, so the pastor said, "Let's allow the church members to vote."

A member of the board, however, called every family and said, "Be sure to vote NO."

When the pastor heard of this, he wanted to call the people back and tell them, "Vote YES."

But God assured the pastor, "This is My battle. Stand still and see the salvation of the Lord." At the meeting that night, the pastor said, "Don't vote by what I say or by what others say. Just vote according to the voice and direction of the Holy Spirit."

He prayed with the people, and a secret ballot was taken. That night the majority voted to build the church! The head deacon was furious with the results, so he started his own church in one of the city's suburbs. His church never amounted to anything.

We cannot come against God's work and not suffer the devil's attacks. When we enter the devil's territory of strife, we are open to his work.

Dear heavenly Father, open our eyes to see that we are here to edify Your work. Lift the blinders from our eyes in any area that needs Your revelation. In Jesus' name, amen.

Day 260

"Mark the perfect man, and behold the upright: for the end of that man is peace" (Psalm 37:37).

Some years ago we had a beautiful young woman on our staff. She really loved Jesus, and her greatest ministry was probably that of mercy. She was extremely merciful to the downtrodden. She began dating a young Christian man who had many problems from his past. He loved the Lord, but he was very insecure.

The couple became engaged, but it was not an engagement directed by the Holy Spirit. My husband and I saw that the enemy was attempting to manipulate the mercy and compassion in that young woman's heart. We prayed and counseled with her and then submitted the situation to God's hands.

Soon the woman realized that she had been moving in pity for the young man. The woman said, "I am going to serve the Lord with all my heart. I know He will, in His own time, direct the right man to me." In six months God brought her the right husband. They have a beautiful marriage centered upon God's Word and the leading of His Spirit.

Dear heavenly Father, we thank You for the inward dealing of the Holy Spirit. Direct us and guide us to make right decisions. In Jesus' name, amen.

Day 261

"But the salvation of the righteous is of the Lord: he is their strength in the time of trouble" (Psalm 37:39).

Every time I went to a certain city in the midwest, there was one young man and his wife who would be available to help in any possible way. They had really taken hold of God's Word for their needs. They both came from poor backgrounds. Neither had extensive education, but they believed God to meet their needs.

They lived with four children in a tiny apartment and desperately needed a house. To buy a house, they needed at least $10,000. They asked me to agree with them for God to meet the needs.

We agreed together, thanked God for His provision, and continued to praise Him. Nothing happened immediately. Then one day when the man was driving to his Bible study, the enemy harassed him about his lack of funds. But he replied, "My miracle must be close, or I wouldn't have such a harassment."

After the Bible study he picked up his tape recorder and Bible and found a small envelope with his name on it. At home he opened the envelope and found $10,000 in cash—the exact amount needed as a down payment for a home!

Dear heavenly Father, when we are faithful about Your business, You are certainly faithful about our business. Meet us in our areas of need. In Jesus' name, amen.

Day 262

"The steps of a good man are ordered by the Lord: and he delighteth in his way" (Psalm 37:23).

When our church was young and small, we desperately needed an assistant pastor. Our number-one goal was to find THE person whom the Holy Spirit had designated.

We called a friend of ours who traveled a great deal and asked, "Can you recommend anyone?"

He said, "No, but I have a scripture for you. 'That which is in darkness shall be revealed. That which is hidden shall be brought to light' [I Corinthians 4:5]." He said, "It's someone who's in hiding."

We thought his words sounded so strange! How would you find someone in hiding? But shortly afterward my husband asked me to call a friend of his. I called the pastor, and he said, "It's strange that you would call me! I've been in hiding for one year." His words stunned me! Then he said, "I might be interested in the position."

That night the friend called my husband, moved to Denver shortly afterward, and ministered beautifully in our church.

Dear heavenly Father, remind us that not only do You prepare our hearts, but You prepare the hearts of others to correspond with ours. Help us not to force circumstances, but be submissive to Your will. In Jesus' name, amen.

Day 263

"Cease from anger, and forsake wrath: fret not thyself in any wise to do evil" (Psalm 37:8).

A young man on my staff shared a marvelous testimony with me. He had purchased an expensive bicycle that he absolutely loved and rode to work whenever possible. But one night someone broke into his house and stole his bicycle. He was very angry because he had saved for the bicycle, and now it was gone.

The Lord really dealt with my staff member to cease from anger, forsake wrath, and trust God. The man called the police, filed a report of theft, and said, "Father, I trust You."

One year later a bicycle repair shop employee called my staff member and said, "I remember selling you a bicycle. Today someone came into my shop with the same bike. The numbers even match! I suspected that the bicycle was stolen, so I called the police, who still had the theft record." The man's bicycle was returned to him one year later—in perfect shape!

God will fight for us. We need to seek His wisdom in trials and then expect a miracle!

Dear heavenly Father, today we thank You that You are a God of the miraculous. Anger only harms us and causes us to miss Your supernatural. Help us to forsake wrath and walk in Your wisdom. In Jesus' name, amen.

Day 264

"And the Lord turned the captivity of Job, when he prayed for his friends" (Job 42:10a).

Many people feel that Job's trial was a blessing in disguise from God. I do not believe that. According to the Word, it was the devil who took from Job. His affliction was called a "captivity," not a "blessing." In the hedge of Job's life, there existed a gap that made him susceptible to Satan's attack.

When you read the book of Job, you find that Satan, not God, robs Job. And in the end we find that God gives much to Job. Satan is always a thief; he takes away. But God is a giver.

If there is an area of fear in your life, Satan can use this as an opportunity to rob from you, just as he robbed from Job.

People have often emphasized Job's trials, rather than the story's ending. But the book of James tells us, "Consider his end" (James 5:11). Job's trials lasted only about nine months, but he lived for 140 years. Let's "major" on his blessings and "minor" on his trials.

Dear heavenly Father, thank You today that whatever the trial or affliction we may face, You have a supernatural way for us to be victorious. We give You praise and glory for what You are doing in our lives. In Jesus' name, amen.

Day 265

"He that is of a proud heart stirreth up strife: but he that putteth his trust in the Lord shall be made fat" (Proverbs 28:25).

Strife always brings problems. Out of it comes every evil work. Sometimes it is very difficult not to respond to people who speak against us. One time I was very upset because a woman had told some terrible lies about me. I wanted to respond by telling her off, but the Lord said, "Vengeance is mine."

The Lord told me that He would fight for me and that I should bless my enemies. I made the decision not to enter into the strife. It was the Lord's problem, not mine. If any fighting were to be done, the Lord would have to do it for me.

God prospered me in that situation. I will never forget it, and I remind myself of it when I have new opportunities for strife. Strife is a luxury you cannot afford; it is too expensive. Strife will cost you time, energy, and your mental peace and well-being. If you want to be a victorious Christian, stay out of strife.

Dear heavenly Father, help us today to see the pitfalls of strife. Help us to rebuke and resist strife with all of our hearts. You said, "Blessed are the peacemakers." Help us to see that we cannot be a part of strife. In Jesus' name, amen.

Day 266

"But know that the Lord hath set apart him that is godly for himself: the Lord will hear when I call unto him" (Psalm 4:3).

*Y*ears ago a small group in Estes Park asked whether we would be willing to take them under the umbrella of our corporation so that they could begin a new work and, at the same time, offer their people a tax credit for their gifts.

The group was very small, and my husband felt "led of the Spirit" to agree. At that time a young man on our part-time staff was attending Bible school. When he completed his training, he felt led by God to pastor that church in Estes Park.

While Dave was pastoring the church, a young cowboy came in, was born again, and Spirit-filled. He later moved to Denver and began to attend our church. Little did we know the wonderful fruit that we would reap from that small church.

This young man later became an assistant pastor—and an excellent one at that! He and his wife were with us for six years and have now begun a work in San Diego.

Dear heavenly Father, show us today that when You call us to perform certain tasks, we are set apart for Your purposes. By sowing seed in Your purposes, we will reap during our times of need. In Jesus' name, amen.

Day 267

"Bless the Lord, O my soul, and forget not all his benefits: who forgiveth all thine iniquites; who healeth all thy diseases" (Psalm 103:2,3).

The word BLESS is a very powerful word. However, if we do not mix blessings with faith, then we lose the benefits promised to us. Basically, the Bible tells us that we are to bless three things: 1) We are to bless our circumstances. Never murmur against them. What we bless will bless us.

2) We are to bless our enemies. Never talk against them or criticize them. Never do evil to them. When we bless them, then, in turn, they will bless us. When a man's ways please the Lord, He will make his enemies to be at peace with us. 3) We are to bless the Lord. You might say, "The Lord doesn't need to be blessed. He is already blessed." But when we bless the Lord, He blesses us back.

Remember, when we bless the Lord, He forgives all of our sins and heals all of our diseases. Spend time blessing the Lord today! If you sow blessings, you will reap them. He will bless you back!

Dear heavenly Father, help us today not to murmur against our circumstances, but to bless them. Help us to not murmur against our enemies, but to bless them. Above all, help us to bless You. Throughout the day we will take time to bless You, Father, with our hearts. In Jesus' name, amen.

Day 268

"Two are better than one; because they have a good reward for their labour. For if they fall, the one will lift up his fellow:...And if one prevail against him, two shall withstand him; and a threefold cord is not quickly broken" (Ecclesiastes 4:9,10,12).

Several years ago a dear friend asked me if I would befriend a certain pastor's wife. I asked "Why?"

He told me, "Marilyn, I feel led of the Spirit that you should be friends with this woman." The woman and her husband pastored a church thousands of miles away. I felt awkward calling up to say, "I want to be your friend." However, my friend was adamant, so I called the woman and initiated a friendship.

The situation was initially awkward. Nevertheless, I continued. In the next six months, a tremendous crisis fell upon her marriage and her church. I told her, "I am going to stand with you as your friend during this time." The marriage did not collapse, the church continued, and today this couple is serving God in a beautiful way.

We need friends who will stand with us in the times when the enemy would like to pull us under. We need to wrap our love around our friends with the power of the Holy Spirit.

Dear heavenly Father, we always want someone to minister to us. Show us opportunities to minister to others during their times of need. Help us see how we can bless, build up, and edify others. Amen.

Day 269

"And be not conformed to this world: but be ye transformed by the renewing of your mind, that ye may prove what is that good, and acceptable, and perfect, will of God" (Romans 12:2).

When we act like people in the world, we CONFORM to their standard. But the Word of God TRANSFORMS us: It renews our minds and causes us to think like Him. The word for TRANSFORM is the same word as "transfigure." When Jesus spoke with Moses and Elijah, He was transfigured. There was a glow from within.

When your mind is renewed with God's Word, your mind also begins to glow from within from God's Word. Then, because of the renewing of your mind, you will know what is good, you will know what is acceptable, and you will know the perfect will of God.

It is very important to have a continual process of renewing your mind. Renewal can be achieved by reading, meditating, and "chewing" on God's Word in a daily way. Then we make right decisions. Because we live in and associate with the world, our thoughts can, at any moment, conform to the world. That's why it is so important to meditate on God's Word daily.

Dear heavenly Father, help us today to meditate on Your Word and to keep our minds renewed with a daily reading of Your Word. In Jesus' name, amen.

Day 270

"...be instant in season, out of season"
(II Timothy 4:2a).

When my husband and I were in Santa Fe, New Mexico, for a yearly vacation, we inquired one day about finding a Spirit-filled church to attend. We wanted to be refreshed in the Lord.

We found a church near our motel and slipped into the back of the church for the service. Suddenly the pastor called our names and asked us to come to the platform. We felt somewhat uneasy because we really just wanted to rest and take in God's Word. But we went to the platform, and the pastor asked me to discuss my upcoming trip to Ethiopia.

I shared with the congregation. Then God moved upon my husband to give the congregation a beautiful prophecy concerning the future of that church. We sat down, the pastor preached, and we thoroughly enjoyed his message. He closed the service by asking the people to give financial gifts for my trip to Ethiopia. That morning we received a check for $3,700. I was absolutely overwhelmed by the generosity of a church that I had never attended! It truly pays to be instant IN and OUT OF season.

Dear heavenly Father, help us not to be "seasonal" Christians. Help us to be available Christians who know that You have many open doors for us. We bless Your holy name today. In Jesus' name, amen.

Day 271

"A fool's voice is known by multitude of words" (Ecclesiastes 5:3b).

One winter when I first began to travel, I was invited to speak in a distant city. When I arrived, I was told that I would stay at a church member's home. But I soon discovered that my room did not have heat! Not only was it extremely cold, it also was dirty and "buggy." Of all things, I was upset because some bugs got into a wig of mine! It was just a horrendous situation!

I voiced my complaint to some people in the church, and my complaint came back to the hostess. It was a very negative and embarrassing situation, and I had to apologize.

Sometimes we can say foolish and unthinking things. When we try to straighten out the damage, it often becomes worse, not better.

I should have simply asked for two more blankets, shaken the bugs from my wig, and never opened my big mouth.

I have learned from such situations, and I'm sure that you are learning too.

Dear heavenly Father, help us to watch our mouths and speak good words in bad situations. Fill our hearts with Your Word that we might speak its abundance from our hearts. In Jesus' name, amen.

Day 272

"That the communication of thy faith may become effectual by the acknowledging of every good thing which is in you in Christ Jesus" (Philemon 6).

Several years ago we had an emergency call from Poland requesting another $20,000 worth of Bibles for a church. It was a door opened by God to bring His Word into a communist country. However, this was also a tremendous challenge to my faith because we were facing extremely tight financial circumstances due to the mail theft I have mentioned earlier.

The Lord dealt with me to communicate my faith by acknowledging Who Jesus was IN me. I acknowledged faith, not fear. I had a witness in my heart that we could do it. We believed God to send us $20,000 in ten days for those Bibles. We didn't know how He would do it, but we continued to communicate that Jesus in us was providing faith for a miracle.

Within ten days we had $20,000. To give $20,000 in Bibles to Poland was a sowing of a tithe on the amount that had been stolen. God soon redeemed what had been lost and supernaturally lifted us out of the financial crisis. We need to acknowledge Who He is in us during times of crisis.

Dear heavenly Father, help us to communicate verbally the good things that Jesus is in us. We praise and thank You for it. In Jesus' name, amen.

Day 273

"Who despiseth the word shall be destroyed: but he that feareth the commandment shall be rewarded" (Proverbs 13:13).

Sometimes in Spirit-filled circles, we see people so thrilled and excited about the baptism of the Holy Spirit that they begin to put the "leadings of the Spirit" over the directions in God's Word. God esteems His Word more than His name. We should always test our leadings with the Word of God. If they do not get in line with God's Word, then we need to discard them.

When we started Happy Church many years ago, we had one member who had many "leadings" that she felt were directed to our church and my husband Wally. She would call Wally up and tell him what the Holy Spirit had "told her" that our church was supposed to be doing. My husband would ask her if she had some related scripture, and she would say, "I don't have to read the Bible. I have the direct leading of the Holy Spirit."

Of course, we did not follow her leadings. She became very offended at us and left the church. She also left every other church she had ever attended because of refusals to listen to her leadings. Today she is in horrible confusion. None of her children serve the Lord.

Dear heavenly Father, help us today to esteem Your Word and give it the right place in our lives. In Jesus' name, amen.

Day 274

"Charity never faileth" (I Corinthians 13:8a).

This scripture has also been translated as "Love never fails" (New International Version). Love doesn't fail. It always wins!

I was 19 years old when my mother received the baptism of the Holy Spirit. Her life was so changed and transformed—and so was our home! I will never forget the first weekend I came home from college. There were Bibles on all the end tables in our living room. Scriptures were posted by the kitchen sink and even on the refrigerator.

My brother and I began verbally to harass my mother. When she would try to witness to us, we would say to her, "Who put a nickel in your soapbox? Don't preach to us." But she continued to love us and give us the Word.

Even though her children refused the most wonderful gift (Jesus), my mother continued to be strong in her love and charity toward my brother and me. Her love had the strength of the love of Jesus Christ.

As the scripture says, "Love doesn't fail." Love wins, and it was the love of Jesus in my mother that overturned the rebellion in us. Today we are both saved and Spirit-filled.

Thank You, Father, for showing us that we must let Your love flow through us. Worldly, natural love runs out so quickly. But we have the sustaining power of Your supernatural love through Jesus. Amen.

Day 275

"A lover of hospitality" (Titus 1:8a).

Years ago an evangelist and his wife stayed with us while they held a four-week series of meetings in our church. The meetings were excellent, but our guests were very demanding.

The couple held two daily services, which I attended. In addition, I was caring for my tiny baby and waiting hand-and-foot upon our guests. The evangelist's wife never offered to help serve a meal and, instead, demanded service. I soon found myself murmuring consistently.

The Lord finally dealt with me. He said, "If you sow hospitality, you will reap it. To be a lover of hospitality is not always to be a lover of your guests' ways."

Many, many times I have reaped abundant hospitality from the sowing of seed during that difficult time of my life. God gave me a love for my guests and helped me to see myself as a servant—His servant.

God doesn't always call us to perform easy or pleasant tasks—but we like the harvest from the seed that we have sown!

Dear heavenly Father, help us to be lovers of hospitality. Cause our homes to be evangelistic centers that are filled with the love of Jesus. We ask in Jesus' name, amen.

Day 276

"Forgetting those things which are behind, and reaching forth unto those things which are before" (Philippians 3:13).

Once we forget the past, we can then reach forth to the things that are ahead. If we continue to remember the past, it will press against our "present" and keep us from the future that God has for us. We can't look backward and forward at the same time.

The Lord tells us that He puts our sins as far from us as the east is from the west. I'm glad He didn't say north from south because then we would meet our sins again! If you start walking south, eventually you'll reach the south pole, and then you'll be going north. North and south can meet each other, but east and west can never meet! There is no east or west pole.

When God forgives us of our sins, He forgets them. He never meets them again, and He doesn't intend for us to meet them either. Therefore, we leave the past sins behind and look to the future glory.

Don't let yourself be burdened down with the memory and guilt of past sins. Christ shed His blood on the cross so that we might no longer be bowed under with the weight of all our sins. Hand them to Him!

Dear heavenly Father, we thank You today that we can forget the past. It cannot exercise power over our present or future. We reach forth for the things that You have for us today. In Jesus' name, amen.

Day 277

"For he shall give his angels charge over thee, to keep thee in all thy ways" (Psalm 91:11).

*T*he first time I ever went to Rome, I was overwhelmed with how the Italians handle their traffic. Basically, they don't handle it! Cars go in every direction, while the people honk very aggressively at each other.

Once while in Rome we had just finished visiting a beautiful church, and it started to rain. So about ten of us dashed for shelter across a busy street. Suddenly a city bus turned the corner. Because the streets were wet, the bus could not stop in time. I was hit on my right hip, flew into the air, and landed on my left hip. The bus driver and the passengers got out, and in true Italian nature, they began to get very excited over this "poor" American. But much to their surprise, I stood up and wasn't injured at all! I wasn't even bruised where the bus hit my right hip, and I was not even wet.

I believe with all my heart that God had given His angels charge over me. My daily prayer for myself and my loved ones is that God will give His angels charge over us and keep us in ALL our ways.

Dear heavenly Father, thank You for appointing angels to be in charge over us. We ask that today our angels would protect us and our loved ones and keep us in all our ways. In Jesus' name, amen.

Day 278

"So then faith cometh by hearing, and hearing by the word of God" (Romans 10:17).

Faith DOES come by hearing God's Word. But many people hear God's Word and don't believe it, so they don't get its benefits.

Do you remember Rahab (Joshua 6)? She, along with all of Jericho's inhabitants, had heard about the God of the Hebrews. The people of Jericho all heard the same report; but Rahab alone heard AND BELIEVED. Not only did she believe in her heart, but she confessed it with her mouth and acted out her faith by hiding the Israelite spies.

Because of Rahab's willingness to believe what she had heard, she was rewarded beyond her wildest imagination. When the rest of Jericho was destroyed, the walls of Rahab's dwelling remained standing—as a testimony to her belief in God's Word.

We can hear God's Word continually, but until we believe what we hear and then act on it, it is not profitable to us.

When you hear the Word, don't just casually receive it in your mind. Meditate on it. Accept it and receive it as a special message from God to you. Then use it to benefit your life.

Dear heavenly Father, help us to mix our faith with Your Word, to take Your Word and use it in our lives, and to know that it is Your personal message to us. In Jesus' name, amen.

Day 279

"Let the Lord be magnified, which hath pleasure in the prosperity of his servant" (Psalm 35:27).

Many years ago Oral Roberts came to town for a large citywide crusade. Many people were born again in that crusade, and Wally and I later called upon each one individually.

Several families came to visit our church on the Sunday after we had called. At the evening service our new visitors had an unsettling experience: five men were causing confusion during worship. We wanted to impress these brand-new converts. But these five men were doing really nutty things—like prophesying in the name of Jeremiah and getting up and running out of the service. (Our church was just a small building—so it was very obvious.) My husband corrected the men and hoped for the best.

The next day we went to call on our new visitors to see how they had reacted. In every case, they said that a "voice" deep inside had warned them that something was wrong with these men and that their actions were not clean nor purely of God. The new converts were not at all upset or overwhelmed by Satan's tricks! God was, indeed, watching over His new servants!

Dear heavenly Father, we thank You today that You delight in taking care of us, watching over us, and guiding and directing our steps into truth. In Jesus' name, amen.

Day 280

"For whosoever shall call upon the name of the Lord shall be saved" (Romans 10:13).

Many people think that it's difficult to be saved. They say, "You mean, all I have to do is to call upon God? That's too easy—too simple." It IS simple to be saved—for one reason: Jesus has done what is necessary. It is not what we have done. It has already been done. We must simply believe that He has done it for us.

Today's scripture can transform any life—if it is mixed with faith. If we call upon the name of the Lord, repent of our sins, invite Jesus into our hearts, and confess it boldly with our mouths, the Bible says that we will be saved. Jesus did it all. He paid it all so that we might have it all.

Today, ask the Lord to lead you to someone who needs Him. Ask God to open that person's heart and show him how he can call upon the name of Jesus and receive the cleansing of Christ's blood for all sins. Let Jesus be acknowledged as the Lord of that person's life.

Dear heavenly Father, we thank You that every one of us is called to be a soul winner. Each of us is called to be light wherever there is darkness. Lead us to a hungry soul in Jesus' name. Amen.

Day 281

"My soul, wait thou only upon God; for my expectation is from him" (Psalm 62:5).

Sometimes it takes time to receive the wisdom that we need and to have our expectations fulfilled by the Lord. One time as I was sitting on a plane, the stewardess came to me and shared that she was a born-again believer. Then she asked me my advice, "You know, I receive many opportunities to witness on these planes. Many people open up and tell me their problems, and I'm able to lead them to Christ or pray with them. But I DO have to serve liquor. Do you think I'm missing God's will for my life?"

I meditated for a moment, and it seemed that the Lord quickened something to me that I had never thought about in my whole life. I said, "Nehemiah was a cupbearer to the king, and God used him to rebuild the walls of Jerusalem. Nehemiah had to carry liquor, and God never condemned Nehemiah. That seems to have been his special position."

This was the answer that she needed, but it was not an answer that came from Marilyn Hickey. It was an answer that came from the throne of grace. The stewardess had waited on the Lord for an answer, and she was not disappointed. You won't be, either.

Dear heavenly Father, today help us not to be impatient when we need answers, but to wait on You and know that our expectations will be met by You in due time. In Jesus' name, amen.

Day 282

"He maketh peace in thy borders, and filleth thee with the finest of wheat" (Psalm 147:14).

God will give us an abundance of revelation knowledge—the good seed out of His Word. As an adult, I received some of my best advice on studying the Bible from...a TEENAGER!

When our church was very small, I was the leader of our teens. One young man had a tremendous hunger to study God's Word. He showed me a small indexed notebook where he wrote the scriptures according to topics. Whenever people had questions about healing, he would immediately refer to that category. Many times he would also jot down special revelations that the Holy Spirit gave him.

At that time I also taught a small home Bible study. Sometimes I did not have specific answers to questions. But with a small indexed notebook such as my student's, I began keeping scriptures and applying them to specific situations where needed.

Today I have many such notebooks on alphabetized topics, Bible characters, and even whole books of the Bible—all supplemented with revelation knowledge. It is a valuable reference resource that I constantly use to teach the Bible on radio and television.

Dear heavenly Father, help us to be consistent and stable in our study of Your Word. Then You will be consistent and stable in giving us revelation knowledge. In Jesus' name, amen.

Day 283

"The Lord is my light and my salvation; whom shall I fear?" (Psalm 27:1a).

When I went to Poland, I asked the pastor of the church where I spoke whether it would be all right for me to teach people how to receive the baptism of the Holy Spirit. He said, "No, It would take hours for people to receive the baptism of the Holy Spirit, and we have to vacate the building promptly after the service."

I told him that I could give them instructions and they could be Spirit-filled in 10 minutes. He said, "I cannot believe it, but go ahead and try."

I felt that some of these men and women had been seeking an infilling of the Spirit for years. They knew God's Word, and faith comes by hearing the Word. I gave everyone brief, simple instructions from the scriptures. These people had no fear or hesitation about receiving this wonderful, new gift—for the Lord was their light and salvation. They acted on the Word, and many were immediately filled with the Holy Spirit. It caused quite a stir in that church!

The Lord is our light, and He will help us to walk in the light.

Dear heavenly Father, thank You that the light of Your Word leads us in the path that You have chosen for us. We have no fear because we trust You completely. Amen.

Day 284

"If any man among you seem to be religious, and bridleth not his own tongue, but deceiveth his own heart, this man's religion is vain" (James 1:26).

One day the Lord spoke strongly to me about my tongue. He told me that I had begun to listen to bits and pieces of gossip about people and then repeated it all to my husband. I had developed a critical attitude. Instead of praying for these people, I was gossiping about them.

God directed me to the scripture in Ezekiel that says the Lord was looking for a man to stand in the gap of the hedge. God chastised me for becoming a "gap finder," rather than a "gap stander." Then He reminded me about some people with whom I had been very angry. These people had gossiped and said untrue things about my ministry. God said, "You reap what you sow. You have gossiped about others; now others are gossiping about you."

I repented deeply and asked the Lord to help me daily with my tongue. The sins of the tongue are among the most serious that we commit. The tongue can build up or tear down. It is so important to ask God for help in bridling our own tongues.

Dear heavenly Father, help us guard our mouths today. Check us if we begin to gossip or criticize. Remind us that when we sow gossip or criticism, we also will reap it. We cannot afford such an expensive harvest. In Jesus' name, amen.

Day 285

"When my heart is overwhelmed: lead me to the rock that is higher than I" (Psalm 61:2b).

When my husband Wally was a child, his sister Shirley was burned severely in an accident. She died a few days later. Shirley had been the "baby" of the family, and she was very much adored. My husband's father became very bitter, and he spoke harshly against the Lord.

But one day Wally's mother said to her husband, "Albert, we cannot afford to be bitter against the Lord. We need Him too much right now."

I believe with all my heart that it was the devil who destroyed Shirley's life. But she's in heaven today, and we cannot let the devil destroy us, too, with bitterness down here. Bitterness is a poison that can seep into all parts of your body and soul. It can taint the way you view life and the way that you live your life. Bitterness can multiply and feed upon itself until it overwhelms everything else.

Don't let bitterness overwhelm you. Go to the Rock that is higher than you, and let Him remove any bitterness in your situation.

Father, we thank You that when we feel overwhelmed by circumstances, Your Holy Spirit will lead us to the Rock, Jesus Christ. In His name we pray, amen.

Day 286

"Above all, taking the shield of faith, wherewith ye shall be able to quench all the fiery darts of the wicked" (Ephesians 6:16).

*T*he devil plays dirty. He is ugly, mean, and full of hate. When God finally opened the door for me to teach the Bible on an educational channel here in Denver, an atheist group picketed the station that broadcast my program. The atheists felt that the Bible should not be taught on an educational channel.

When picketing didn't force the cancellation of my program, the group approached the Denver school board, which controls the station. The leader of the group of atheists planned to appear before the school board to protest my program. We prayed that the devil's tools would be put to confusion that night.

When the leader of the atheist group stood up, he couldn't speak his sentences correctly. The school board couldn't understand what he was saying. The school board chairman pressed him with questions, but the answers made no sense. Finally he said, "Just sit down and be quiet. You're so confused that we don't understand what you are saying. Marilyn Hickey's program is going to stay on the air." If God is for us, who can be against us (Romans 8:31b)!

Dear heavenly Father, in the name of Jesus, we call forth the supernatural for today's situations and circumstances. The enemy is defeated, and we are victorious. Amen.

Day 287

"The sufferings of this present time are not worthy to be compared with the glory which shall be revealed in us" (Romans 8:18).

Many of our Christian brothers and sisters suffer severe persecution for their faith in Jesus. When ministering in Honduras, we went to a refugee camp for Nicaraguan refugees. One pastor told us a story of how he and 800 of his church members fled on foot so that their lives might be spared. If they had stayed, they would have been forced, upon threat of death, to join the communist political movement in their country. They fled at night and hid during the day.

On his shoulders the pastor carried his 16-year-old crippled son—for over 150 miles. But the pastor had no pity stories to tell! He was sweet, warm, and full of praise toward God, Whose protection brought safety. The pastor and the church families had forsaken every possession. But they were experiencing God's glory in the camp. Many were being saved and Spirit-filled.

Sometimes our sufferings seem almost too difficult to bear. If we are not careful, these sufferings can overwhelm us and become a stumbling block in our pathway. We must remember that God's final glory will make all sufferings seem like nothing!

Dear heavenly Father, remind us to pray continually for our suffering brothers and sisters. Give us compassion and a desire to minister to their needs. In Jesus' name, amen.

Day 288

"The Lord is not slack concerning his promise, as some men count slackness; but is longsuffering to us-ward, not willing that any should perish, but that all should come to repentance" (II Peter 3:9).

On our first trip to Israel, we changed planes in Cyprus. I sat next to a man who was traveling to Israel on official business.

As we talked, I prayed silently that the Holy Spirit would open this man's heart. I asked him what church he attended. He told me that he attended a large, old-line denominational church. He said, "I go to church every Sunday, but my heart is empty."

I asked him, "Do you feel that you have the Author of the Bible in your heart?"

He said, "No."

He was so open! Right there on the plane, we joined hands and prayed, and he invited Jesus into his heart. When we landed in Tel Aviv, I introduced my friend to the members of our tour group. He openly told them that he was born again—that he had received Christ in his heart.

Since that time my husband has corresponded with this man and sent him Christian books. Isn't it wonderful to see God work in the lives of others!

Dear heavenly Father, help us today to be bold witnesses for Jesus Christ so that all can come to repentance. Give us mouths full of wisdom that the enemy cannot gainsay or resist. In Jesus' name, amen.

Day 289

"Wherewithal shall a young man cleanse his way? by taking heed thereto according to thy word" (Psalm 118:9).

The Word will not only TAKE you out of trouble, but it will also KEEP you out of trouble.

When I was growing up, my mother would always say, "I never want you to smoke. If you begin smoking, it will just break my heart." My father was a heavy smoker, and smoking had really affected his health.

When I was 16 years old, my very best friend began to smoke. I decided to start smoking secretly with her. But when I lit up my first cigarette, my mother's words came back to me. I never smoked again because I would always think, "I am breaking my mother's heart." My mother's prayers kept me out of trouble many times.

I once heard of a young woman who was extremely depressed. Her mother called upon God to release her daughter from this wretched condition, and today this daughter is healed and a leader in a Spirit-filled church.

Dear heavenly Father, help us to know that Your Word will not only take us out of trouble, but it will keep us out of trouble. In Jesus' name, amen.

Day 290

"Take therefore no thought for the morrow: for the morrow shall take thought for the things of itself" (Matthew 6:34a).

We never know exactly where God will lead us or what wonderful things that He has in store for us.

Years ago my husband and his assistant pastor drove by an older denominational church in our city. It had beautiful architecture, so my husband said, "Let's run in and have a look. I'd love to see the stained glass windows."

When they entered the church, a woman from one of my Bible studies ran up to Wally and said, "I can't believe you're here in this building! Today we were having our women's meeting, and Ruth [another woman from one of my Bible studies] had a heart attack. Will you come and pray for her?"

Wally went into a small Sunday school room where women were gathered around Ruth. Wally and his assistant laid hands on Ruth and asked God for a miracle. That's exactly what Ruth received, and she lived for many years afterwards.

Dear heavenly Father, we thank You that You are leading us by Your Spirit. We don't have to worry about what tomorrow holds because we know that You hold all our tomorrows. In Jesus' name, amen.

Day 291

"But the Lord is faithful, who shall stablish you, and keep you from evil" (II Thessalonians 3:3).

*T*hrough the years I have watched God transform miserable, cursed situations into blessings. We once has a wonderful schoolteacher in our church. He had even initiated Bible studies in the public school where he also taught. Many teenagers were saved and Spirit-filled. His own teenagers attended the same school and witnessed to their classmates.

Eventually some of the parents became irate about their children's born-again experiences. This teacher was, as a result, suspended from his job for one year. But he remained established in faith and did not become bitter. Later that year a man from Oral Roberts University spoke at our church. Upon meeting our teacher, the ORU speaker suggested that our friend apply for a teaching position at the university. He was accepted and has taught there for many years.

When the devil closed one door, God just opened a better one! When we pray in the Spirit, all things work together for good. If you are ever in a "closed-door" situation, pray in the Spirit. God will turn your curse into a blessing!

Dear heavenly Father, we pray that what the devil has intended for evil will turn for our good because of Your supernatural power toward us. In Jesus' name, amen.

Day 292

"And what is the exceeding greatness of his power to us-ward who believe, according to the working of his mighty power" (Ephesians 1:19).

One night in our church we showed a film about a young man's dramatic deliverance from the occult. When my husband gave an altar call, one young woman began to scream and cry. Her screams came from the demon power within her.

I knelt beside her and began to command the devil to come out of her. Nothing happened. In fact, she screamed louder.

I asked, "Lord, what's wrong?"

He replied, "Tell her to command the devil to leave in Jesus' name."

I whispered that into her ear, but she said, "I cannot do it."

Very boldly I said, "You can do it. Do it!"

She said, "I can't."

"Then just leave," I said. "You don't sincerely want deliverance."

When I said that, she spoke boldly, "Go, in Jesus' name!"

Instantly her countenance changed. She was absolutely transformed.

Dear heavenly Father, thank You today that the devil cannot assert authority over us unless we allow it. We choose to use the power in the name of Jesus to triumph in every area of our lives. In Jesus' name, amen.

Day 293

"I shall be satisfied, when I awake, with thy likeness" (Psalm 17:15b).

My husband and I have often asked the Lord to help us witness to his family. One summer we traveled to visit them. On our way we met a young man at a rest stop. We asked him to share our lunch. He accepted and told us about his travel plans.

As we talked, it became evident that his heart was ready for Jesus—he was hungry for something spiritual in his life.

My husband told the young man that we had been reading a Christian book aloud to one another while we drove. "Would you like to hear some special things that I just read to Marilyn?"

The young man replied, "Yes, I would like that."

The words touched an empty spot in his soul, and he began to weep.

My husband said, "Would you like to have Jesus in your heart?"

The young man nodded. Right there beside the highway, he received Jesus as his personal Savior.

We had hoped to lead people to Christ at our trip's end, but God gave us a precious soul at the beginning.

Dear heavenly Father, we thank You that the likeness of Jesus is formed in us at the new birth. Thank You for leading us to those who hunger for You. In Jesus' name, amen.

Day 294

"Keep thyself pure" (I Timothy 5:22b).

We are encouraged to keep ourselves pure. The most important place for purity is in our thought lives. If our thought lives are clean, our actions and words will be pure.

When we began to work on our television special, God sent us a writer who had written for many Christian programs and has an excellent reputation. During our first meeting I noticed that she said the right things, but her words lacked purity. I wondered whether she was born-again.

That night one of our staff members brought the writer to our Bible study class. I could tell that the writer's heart was open, tender, and sensitive to the Holy Spirit. Later my staff member gently asked her, "Have you ever received Jesus as your Savior?"

The writer said, "You are the first person ever to ask me that question. No, I haven't received Jesus, but I would like to do so."

Right there in the car, this woman received Jesus as her personal Savior. Her thought life changed and the Lord's purity entered her life.

Dear heavenly Father, we thank You today for Your purity. To be pure is to have Jesus, the Living Word, in our hearts. Amen.

Day 295

"With everlasting kindness will I have mercy on thee, saith the Lord thy Redeemer" (Isaiah 54:8b).

Shortly after I was married, my father had a nervous breakdown. My mother accompanied us to Dallas for a healing convention. One night the evangelist called forth my mother out of the thousands of people present.

He said, "You are weeping not for yourself, but for your husband, who has had a nervous breakdown. Take the handkerchief in which you have shed your tears. Place it on his body, and he will be healed."

How merciful God is! My mother took the handkerchief, followed the Lord's instructions, and my father began to recover. No, it did not happen overnight, but one day he improved.

Our heavenly Father has promised us that we will always have His lovingkindness and mercy. When we became born-again believers, we became vessels to extend God's mercy and love to others—including our loved ones. We must reach forth, in faith, to touch and minister to those we love. When we reach out, with our hands securely grounded in God's mercy, we will surely know how to meet the needs of others—no matter what their suffering may be.

Dear heavenly Father, we thank You today that You care about our loved ones. Show us, by the Spirit, how to minister to those we love, how to touch them, and how to meet their needs. In Jesus' name, amen.

Day 296

"And the Lord make you to increase and abound in love one toward another, and toward all men" (I Thessalonians 3:12a).

I have a cousin who lives here in Denver. I have loved her dearly since her childhood, but I have had little time to spend with her lately. I have continually asked God to send laborers to her because many times I, like other people, am not always able to reach out to all my loved ones.

She works near our church, and one day she drove into our parking lot just to turn around. Some women asked her for directions to a motel. She drove them to her office to consult the telephone directory for a nearby motel.

The women found favor with my cousin. In fact, her husband even offered to pay for their first night at the motel! The women then took the opportunity to pray and minister to my cousin and her husband.

It was such a shock to me when I heard the whole story. I marveled at God's love. He knows how to abound in unusual circumstances.

Dear heavenly Father, we thank You today for sending laborers to our loved ones. We pray that they might see Jesus and know His wonderful love. In Jesus' name, amen.

Day 297

"They cried unto thee, and were delivered: they trusted in thee, and were not confounded" (Psalm 22:5).

One Sunday morning years ago, I felt a strange pain in my index finger. When I pressed the fingernail, pain shot up and down that finger. Upon closer examination I noticed a growth under my nail. Within a week the growth darkened and had begun to grow larger.

The next Sunday morning I went forward and asked the congregation to lay hands on me for healing. I returned to my seat, and the woman beside me said, "Let me see that growth under your fingernail." She looked and said, "Oh, I had a friend with the same type of growth."

"What happened to her?" I asked.

"She's dead," the woman replied.

Immediately the devil said to me, "You will die too."

But I refused to believe the devil's lies. Believers had laid hands on me, and the Bible said that I would recover. I focused on my recovery. I believed that I was recovering, and in three days that ugly growth fell out from under my nail.

Dear heavenly Father, we choose to trust in You each day. We choose to believe that angels encamp round about those who fear You. You are taking care of every step we take. In Jesus' name, amen.

Day 298

"In all thy ways acknowledge him, and he shall direct thy paths" (Proverbs 3:6).

When I first began my radio ministry, I taped my programs in the basement of our home. I always waited until my family was gone because any background sounds would put noise on my radio tape. One day as I taped, a cricket chirped—right in the middle of my tape. I couldn't locate the cricket, so I restarted the tape. The cricket chirped again and again, yet I could never find it.

One woman later heard those tapes and asked to buy the entire series. She commented, "I loved the tapes. But the day I listened to them, there was a cricket in my house that I could never find." We laughed and laughed!

A week later we received a letter from another woman who said, "I have been in a mental hospital for two years. I heard a cricket on your radio program, and it was the first time I'd heard a cricket in two years. How refreshing it was!"

I thought, "How good God is; He is so economical that He gets precious mileage out of everything." When we acknowledge Him, He will direct our paths.

Dear heavenly Father, we choose to acknowlege You in every step that we take. You will lead and guide us into victory and triumph. In Jesus' name, amen.

Day 299

"Watch ye therefore:...Lest coming suddenly he find you sleeping" (Mark 13:35,36).

We never know what each day will hold. Could today be the day of the Lord's return? We must keep a sharp lookout for His presence and the special manifestations of His presence toward us.

For many years my husband had an all-night prayer meeting on Friday nights. Late one Friday, about 2:00 A.M., the group was singing and worshiping the Lord. As they sat down at the front of the sanctuary, God suddenly gave my husband a new song. He began to sing in the Spirit, and then he continued with beautiful, beautiful words in English. Those seated beside Wally heard someone sing the same words, in perfect harmony from the balcony. But no one was in the balcony! Even if there had been someone in the balcony, how could that person have known the words or the melody? It was a new song, even to my husband.

God had sent an angelic choir to join my husband in singing beautiful praise to the Lord. Be sensitive and keep a sharp lookout. Who knows what very special, supernatural manifestation God has in store for you today!

Dear heavenly Father, we thank You today that the Holy Spirit lifts the blinders from our eyes so that we may be sensitive to the good things that You are doing in our lives. In Jesus' name, amen.

Day 300

"He that spared not His own Son, but delivered Him up for us all, how shall He not freely give us all things?" (Romans 8:32).

God freely wants to give us all things. When He first called me to provide food for the hungry children of the world, I didn't know how to do it! But God always has a variety of ways and creative, witty innovations for following His will.

One day a pastor called me from Texas and said that he knew a wealthy oilman who had purchased a ship, but didn't know what to do with it. He said "I feel led to have him call you. Would you mind?"

The oilman called me and said that if I would fill the ship with food, he would take it to any part of the world!

Not only did we send one huge load of food to Haiti, but we also started a special new campaign called "Fill the Ship." The oilman's initial donation multiplied to include the time, money, and efforts of hundreds of other people. Our food shipments then extended down into Central America. We later sent supplies to earthquake victims in Mexico City.

We don't always know HOW God will provide, but we know that He freely gives us all things.

Dear heavenly Father, we thank You that when You call us to do something, You also bring the people and circumstances to fulfill Your call. We praise You for it! In Jesus' name, amen.

Day 301

"For it is not ye that speak, but the Spirit of your Father which speaketh in you" (Matthew 10:20).

In 1978 I taught a seminar at PTL. During the seminar the Lord told me that He was going to heal a woman's back. I invited people who had back problems to stand for special prayer. My attention was drawn to one woman who stood up. I quoted the Word and asked God to heal those backs.

I saw the woman leave the room. In a little while she returned, raised her hand excitedly, and asked to speak. She said that the bones in her spine had been disintegrating. When we had prayed, she had felt the warmth of the power of the Lord go through her. She checked her spine, and it was completely normal! She wrote to me later and told me that she had gone to a doctor, who had x-rayed her back and confirmed her miracle.

When God wants to speak and act through us, it doesn't matter what our abilities or strengths are—all that matters is the supernatural ability and strength of our Lord Jesus Christ!

Remember, when we speak God's Word, His Spirit speaks through us and brings miraculous results!

Dear heavenly Father, we give our thanks to You today. Help us to speak Your oracles to minister with the ability that only You can give. In Jesus' name, amen.

Day 302

"Thy mercy, O Lord, is in the heavens; and thy faithfulness reacheth unto the clouds" (Psalm 36:5).

God's love is great. He has so many ways to manifest it to us. For years we have prayed for my mother's family of 11 children, plus all her many nieces, nephews, grandnieces, and grandnephews. We have believed God for their salvation, but sometimes it has looked so discouraging. I know that many of my relatives have thought that we are just "holy rollers" and the nuts in the family tree! But God is always so faithful.

Not long ago a cousin whom I had never met called me. She was a member of a well-known, liberal church. But she had been born again and wanted to know if she could come ask me some questions about my ministry. She felt that God had His hand on her life too. I almost fell over when I received the letter!

When she arrived in Denver, she said that she came to ask some questions about ministry, but she also wanted to receive the baptism in the Holy Spirit. My heart just overflowed! I thought, "Look no further!" She soon beautifully received the baptism in the Holy Spirit!

Dear heavenly Father, we thank You today that, no matter what we see with our eyes, our hearts are fixed, trusting in You to bring in our loved ones. In Jesus' name, amen.

Day 303

"Whosoever shall deny me before men, him will I also deny before my Father..." (Matthew 10:33b).

When my husband and I were first married, I taught a junior high class in the Denver public schools. My subjects were Spanish and English, and the opportunities to witness were very exciting. However, the schools told us that we could not speak on any religious matters during class time. (What we did after hours was our business.)

My husband and I started a home Bible study for teenagers. That year, out of 37 students in my class, 34 were born again. I'll never forget the first student who wanted to be a witness. She and another Christian were talking with one of their class officers. One Christian girl told the other, "I wished that I could have gone to heaven the other night."

The other said, "I understand what you mean—because you're ready to meet Jesus."

The unsaved girl said, "What do you mean, you're ready to meet Jesus?" Then they shared their faith. In a short time she was born again, too, and later that summer won seven young people to Christ. God will open many doors for us to witness.

Dear heavenly Father, help us today to be a witness for Jesus. Give us boldness in heaven, on earth, and in hell. In Jesus' name, amen.

Day 304

"Whoso trusteth in the Lord, happy is he" (Proverbs 16:20b).

God can open unusual doors where all doors seem to be closed. Once God told me to pass out Bibles to Jewish people. But I soon discovered that a national Israeli law forbids Bibles to be passed out in that country. Yet I felt very strongly that God wanted me to proceed with this plan.

Sometimes I think that God is a little sneaky, or at least He is very creative in His ways of overcoming obstacles. At that time 30,000 Jewish soldiers were stationed in Lebanon. The Lord told me, "Cross the border. Lebanon has no such laws." We crossed the border and passed out Bibles to all those soldiers! It was such a blessing to watch young men sitting on tanks and reading the New Testament.

Have you ever faced obstacles so big you could see no way around them? Just remember, no matter what the obstacle may be, God has prepared a miracle for you that will push your "problem" out of your way, so you may go FORWARD and UPWARD in faith. "And nothing shall be impossible unto you" (Matthew 17:20b).

Dear heavenly Father, when our trust is in You, we will always end up being happy. You will do miraculous things in our situations. Thank You for doing so today. In Jesus' name, amen.

Day 305

"Let us therefore come boldly unto the throne of grace" (Hebrews 4:16a).

*T*here are times when we need great boldness as we come before God. Otherwise, we'll be wiped out by the enemy's devices.

One day a young girl was out riding her tricycle. Some distance away a man was doing target practice with his gun. One of the bullets missed the target completely and struck this tiny girl's head. She fell from her tricycle to the earth. Her parents found her unconscious and rushed her to the hospital. Little hope was given for recovery. Even if she did recover, the doctors warned that she would probably be in a hopeless, vegetable-like condition.

The girl's parents had a "miracle promise" book that our ministry had sent to all pledge partners. All night her parents prayed the promises listed for healing and for the miraculous. They also prayed in the Spirit. The doctors removed the bullet, and the girl's life was miraculously spared. Today she is a straight-A student. Like those parents, we need to be bold in coming to God. Be bold in claiming His Word!

Father, thank You that when we come before You, we come before a throne of grace. It doesn't come to us because we have earned it. It comes through the provision of Your Word in the name of Jesus and the power of Your Holy Spirit. We boldly take hold of what belongs to us for this day. In Jesus' name, amen.

Day 306

"But they that wait upon the Lord shall renew their strength" (Isaiah 40:31a).

When my husband Wally and I first encountered a demon-possessed person, my husband felt led to go on an extended fast. After seven days we brought the young woman out of a mental hospital and began to pray and cast evil spirits out of her. The girl was delivered and set free miraculously.

But my husband had a horrible demonic attack that we never expected—and we didn't know what to do! His mind went blank, and he could almost feel his senses "slipping away." He said that he had lost all will to make decisions or even to live! When I would ask him to pray in the name of Jesus, it was as though Wally could do nothing.

Some Christian friends immediately rushed over and prayed that God would refresh my husband and renew his strength. For several nights my husband would jerk and jump in his sleep. He would waken and scream out. But I would lay my hand upon him, in the name of Jesus, and speak peace to my husband.

Within two days he was refreshed and fine. I told the devil, "You will never do that to us again when we come against your kingdom." And he didn't.

Thank You, Father, that today our strength will be renewed through a fresh supply of Your anointing. In the name of Jesus, amen.

Day 307

"In the world ye shall have tribulation: but be of good cheer; I have overcome the world" (John 16:33b).

Sometimes we can get into a great deal of trouble without even trying! When our church had a membership of two or three hundred people, a certain young woman and her son decided to surprise my husband and me by painting some of our Sunday school classrooms. She was a perfectionist in all of her work, so each room was painted perfectly. However, we were caught by surprise, and when we walked in and saw the color, we made a comment that should never have been made. "Who selected this horrible color?" we asked.

My husband and I hurt the woman and her son's feelings. I felt rude, crude, and uncouth in being so insensitive to her generosity. I called to apologize, but she refused my call. When I finally DID get through, she cried and then hung up on me. Certainly it was tribulation, but it was of our own making!

One day the Lord spoke Colossians 1:20 to me: "Jesus can bring reconciliation." I began to pray that scripture. Within that very day the woman called to ask for prayer for her dying father. Our friendship was restored, and God received the glory.

We can overcome tribulation with God's Word!

Dear heavenly Father, even when we blow it, help us to receive and act on Your wisdom. In Jesus' name, amen.

Day 308

"The Lord thy God in the midst of thee is mighty; He will save, He will rejoice over thee with joy" (Zephaniah 3:17a).

*Y*ears ago a man called to ask if we would pray for a friend. He had found this woman slumped over the wheel of her car in front of his house, and he had driven her home. She lived in a mansion in one of Denver's most prestigious sections. She was later hospitalized for drug abuse. The man asked us, "Will you go witness to her?"

My husband and I talked to her, prayed with her, and gave her a New Testament with our telephone number. But later we read in the society column that she and her husband had been divorced.

We moved away from Denver for several years. When we returned, we would occasionally drive by that lovely mansion and pray over the people who lived there. One day I was holding a Bible study in an affluent part of town. A woman came to the study and received Christ in her heart. She asked, "Can someone take me home?" I offered.

Her home was that lovely mansion that my husband and I had prayed over for years! The woman was the husband's new wife, and she had received new life in Jesus.

Dear heavenly Father, help us to be obedient to Your call and to be trusting for the results that shall come forth. In Jesus' name, amen.

Day 309

"I, even I, am he who comforteth you" (Isaiah 51:12a).

*T*oday's devotion is a continuation from yesterday. After this lovely new wife received Christ in her heart, we began to pray that her husband would be born again. Not long afterward he also invited Christ into his heart.

One evening we were invited for dinner at their home. Two teenagers from the former marriage lived there. The young man brought me a New Testament and asked, "Marilyn, what is your name doing in my mother's Bible?" He held out the New Testament that we had presented to his mother while she was hospitalized for drug abuse. Within was the prayer that we had written to encourage her to receive Jesus in her heart.

I shared the story with the young man, and he was greatly comforted. He, too, received the Lord as his personal Savior.

God has many ways to comfort and bless us. I praise Him for every one of them!

Dear heavenly Father, help us not to look for comfort through people or circumstances, but to look to You. You have sent us the Comforter. In Jesus' name, amen.

Day 310

"I beseech you as strangers and pilgrims, abstain from fleshly lusts, which war against the soul" (I Peter 2:11).

Drinking is one of the most evil pleasures that is attacking this world. It has become socially acceptable to drink—even in Christian circles! Many Christians serve wine with their meals and drink alcoholic beverages on airplanes when they travel. They see nothing wrong with it. Many people excuse their behavior by saying that when out in public or in a foreign country, to not drink wine or beer with people will offend them.

The Bible tells us clearly that drinking is NOT for Christians! Why do we drink? Most people will tell you that they drink to get a "buzz" or stirring inside. This is an ungodly imitation of the Holy Spirit, for the Bible tells us, "Do not be drunk with wine wherein is excess, but be filled with the Spirit."

The buzz you receive from natural alcohol is a counterfeit of the true lift received from being filled with the Spirit. Don't accept the devil's counterfeit. Take the reality of the Holy Spirit. Drinking is not for Christians. It causes others to stumble and can keep our minds from being alert to God. Turn alcohol down. It's not for you.

Dear heavenly Father, help us not to fall into the pitfalls of the world's system, which can only hurt us. Help us stand in Your Word and walk in freedom and liberty. In Jesus' name, amen.

Day 311

"He that shall humble himself shall be exalted" (Matthew 23:12b).

A Christian woman in our church was very unhappily married. Her husband abused her physically, drank a great deal, and was certainly not loving or understanding.

She then became "involved" with another man. It was a bad situation because there was no question of her guilt—or of her husband's. But sin is sin. If you sow to the flesh, you will reap from the flesh.

We prayed with this lovely Christian woman and encouraged her to humble herself before the Lord, as well as before her husband. She broke off her relationship with the other man, and then she humbled herself before her husband. She said, "I have done wrong, and I do not deserve to be your wife." In no way did the woman blame him for anything! She humbled herself.

However, he divorced her and would not accept her apology. But one year later God did a work in his heart. My husband had the privilege of remarrying them, and they are married to this day.

Dear heavenly Father, help us to see that humility precedes honor. Help us to see how we can humble ourselves. In so doing, we will be exalted by You. In Jesus' name, amen.

Day 312

"...he hath set his love upon me" (Psalm 91:14a).

God's love is overwhelming. Sometimes it just seems too good to be true! Once, when we were in Ethiopia, we were preparing to leave on a helicopter to enter a drought area. On that helicopter were a number of American congressmen. When they saw me and our cameraman boarding, they said, "Get off and wait for the second flight." We knew that if we went with the second crew, it would probably be too dark to videotape for TV coverage. Thus, it was essential that we leave on the first flight. But the congressmen demanded that we get off the helicopter.

We got off the helicopter, but we didn't get out of faith. We said, "Lord, if You have to tell the sun to stand still for us so that we can videotape, You will do it." In a short time the helicopter returned for us. We arrived at the drought area and discovered that it had rained all during the first helicopter flight. But when we climbed off the helicopter, the sun shone brightly, and we took every picture that we needed in the drought area.

God's love will see us through when the world denies us.

Dear heavenly Father, help us not to hate those who hinder our work. Help us to love them with Your love. Your love will make us overcome because Your love never fails. In Jesus' name, amen.

Day 313

"...let the peace of God rule in your hearts" (Colossians 3:15a).

When we prepared to purchase our first church building, it seemed like a tremedous mountain. The cost was $65,000, and we had to have $15,000 up front. Our congregation had only 75 people, and $15,000 was a staggering amount to such a small congregation, which had just begun to walk in faith.

Piece by piece, dollar by dollar, the money began to come in. We had a millionairess in our congregation, and we thought perhaps she would give $1,000. Instead, she gave ten dollars. But I knew that God was saying, "Don't look at earthly millionaires. Look to Me, because I am your source of billions."

On the day of closing, we were short only $500 for closing costs. At a prayer meeting before the closing, our pianist asked us, "Do you have enough money?"

My husband said, "Almost. We just lack $500." She began to cry. She said, "God spoke to me and my husband to borrow that exact amount and give it to you." We need to stop worrying and let God's peace rule in our hearts. He will take care of every situation in our lives.

Dear heavenly Father, we thank You that You have gone ahead and made a provision for every crisis of this life. Help us to look to You and grasp Your peace. In Jesus' name, amen.

Day 314

"Wait on the Lord, be of good courage" (Psalm 27:14a).

When I was once visiting my aunt in Pennsylvania, we took a trip into a beautiful mountainous region. I enjoyed every moment of that trip. The trees were turning, and nothing is prettier than the fall foliage of the hardwood trees in Pennsylvania.

When we returned from our two-day trip, I noticed that my watch was missing. It was a beautiful watch that my husband had given me. I hated to go home without it. We searched the car and called the motel where we had stayed; but there was no sign of the watch.

I prayed in the name of Jesus. I commanded angels to help me find that watch. Six months went by and nothing had happened. One night my aunt called and said, "Something very unusual happened today. We went out to our car, and when we opened the door, your watch fell out on the sidewalk. It's in perfect shape. I'll mail it to you."

My watch was returned. It took six months, but God answered my prayer! Patience and faith are twins whom we cannot separate.

Thank You, Father, that You will reward our faith if we will wait patiently for Your answer. In Jesus' name, amen.

Day 315

"That ye be not slothful, but followers of them who through faith and patience inherit the promises" (Hebrews 6:12).

Many times God has unusual surprises for His people. And they can be wonderful surprises! My husband has always enjoyed going to New Mexico for vacation. The Indians, their craftwork, and the relaxed environment are very special. As a result of these vacations, my husband has always given me turquoise jewelry for special occasions.

Wally once had a beautiful turquoise cross made for himself. It was one of the most attractive pieces of jewelry I had ever seen. Frances Hunter was holding a meeting in our city at that time, and when she saw the cross, she commented on its beauty.

Several nights later my husband said, "Marilyn, God has spoken to me to give Frances the cross." She cried when she received it because she had prayed that God would give her a cross similar to that of my husband. When he gave her his cross, she was deeply touched.

Sometimes God wants to bless us in unique and wonderful ways—and He wants us to bless others in the same way. Stay open to the Holy Spirit's leading.

Dear heavenly Father, thank You for the generous nature that You have given us. We have the nature of Jesus Christ. It is a giving nature. We are open for the flow of Your gifts, not only TO us, but THROUGH us. In Jesus' name, amen.

Day 316

"O death, where is thy sting?" (I Corinthians 15:55a).

Satan would like to harm Christians, but he has lost his power because of Jesus. Your physical and spiritual life, your possessions, and your family are all things that Satan would like to steal. But he has lost his sting!

I was once invited to a meeting in a large church in Cincinnati, Ohio. I arrived late at night and was waiting in the airport for a number of boxes containing my tapes and books. As we watched the boxes being removed from the luggage carrier, I noticed someone leaving the airport with a piece of luggage exactly like mine. I pursued the man and discovered that he did indeed have my luggage. When I asked him whether it was my luggage, he dropped it and ran. He had meant to steal it, but the Lord quickened this to me. I believe that the Holy Spirit directed my attention to that man so that my luggage could be recovered.

The devil cannot steal from Christians if we will stand in the authority of the Word and be bold to use Jesus' name.

Dear heavenly Father, help us to stand firmly against the devil and his intentions to steal from us. In Jesus' name, amen.

Day 317

"God is no respecter of persons" (Acts 10:34b).

Radio is an excellent way to blanket an area with God's Word. However, there have been several areas that have remained closed to my programs. One of them was a large city in southern Texas. Every time we attempted to buy time on that station, they insisted, "We don't believe in women teachers," and wouldn't let me air my program.

Once when I was holding a crusade in Houston, Texas, a pastor asked, "Are you coming to my city?" It was the city in which the station had refused my program. I told him that I couldn't hold meetings in every city, so I tried to focus my attention on those where I was on the radio.

The pastor asked me why I wasn't on the station, so I shared the reason with him. He began to weep, "God has just spoken to me about making an appeal to the manager of that station."

I had never seen this pastor before! But that day he followed through with his leading from the Holy Spirit. Within 10 days the station called and said that my program would be included on its format.

People may be respecters of persons. But God isn't! Whenever we exercise faith, He will do a miracle.

Dear heavenly Father, protect our emotions from rejection. Teach us not to accept closed doors, but to know that You can open doors for us supernaturally. In Jesus' name, amen.

Day 318

"The effectual working in the measure of every part, maketh increase of the body unto the edifying of itself in love" (Ephesians 4:16b).

It is great to be a praying mother. Perhaps you had one, or perhaps God has called YOU to be one! We don't always have to be a NATURAL, PHYSICAL mother to be a SPIRITUAL mother. In fact, you don't even need to be a woman in order to give that special nurturing and care to your own church. Some of the most dedicated "mothers" of our church are the many deacons and volunteers—both male and female—who give so selflessly of their time.

For years my mother has prayed for our church, and at one time she held a Thursday morning prayer meeting. People were greatly blessed, changed, and transformed during those meetings.

My mother has also taught a "new converts" class. I have noticed that every person who took her class many years ago still loves to pray. Today we have a 5:00 prayer meeting every morning of the week. This is a part of the increase of the seed that my mother has lovingly sown in her prayer life and into the Body of Christ.

Thank God for the "effectual working" of praying mothers in the Body of Christ.

Dear heavenly Father, help us today to dedicate ourselves to prayer in the Body of Christ. Thank You for those who pray for us and help us to be involved in an in-depth prayer program. In Jesus' name, amen.

Day 319

"Behold, I come quickly: blessed is he that keepeth the sayings of the prophecy of this book" (Revelation 22:7).

While ministering in a Catholic parish in Springfield, Illinois, my daughter and I were invited to the priest's house for dinner. He escorted us into his beautiful library where he had the works of many famous religious and philosophical scholars. He began to talk and mention many of their names. He asked me, "Have you read these books?"

"No," I admitted, "I know nothing about them." The priest seemed embarrassed that I was so "unintellectual" and unchallenging. In fact, he told me that I was too heavy on the Bible and not heavy enough in the areas of man's intellectualism.

However, when a parishioner in the priest's parish was miraculously healed in one of our services, the priest said, "God's Word works, and I see it. I have been in man's intellect, when I should have been into God's intellect."

No matter how many radio and TV ministries you watch...no matter how many books and commentaries you read...no matter how many crusades you attend...you still need to be grounded and washed in God's Word.

Dear heavenly Father, reveal today how Jesus is made wisdom unto us. Help us put on the mind of Christ that we might flow in His wisdom. In Jesus' name, amen.

Day 320

"....they seek me daily, and delight to know my ways" (Isaiah 58:2a).

It is really delightful to teach Bible school students who are serious and committed. They are hungry and purposed to know God's Word and His Son Jesus in a personal way.

However, through the years I have watched some people in various Bible schools backslide, and I have wondered, "How can that happen when they receive indepth Bible teaching daily?" But upon questioning some of them and through prayer, I have discovered that Bible students, as strange as it seems, often neglect their own PERSONAL daily relationship with the Lord. They mistakenly think that their classes take the place of personal time with the Lord.

Such thoughts are dangerous. Each one of us, no matter what our call, must have a close, daily relationship with our loving heavenly Father.

Sometimes when we are overburdened with things of the world—work, family problems, relationships, financial difficulties—we tend to "shelve" the reading of the Word. It may make worldly sense to put God "on hold" until we have more time; but it never makes sense spiritually.

Dear heavenly Father, help us to realize the importance of our daily walk with You. We can never treat our relationship with You casually. In Jesus' name, amen.

Day 321

"That it might be fulfilled which was spoken by Esaias the prophet, saying, Himself took our infirmities, and bare our sicknesses" (Matthew 8:17).

*Y*ears ago I was invited to speak in a Lutheran charismatic conference. Before appearing at the conference, I prayed and waited on God. He said to me, "Before you teach, I want you to pray for the sick." I felt as though this would make the Lutherans uneasy, but God assured me that this was His will for the meeting.

When the time came to minister, I asked for people with warts and tumors to stand up for prayer. One man in the very front row had a growth the size of a quarter on his forehead. During the call for healings, the growth fell off—right in front of everyone! This miracle so stirred the people that when I gave the altar call, 250 people came forward to receive the baptism of the Holy Spirit.

Another time, in my own church, God told me to ask people with arthritis to stand up for prayer. One man, whom I noticed in particular, stood up, got healed, and was able to jump around in the aisle. I later found out that this man had been afflicted with arthritis for years and the disease was crippling him, but God stepped in and performed another miracle.

Dear heavenly Father, thank You for the direct leading of the Holy Spirit AND for Your provision for healing. In Jesus' name, amen.

Day 322

"Should a wise man utter vain knowledge, and fill his belly with the east wind?" (Job 15:2).

When I was growing up, I had a wonderful relative who loved me dearly. But she was not very thrilled when I became a born-again, Spirit-filled believer. She had made great plans for me to get my doctorate and had planned to pay for it.

When my husband and I began our ministry, this relative started to call us "Holy Rollers" and wanted little to do with us. Over the years communication between the two of us slowly declined. However, she DID attend one of my crusades when I taught in her city.

Two of her friends came to that crusade, but she didn't know that they were going to be there. When both stood for salvation, her heart was touched, and soon afterward she, too, became a Christian.

Worldly knowledge is nothing without God's wisdom, and we must think on this when we witness to people who are trusting in their intellect, instead of the redeeming power of Jesus Christ. The scriptures tell us NOT to be wise in our own eyes, but to fear the Lord and depart from evil.

Dear heavenly Father, we thank You today that Jesus is made unto us wisdom. We thank You that Your wisdom is perfect and complete and comes from above. We claim that wisdom for ourselves today. In Jesus' name, amen.

Day 323

"Behold, all is vanity and vexation of spirit" (Ecclesiastes 1:14b).

Several years ago a man agreed to fix my hair each week in return for a credit on my television show. He felt that this credit would help advertise his already successful beauty shop.

One day when I was in his shop, he was feeling very depressed so I asked him what was wrong. "Are you having problems with your wife or children?" No, his wife and children were fine. His health was fine.

I then asked, "Have you ever received Jesus as your Savior?"

"No," he answered. He had been raised with a mother who was involved in witchcraft, and his experience with Christianity was limited.

"One third of your life is missing," I told him. "Physically and emotionally you have fulfillment. But spiritually you are dead. You are one-third empty." He and his wife soon became born again and Spirit-filled, and, at last, found completion in Christ.

Dear heavenly Father, help us to see that this world alone is vanity and vexation of the spirit. But in Jesus we have abundant life and total completion. Help us see that without You, our lives are empty. In Jesus' name, amen.

Day 324

"Praise ye the Lord: for it is good to sing praises unto our God; for it is pleasant; and praise is comely" (Psalm 147:1).

Praise is wonderful and full of power. Praise does wonderful things in your heart—things of which you've only dreamed!

One Sunday a friend of ours brought a very sophisticated woman to our services. Before our friend came to church, she prayed that the woman would not be offended by our praise and that it would not be too lively that morning because the woman had very conservative attitudes.

However, upon their arrival, the praise was very, very free. One woman spontaneously danced down the aisle. As she did, she reached out her hand to touch this very sophisticated woman. When their hands met, the power of God struck our visitor, and she fell upon her knees and received the Lord into her heart.

This was such a wonderful and unusual demonstration of the Holy Spirit! Praise is very important and causes the supernatural power of God to be present. Praise is a way of life, not just a service.

Dear heavenly Father, help us to live in praise and worship. Teach us to walk in a spirit of thankfulness. In Jesus' name, amen.

Day 325

"But that on the good ground are they, which in an honest and good heart, having heard the word, keep it, and bring forth fruit with patience" (Luke 8:15).

Sometimes we forget that patience and faith are like Siamese twins. We have faith, but at times we can run out of patience. But it is very important that we never give up before we see the manifestation of the promise for which we are believing.

For years I had desired an article in a certain fundamental magazine, which was very anti-Pentecostal. I felt in my heart that God wanted me to write a special piece for this particular reading audience. But five years passed without any success in obtaining an article.

Then I had an invitation to speak in a large church in Illinois. Afterward a woman came up to me at our book and tape table and said that she was one of the contributing editors of that particular magazine. She said, "I feel led for you to write us an article."

God does things so uniquely. We cannot afford to give up because sometimes the last 30 minutes of our faith are the most important!

Dear heavenly Father, help us to hold on to our faith and to know that, in due season, we will reap if we faint not. We commit ourselves not to fainting, but to reaping. In Jesus' name, amen.

Day 326

"Behold, what manner of love the father hath bestowed upon us, that we should be called the sons of God" (I John 3:1a).

Before Sarah was born, a sudden fear came over me that I would not love my child as I should. How would I feel when I saw that baby? I had waited so long for motherhood that I wondered, "Will I be a good mother?"

I expressed these fears to my family doctor, and he assured me, "When your baby is born, many new hormones will rush into your blood and overwhelm you with love for your child."

There was no question of my love for Sarah from the very first moment that I looked at her. I simply fell in love with her.

I'm sure that our love for our children is nothing compared to the strong love that the Father has when He looks at us. Certainly He has begotten us in love.

He has shown His love to us over and over again as He comforts us in trials, as He reveals spiritual truths to us, and in all ways meets our daily needs.

Dear heavenly Father, give us spiritual revelation of Your love today. Help us to know Your love so that we will be free from fear. In Jesus' name, amen.

Day 327

"And when he was in affliction, he besought the Lord his God,...and [the Lord] heard his supplication, and brought him again to Jerusalem into his kingdom" (II Corinthians 33:12a,13b).

Years ago I was invited to speak in a large Baptist church in Phoenix, Arizona. At the meeting there was one woman whom I had known for years. In fact, she had been in the first adult Sunday school class that I had ever taught.

I knew that this woman's life since that time had been wretched. But I had not seen her during the interim. She had divorced her Spirit-filled husband and fallen into a life of sin and debauchery.

That day when we met, I saw the signs of past distresses written on her face. But I also saw the signs of a new beginning. After all of her many sinful mistakes, she had finally come back to the Lord and found a fresh, new life in Him.

Today she is remarried—to a wonderful Christian man. She is restored in spirit, living for Jesus, and active in the kingdom.

Never think, "It's too late." As long as you have breath, you have hope in God's love. Seek out God, ask His forgiveness, and receive His blessed grace.

Dear heavenly Father, our hope is not in ourselves or others. Our hope is in You. Today we lay hold upon our hope that this will be a supernatural day. In Jesus' name, amen.

Day 328

"So shall my word....accomplish that which I please, and it shall prosper in the thing whereto I sent it" (Isaiah 55:11).

God once gave our fellowship group an opportunity to witness to a woman who was a stripper in a bar. In fact, she had even used a snake in her act. She wore a great deal of heavy makeup and very revealing costumes.

One day, as that woman was on her way to work, a young man from the Campus Crusade Ministries approached her and said, "Do you know that Jesus loves you?" The woman was offended.

That night as she handled her snake, she reflected with contempt on how rich her life was compared to that of a Christian. But only six months later, the man with whom she lived was dying from a drug overdose. The words of the young man came to her, "Hey, lady, do you know that Jesus loves you?"

That night she cried out for Jesus' love to be manifested to her lover so that he would not die. She received Jesus as her Savior and very shortly afterward her lover became her husband—as a born-again believer. Today they are serving Jesus wholeheartedly.

Dear heavenly Father, we do not see people as impossibilities for You. We look at all people as possibilities for Your kingdom. Your love will reign supreme in their lives and give them the turnaround they so desperately need. In Jesus' name, amen.

Day 329

"Sing praises to God, sing praises: sing praises unto our King, sing praises" (Psalm 47:6).

On our first trip to Mexico, we witnessed to many people. They asked us, "What kind of Christians are you? Are you Baptists? Are you Catholics or Methodists?"

We said, "We are Pentecostals," but they could not understand what that word meant. In my limited Spanish I tried to explain about the born-again experience and baptism in the Holy Spirit.

Finally one person said, "You are a HALLELUJAH!" (We then discovered that's what Mexicans call Spirit-filled people since most Pentecostals in Mexico use the word "hallelujah" many times throughout their praise and worship.)

The word HALLELUJAH is derived from three Hebrew words: HAL, meaning "hail", EL, meaning "God the Creator," and JAH, meaning "Jehovah the Redeemer." Together it means "Hail to God, the Creator, and Jehovah, the Redeemer!" Isn't that the glorious truth!

I'm glad we're called "Hallelujah's," aren't you?

Dear heavenly Father, we thank You for the opportunity to live in praise and worship for a wonderful, loving Father. Order the events of our day to glorify Your name. In Jesus' name, amen.

Day 330

"Break forth into joy, sing together....The Lord hath made bare his holy arm in the eyes of the nations: and all the ends of the earth shall see the salvation of our God" (Isaiah 52:9,10).

Several years ago when our children were smaller, we took a vacation to Mexico City. In our hotel we kept meeting an Argentinian couple who was taking a family vacation. They spoke no English, so any communication had to be through what Spanish I could remember.

We soon traveled on to another city, Taxco, and again we met the same couple from Argentina! We believed that God had brought them across our path for a divine reason. One day at lunch we shared with them our faith and love for Jesus Christ. They told us that they were Jewish. They also shared that they had just begun to SING the psalms in their synagogue.

We had a beautiful opportunity to share Psalm 22, a prophetic psalm written by David about Jesus' death. The couple was hungry and open for God's Word.

Wherever we go, we meet people who are hungry for Jesus' love. Let's be available to them.

Dear heavenly Father, lead us to people to whom You want us to witness and minister. Help us to bare the holy arm of the Lord to all who hunger for His Word and mercy. In Jesus' name, amen.

Day 331

"Through God we shall do valiantly: for he it is that shall tread down our enemies" (Psalm 108:13).

Right after my mother became a Spirit-filled Christian, a large cottonwood tree in our backyard became simply plagued with worms. They were ugly things that would fall from the trees into your hair, and when you'd walk, they would squish on the sidewalk. All over the neighborhood, cottonwood trees were being ruined by these worms.

One day my mother told me, "God has given me authority in Jesus on this earth, and I am going to take my dominion." I could not imagine what she was talking about. But she went out, laid her hands on our tree, rebuked the devil, who was destroying cottonwood trees, and commanded all the worms to die.

The next day dead worms were all over our yard. All of our neighbors' cottonwood trees eventually died, but not ours. We never saw another worm on our cottonwood tree.

Dear heavenly Father, we thank You for our authority in the name of Jesus, and we choose to take His name to rule over sin, sickness, and disease today. In Jesus' name, amen.

Day 332

"Yet count him not as an enemy, but admonish him as a brother" (II Thessalonians 3:15).

Many years ago God dealt with me to pray for people in the Mafia. God said that He would send revival among them and bring confusion to their order and that their money would be lost to go into the kingdom. (The wealth of the wicked has always been laid up for the righteous.)

Whenever God takes wealth from the wicked, this money, in a sense, returns to its owners when it is used to spread God's Word—through television, radio, or whatever means. When the enemy hears the Word, they are getting a return on their money!

From time to time I hear testimonies of men or women who were previously active in the Mafia. And it reminds me that no situation nor sin is too difficult to be transformed by God's love, because He is much greater than sin.

We should look at our enemies as brothers. Then we can extend forgiveness, no matter what their past may be. Likewise, we should never give up hope for the rest of our "family"—the family of mankind.

Dear heavenly Father, we pray for the people in the Mafia today. Put the whole organization to confusion. Let the men and women involved in such tremendous sin and darkness turn their lives to Jesus Christ. In Jesus' name, amen.

Day 333

"Behold, all things are become new"
(II Corinthians 5:17b).

*M*any times we need a new beginning, a fresh start. We must always be aware that God can create new beginnings for us.

When Sarah was born, I was 36 years old. Believe me, it was a new beginning for me: to be a mother at 36, to have never before been a natural mother, and to know it was a miracle!

We painted Sarah's bedroom, refreshed it, bought new furniture, and had new clothes in her chest of drawers. Everything in her room smelled fresh and brand new. It was made especially NEW and pretty for a NEW being.

God also prepares new things for us: He gives us a new nature, a new life. He makes us new creations. And all of this was prepared for us when we made the decision of faith to be saved.

When we are born again, we are just like new babies. That's why some people refer to new believers as "baby Christians." Let's rejoice in our new life in Christ!

Dear heavenly Father, remind us today that You have made all things new for us. You still have new things awaiting us, things that have our names on them, things that we haven't yet experienced. Help us to enter into Your Spirit and claim what You have for us. In Jesus' name, amen.

Day 334

"The blueness of a wound cleanseth away evil" (Proverbs 20:30a).

Some people worry about the black and blue marks of a bruise, but these marks are actually symptomatic of the healing process. The blue is the rich oxygen of the arterial blood that brings in new supplies and healing materials of the body's "first aid" kit. Then red venal blood carries out the damaged cells, refuse, and waste products.

Have you ever realized that Jesus' blood also has a twofold healing purpose? It cleanses us of sin and waste, and it also brings the freshness of His love into our lives.

Christ's blood is one of the most powerful cleansing agents known to mankind! His blood does more that whitewash our hearts—it purifies them from the inside out. Christ's precious blood purifies our hearts so completely that we become temples of God.

When Jesus was confronted with the wrong-doings of the Pharisees, he warned them, "You are clean on the outside, but your hearts are like the insides of tombs—filled with death." What do you want to be? A tomb of death or a temple of God?

Dear heavenly Father, we thank You today for the life of Jesus that flows through us. We thank You for the dealings of Your Spirit to remove the garbage from our lives; and we thank You for Jesus' love that brings us freshness. In Jesus' name, amen.

Day 335

"Hold thou me up, and I shall be safe"
(Psalm 119:117a).

When Mike was six years old, he was kidnaped from a playground by a mentally disturbed woman. It was a very frightening experience! At the very moment we realized what had happened, my husband grabbed my hand to pray. He said, "Marilyn, we're going to believe that Mike will be safely returned to us in one hour."

The police called and told us that they had a report of a woman taking a little boy from the playground where Mike had been. We met a policeman at the playground. I looked down the street alongside the playground, and three blocks away I noticed a woman walking with a small boy. I told the policeman, "That's our son." He told us to wait, jumped into his car, drove down to pick up Mike and the woman, and then returned with our son.

When Mike climbed out of that police car, I looked at my watch—it had been exactly one hour!

When we pray, God is faithful to hear and answer our prayers.

Dear heavenly Father, today we thank You for Your faithfulness to keep us and our loved ones safe. We know that through Your lovingkindness and mercy, we AND our loved ones shall be eternally held up by You and kept safe. In Jesus' name, amen.

Day 336

"That whosoever shall say unto this mountain, Be thou removed, and be thou cast into the sea; and shall not doubt in his heart, but shall believe...he shall have whatsoever he saith" (Mark 11:23b).

Several years ago a pastor in Niagara Falls told me of a time when his area desperately needed rain. Many of the men in his congregation were farmers, and their situation had been growing steadily worse. If it didn't rain, all of the crops would be ruined.

The pastor felt impressed to tell his congregation to speak to the weather, just as God told us that we should speak to the "mountain." He said, "Speak God's grace to the clouds and wind."

The congregation began to speak to the clouds and to call forth wind. And the rain came and their crops were saved.

God will save us when we speak words of faith.

Do not let doubt creep into your heart; but, instead, believe! Believe even with just a drop of faith no bigger than a mustard seed. Then you SHALL HAVE whatsoever you say! What a wonderful promise God has made—and all we have to do is believe.

Dear heavenly Father, today we thank You for our authority to speak Your Word in the name of Jesus. That authority will bring the miraculous to us. We praise You in Jesus' name, amen.

Day 337

"And he that is feeble among them at that day shall be as David...." (Zechariah 12:8b).

Some of today's greatest ministers came from "feeble" beginnings. Just because one graduates from a Bible school doesn't mean that he or she immediately steps out and becomes the number-one minister of the hour. Many of the people whom God has used and is using today will tell you that they have come from very lowly positions and have been through tremendously difficult struggles.

One of the most beautiful ministries I know is that of a young woman who was sexually abused by her stepfather. She grew up and became a prostitute. But someone brought her the message of Jesus Christ. Today she ministers to the women in prisons and jails. She especially feels led to reach out to prostitutes with the love of Jesus Christ. Literally hundreds of women have been affected by the gospel message from this woman's lips.

Dear heavenly Father, encourage us today that, wherever we are, we can enlighten the darkness around us. Those who are doing things for God aren't "big names." There is only one big name, and that is Jesus. We take His name into our circumstances today. In Jesus' name, amen.

Day 338

"Open thou mine eyes, that I may behold wondrous things out of thy law" (Psalm 119:18).

I was a rebellious Christian at the time when my husband and I first met. I was especially rebellious against the baptism of the Holy Spirit and God's perfect will for my life. I just wasn't interested—there seemed to be so many more exciting things to do in life.

I loved to be with Wally and wanted to do exciting things with him. The only place, however, that he ever went was to church or out for dinner. He wouldn't take me dancing. He really didn't even take me to movies! I wanted to see him, so I had to go to church—even if I didn't want to!

Church was dull. But Wally was exciting. Little did I realized that God would use the Word from those supposedly dull services to give me a hunger for the baptism of the Holy Spirit! Wally was also fasting and praying for me, so my rebellious nature was soon broken. I was then baptized in the Holy Spirit.

Each day I grew more and more in the wisdom of our Lord. How I delight today in His Word.

When you begin to hear God's Word, it works its way into your heart!

Dear heavenly Father, we pray that today, as we read the Word, You will open our eyes to behold wonderful wisdom from Your law. Speak to us personally. We are Your sheep; we know Your voice. Speak to us according to our needs. In Jesus' name, amen.

Day 339

"The man departed, and told the Jews that it was Jesus, which had made him whole" (John 5:15).

My husband loves to restore old furniture. He brings home furniture that looks like junk and then piles it all on our back porch or in our garage. The furniture looks ratty, dirty, old, and worn.

When all that old furniture collects in the backyard, I sometimes wonder how it can ever be restored to something worthwhile. My first instinct would be to say, "Call the trashman! Let's give it to the Salvation Army!" I don't possess Wally's special insight to see the beauty that lies beneath the tattered surface.

But Wally knows that he can use paint remover and all sorts of tools to restore this furniture. As he works with each piece and rubs oil into the wood, the broken-down furniture is transformed into a beautiful piece—and some of them have even ended up in our living room and foyer.

Restoration is what our heavenly Father does for us. He takes us from our ratty, dirty ways and restores us. He makes us new and puts us in a special position in His kingdom.

Dear heavenly Father, we thank You for the work of the Holy Spirit that is restoring us into everything that is Your will for us. Help us to discard all our old, dirty, and worn ways so that we, too, can say that it was Jesus Who has made us whole. In Jesus' name, amen.

Day 340

"But he that putteth his trust in me shall possess the land, and shall inherit my holy mountain" (Isaiah 57:13b).

When God gave us our new church building, He also told me, "I want Kenneth Copeland to dedicate your church."

Kenneth Copeland didn't know us, and he certainly wasn't in the business of dedicating churches! But the desire lay so heavily on my heart that I called the Copelands' ministry. But I was informed, "He never dedicates churches."

I had, however, heard Kenneth's teaching that we were to "hold fast the confession of our faith without wavering," for God is "faithful that promised." I held fast to my confession for almost eight months.

Then Kenneth Copeland appeared in Denver for a crusade. He invited Wally and me out for coffee after a service, and then he shared, "God has called me to dedicate Happy Church. At first I was disobedient and said, 'No.' But I'm glad that the church hasn't yet been dedicated. I will do it!"

Just because you receive a "No," don't call the game "over." Hold fast to your faith without wavering because God is "faithful that promised."

Dear heavenly Father, we trust in You today. We don't look for answers from ourselves, others, or circumstances. We look to You to do supernatural works in our lives! In Jesus' name, amen.

Day 341

"And he spake a parable unto them to this end, that men ought always to pray, and not to faint" (Luke 18:1).

Sometimes our circumstances make us want to "faint" or give up! At one of Sarah's basketball games, her team was losing dreadfully. I had prayed beforehand that they would win—but they trailed 30 points. It seemed that my prayers were not working.

The Lord impressed me (if you can imagine this in a basketball game!) to pray in the Spirit. He said, "This will steady your confidence in Me."

I looked around and thought, "How can I pray in the Spirit at a Lutheran high school gym?" But I just cupped my hand over my mouth, and no one knew what I was doing! I then remembered that the woman beside me was a Spirit-filled Lutheran, so I shared the Lord's Words with her too....and then with another woman at the end of the row. Soon the three of us sat together, with our hands cupped discreetly over our mouths, and prayed in the Spirit. The game ended in a tie. Seven overtimes occurred, and at last Sarah's team was the victor by one point!

Don't faint. Keep praying. Your answer is on its way.

Dear heavenly Father, we know that we shall reap in due season if we don't faint. We do not believe in fainting. We DO believe in reaping Your precious promises. In Jesus' name, amen.

Day 342

"For promotion cometh neither from the east, nor from the west, nor from the south. But God is the judge: he putteth down one, and setteth up another" (Psalm 75:6,7).

Sometimes we find ourselves in positions where God didn't call us. We always need to be sure and secure that we are in God's will.

When Wally and I first began full-time ministry, we were assistant pastors in Amarillo, Texas. A beautiful woman in the church loved to intercede and had a beautiful ministry of intercession. I admired the woman so much that I decided, "God has called me to be an intercessor too." Notice my words, "I decided...."

I shared my decision with the woman, and she studied me seriously and then said, "Marilyn, I don't believe that. I think that YOU made the decision, not the Holy Spirit."

She was so right! God has called upon us all to pray and intercede. But my sure and secure calling has been to teach God's Word.

Sometimes we make decisions that are not born of the Spirit. They are decisions born of the flesh and sense knowledge. Learn to know God's voice. Listen to it and let Him promote you to your special place.

Dear heavenly Father, we thank You today that we don't have to seek promotion from people. Our promotion comes from You. In Jesus' name, amen.

Day 343

"That in every thing ye are enriched by him, in all utterance, and in all knowledge" (I Corinthians 1:5).

I know of a farmer whom one day God called to pastoring. The farmer went home and pleaded with his wife, "How can I possibly be a pastor? I can't even read!"

The man went to his pastor and volunteered to teach Sunday school. Each night his wife would read to him a quarterly pastors' journal and some scriptures. The man practically memorized his lessons by ear and then taught them on the next Sunday. But one day the Lord dealt with the man, "I didn't call you to teach Sunday school. I called you to be a pastor."

The farmer was distraught and cried out to God. In doing so, he was suddenly immersed in God's peace. That night when the man's wife began to read for her husband, she stumbled on a word. He looked at the word and pronounced it. Later the same thing happened again. Immediately the man realized, "These are not words that I have memorized. I am reading God's Word!"

Today this man pastors a church and speaks God's Word by the divine utterance of the Holy Spirit.

Dear heavenly Father, help us to speak Your Word today. Enrich us with the utterance of the Holy Spirit and with His power. In Jesus' name, amen.

Day 344

"Favour is deceitful, and beauty is vain: but a woman that feareth the Lord, she shall be praised" (Proverbs 31:30).

This world puts a great deal of emphasis on our exterior appearance and very little emphasis on the "hidden man of the heart."

This outward emphasis on looks can be particularly crippling to women. Not only is a woman judged and valued today for her beauty and attractive appearance, but also there has been an equally strong emphasis on youth—far beyond what is normal. Thus, many women go on extensive, and possibly damaging diets, or even seek the services of plastic surgeons.

Think how much more valuable it would be to spend the same amount of time on one's inward and spiritual beauty!

Some of the women who are beautifully used in God's kingdom are not OUTWARDLY glamorous. But these women are outstanding in their INWARD beauty.

It's great to LOOK attractive. But it's even greater to BE good. God's goodness—His soul prosperity—is extended to those who seek His kingdom and righteousness first. Which is first in your life? The way you look or the way God looks IN you?

Dear heavenly Father, we thank You today for the great work that You are performing in our hearts and lives. We are daily being conformed to the image of Your Son. In Jesus' name, amen.

Day 345

"He that putteth his trust in the Lord shall be made fat" (Proverbs 28:25b).

My first conference in Ithaca, New York, had only a small attendance. This was somewhat discouraging, yet God impressed me to return the next year. I thought, "Surely this time the attendance will be better." But it wasn't.

Several people told me, "No one ever comes to Ithaca to hear speakers. This place never attracts a crowd."

Many people advised me against returning to Ithaca. But I had a strong impression from the Spirit that I was not to give up. God has taught me to be very persistent when He gives me a desire to serve Him in a specific area. He has also taught me that if He asks me to do ANYTHING, He will surely provide the opportunity.

I was to return again. My daughter accompanied me on that third trip. This time the building was packed, and the meeting brought glory to the name of Jesus.

Trust in the Lord and expect Him to anoint you in every situation. He will prosper you, so don't give up until you see His results.

Dear heavenly Father, today we thank You and appreciate Your prosperity in our lives. You are making us victors, and our confidence rests in You. In Jesus' name, amen.

Day 346

"Now he that planteth and he that watereth are one: and every man shall receive his own reward according to his own labour" (I Corinthians 3:8).

Years ago when my husband and I held home Bible studies in our home, the material on our divan and couches became frayed and worn. The condition of our furniture was somewhat embarrassing, but we absolutely did not have the money to have them reupholstered.

One night when a woman sat on our divan, I could see her fingers pulling the strings of the tattered material as she listened to the Word. I knew that this woman had a very attractive home, and I was sure that ours seemed shabby in comparison. Then one week later the woman called and said, "The Lord has prompted me to give you a gift." It was a gift of money to reupholster our divan and chair! When we called about the cost, her gift was exactly the right amount!

Place your trust in God. He will never fail to reward your labor.

Dear heavenly Father, we thank You that our labor for You on this earth is not in vain, but that You have planned and made provision for every step that we take. We commit our labors in the gospel to You today. In Jesus' name, amen.

Day 347

"For the time is at hand" (Revelation 1:3b).

God once gave me an opportunity to minister in three Catholic parishes in Springfield, Missouri. At the first church I asked the priest for guidelines, and he said, "You can speak for 20 minutes." During that 20 minutes God gave me a scripture for a young man in the congregation.

I asked the man to stand and receive the scripture. I had no idea that this would shock the parishioners beyond all imaginable! The young man later said, "God should not be giving scriptures to you. He gives them to His priests."

I felt troubled because I was sure my message was from God. Yet I also thought that I had been insensitive to this church's protocol.

Three days later the young man called me. The scripture I had offered had caused him to meditate upon his relationship with God. He was subsequently born again and Spirit-filled.

When God's time is at hand, we must move. He is faithful to call us; we must be faithful to listen.

Dear heavenly Father, today we make ourselves available to You and sensitive to Your Holy Spirit. We will, thus, be sensitive to the needs of those around us. We praise You for Your ability in us to meet others' needs. In Jesus' name, amen.

Day 348

"Man shall not live by bread alone, but by every word that proceedeth out of the mouth of God" (Matthew 4:4b).

During the time in Springfield when I visited those Catholic parishes, I took communion. I had asked the priest of the first parish whether I should, and he answered, "Of course, you may take communion in the Catholic church."

I don't know why I also took communion in the second church. I must have thought, "If once is good, twice is better."

When we drove to the third church, the priest said, "Please don't take communion the third time. You should only take it once."

God did such a miracle in the third service that I have often wondered whether taking communion twice wasn't a great blessing to me! A tremendous, miraculous healing took place in that third parish.

Sometimes we need to go over God's Word again and again. It's like communion: we need to take it more than twice. We need to take it hundreds of times to make sure that not only are we consuming the Word, but that it is also consuming us!

Dear heavenly Father, today we consume and read Your Word. As we do, let it become a fire within that consumes us. In Jesus' name, amen.

Day 349

"All scripture is given by inspiration of God, and is profitable for doctrine, for reproof, for correction, for instruction in righteousness: That the man of God may be perfect, thoroughly furnished unto all good works" (II Timothy 3:16,17).

When Sarah began attending a Lutheran school, one of her teachers struck up an argument with her about healing. He informed his class, "Healing is NOT for today." He said that healing only occurred during biblical times—but is not scriptural for today.

Sarah asked me some very pointed questions that night. She said, "Mother, show me the scriptures that prove healing IS for today." I showed her how to look up HEALING in Strong's Concordance. After rehearsing many scriptures, she said, "Mother, let me take this book to school with me."

She carried that concordance with her for the next ten days. At the end of that time, the teacher said, "Sarah, don't bring your concordance any more." Sarah thought that he was angry with her. But he said, "I see in the Word that healing IS for today."

Later the teacher came to our church, had hands laid upon him, and received a healing.

Remember, all scripture is given to man by God for many purposes, including correction and instruction.

Dear heavenly Father, thank You that the scripture corrects, instructs, and blesses us. Thank You for the mighty work of Your Word in our hearts. Amen.

Day 350

"The fear of man bringeth a snare: but whoso putteth his trust in the Lord shall be safe" (Proverbs 29:25).

Once when we were hosting a large convention in Denver, our guest speaker suddenly became nauseous and weak—right before he was going to speak! It was a special privilege to have this well-known and respected speaker at our convention. Over 4,000 people had arrived to hear this man deliver the Word of God.

The speaker turned to me and said, "Marilyn, please, would you take the pulpit?" I knew that I had to accept this responsibility, but my mind went totally blank. It was as though I had never seen a Bible before in my life. I cried out, "Dear God, take away my fear and anxiety." And suddenly my whole mind became as clear as a bell!

That night God gave me such a beautiful anointing in His Word. And many, many people came forward to receive Jesus as their Savior and to recommit their lives.

Sometimes fear can be like a snare that traps our minds. But when we put our trust in the Lord, instead of ourselves, the trap is broken. Crises can then be transformed into some of God's greatest miracles!

Dear heavenly Father, many fears and afflictions can come our way. But as we look to You, daily deliverance prevails in every one of our situations and circumstances. In Jesus' name, amen.

Day 351

"For the perfecting of the saints, for the work of the ministry, for the edifying of the body of Christ" (Ephesians 4:12).

God has given the ministry gifts to Christians to help them accomplish His work. Sometimes we wonder, "Why have pastors, evangelists, apostles, teachers, and prophets?" But they are really here to mature us and to get us involved in ministry.

Once when I planted tomato plants in our yard, I thought that they would grow well because they were in a very sunny area. But my husband transplanted them to another area when I was gone. When I arrived home and discovered the transplanted tomatoes, I asked my daughter what had happened. She said, "Dad thought they were getting too much sun."

I quickly dug them up and transplanted them back into a sunny area. You can imagine what three transplants can do to tomato plants! They didn't bear very many tomatoes...and that's the way it is with some Christians. Instead of staying under one pastor, they are constantly changing churches. They change churches like they change clothes, and those Christians never bear fruit.

Until you plant yourself in one church, you will not bear the fruit that God has for you.

Dear heavenly Father, we thank You for Your plan for us to mature and do well. You have given us people with ministry gifts to help develop our spiritual growth. In Jesus' name, amen.

Day 352

"And I will rebuke the devourer for your sakes, and he shall not destroy the fruits of your ground" (Malachi 3:11a).

*M*any years ago when I was still young in the ministry, a young woman called to ask my husband to pray for HER husband who had just had a heart attack. My husband was gone, so the woman begged me to come. I had never gone on a personal prayer call, nor had I ever laid hands on anyone for healing. In fact, I had just recently been Spirit-filled.

As I drove to the woman's house, the devil told me, "If you touch that man, he'll surely die." When I arrived, I knew that my faith was weak and wavering, so I sat in the car and began to quote scriptures to myself about healing. I began to say, "I can do all things through Christ Who strengthens me."

And I didn't stop there. Then I quoted Psalm 103:3, "Who forgiveth all thine iniquites; who healeth all thy diseases." Isaiah 53:5b, "And with his stripes we are healed." Romans 8:2, "For the law of the Spirit of life in Christ Jesus hath made me free from the law of sin and death."

That night I laid hands on that man and prayed. I rebuked death in Jesus' name. The man lived. That was over 22 years ago.

Dear heavenly Father, we thank You that not only will You rebuke the devourer for our sakes, but we can rebuke him, too, in Jesus' name, amen.

Day 353

"Stretch forth the curtains of thine habitations: spare not, lengthen thy cords, and strengthen thy stakes" (Isaiah 54:2b).

This scripture was given to us at the beginning of our church. When I first heard it—and I heard it from many people, including Kenneth Hagin—I felt that it meant our church was going to grow. I had no idea that an outreach ministry would result.

When our church didn't grow as fast as I had anticipated, I became very discouraged. But later God began to deal with me about doing radio and TV programs. Soon these literally became worldwide ministries or cords extended into the world.

One day God reminded me again of this scripture, "Look: the cords were to be lengthened first, and then the stakes." I'd always felt that the stakes were the church, and the cords were my outreach. I thought the church would grow first, and then the cords would be lengthened. But it was just the opposite! First the radio and television broadcasts were lengthened. Then Happy Church grew as its stakes were strengthened.

God does things in HIS divine order, which may not always be our idea of order!

Dear heavenly Father, we thank You for Your divine order and what You want in our lives. We are asking for Your will to be complete. Amen.

Day 354

"Be not overcome of evil, but overcome evil with good" (Romans 12:21).

Many years ago in our city, a woman's daughter was raped and murdered. That woman became bitter not only toward God, but also toward people. One day the Lord spoke these words to that woman: "If you don't forgive your daughter's murderer, I won't forgive you of your sins."

The woman repented by faith and forgave the man. Later God asked her to send a Bible to this man, who was imprisoned locally. The Bible was to include a personal message stating that she loved him.

A man who worked for Gideons personally presented the Bible to the prisoner and told the man who had sent the Bible. The prisoner's heart melted. He fell to the floor of that prison in prayer and gave his heart to Jesus Christ. He is now an evangelist in that prison.

I never cease to be amazed at what God's Word brings forth when we obey it!

Dear heavenly Father, we thank You for the opportunity to obey Your Word. We choose to walk in love, instead of hate and vengeance. We choose to give our wills to You and walk in the Spirit. Amen.

Day 355

"Casting down imaginations, and every high thing that exalteth itself against the knowledge of God, and bringing into captivity every thought to the obedience of Christ" (II Corinthians 10:5).

Right after our marriage, my husband and I planned to visit some of his relatives in Nebraska. But a woman told us that she had dreamed we would be killed on the way to Nebraska. The dream concerned us, and we wondered whether it was from God. We began to pray.

I finally called my mother about our concern over the dream, and she said, "If God loves you enough to tell another person about you, He loves you enough to tell you personally. You are His sheep. You know His voice. Ask Him if He wants you to go to Nebraska."

We prayed, "God, check us if we aren't to go. If we ARE to go, give us a stronger desire." We received a stronger desire to visit Nebraska, so we went—with no accidents.

ALWAYS check other people's leadings and personal "prophecies" with God's Word. Always check such leadings with your own inner witness. If you do, you will not be led astray by human premonitions that are not the leading of God's Spirit.

Dear heavenly Father, we look to You and Your Word as our guide. Your Word is the most sure Word of prophecy and will direct every step that we take. In Jesus' name, amen.

Day 356

"Great is the Lord, and greatly to be praised: and his greatness is unsearchable" (Psalm 145:3).

One Saturday evening my husband invited a family over for Sunday dinner. I awakened early Sunday morning and put a roast and vegetables in the oven—everything was planned perfectly. When we came home from church, dinner would be all ready.

After the services when we walked in the door, I couldn't smell the roast. When I walked into the kitchen, I realized that I hadn't turned on the oven. My heart dropped! But I remembered that we should praise God, even when circumstances seem against us. I said, "Thank You, Lord, I know You are taking care of this situation."

I told my husband about the mistake, and he said, "Don't worry, Marilyn. We'll just go out to dinner, and you won't EVEN have to wash dishes."

Sometimes everything doesn't fall into place exactly as we had planned. But let's continue to live in praise, trust, and worship. We aren't praising God just for what He does for us. We are also praising Him for Who He is IN us.

Dear heavenly Father, thank You for doing all things well in our lives. We praise You for WHO You are and WHAT You are in our personal lives. In Jesus' name, amen.

Day 357

"Go ye into all the world, and preach the gospel to every creature" (Mark 16:15b).

God has many ways for us to bring the gospel into the world, and I believe that one of those ways is through our TIME WITH HIM Bible-reading plan. When people begin to read the Bible, they begin to receive the good news that God has for them.

A woman wrote me a letter saying that God had told her to follow my Bible-reading plan and to read it aloud to her retarded son. Each day she would mark the chapters indicated for that day's devotions, and then she read them aloud to her son.

After five months the principal of her son's school called and said, "I don't know what has happened to your son, but he is doing normal work. We are going to promote him to a normal class."

The woman later wrote to me and said, "The Word is truly Spirit and life. It is such good news!" Wherever God's Word is preached and heard, it changes the circumstances.

Let each of us remember to share the gospel with others—even if they do not seem to be receptive.

Dear heavenly Father, enable us today to preach Your Word in every possible way: through tracts, through our voices, and however else possible. The light of Your Word is greater than the darkness, and the light will overcome. In Jesus' name, amen.

Day 358

"Through God we shall do valiantly: for he it is that shall tread down our enemies" (Psalm 108:13).

One night after a crusade, a middle-aged woman shared her dynamic testimony with me. The woman's son was involved in deep sin and crime in Chicago. He had been using and selling drugs.

One night his mother felt strongly impressed of the Lord to pray in the Spirit for an hour for her son. At 10:00 p.m. her son called and said, "Mother, what have you been doing for the last hour?" She told him that the Spirit of God had directed her to pray for him.

The son explained that he had recently sold some bad drugs to a man, who had returned that very evening with a gun—and the intent to kill! But the man couldn't pull the trigger. He kept trying to pull the trigger, and finally he threw the gun on the floor and said, "I can't fire this gun! There's something your mother is doing that is keeping me from killing you." The man ran from the room.

Needless to say, the son came home and gave his heart to Jesus. And guess what? He is now preaching the gospel.

Dear heavenly Father, we thank You today that no man or situation is impossible. With Your Word and Your loving support, we shall do valiantly in any situation. We shall tread down our enemies. In Jesus' name, amen.

Day 359

"O my God, I trust in thee: let me not be ashamed" (Psalm 25:2a).

On a recent vacation in Santa Fe, my husband and I ate at a restaurant where we were seated next to a table of Hari Krishna followers. The Lord dealt with me to tell those people, "Jesus loves you." But as I began to think about it, I decided that I hadn't truly heard the voice of the Spirit. Consequently, I absolutely failed and missed God's will.

Later I repented and asked God to send other laborers who would be faithful to bring the message of His love to those people in Santa Fe. But God did not condemn me for my error. Instead, He gave me an opportunity, within two days, to witness to a drunken couple in a Houston airport. As I shared with them about Jesus, God performed a miraculous work in their hearts.

If you have failed, simply repent. God has yet many more doors to open before you. He will give you a second, third, fourth, fifth, and sixth opportunity—plus many others!

Dear heavenly Father, thank You for Your Word that is so real, so beautiful, so wonderful. We trust in Your Word and the leading of Your Holy Spirit to guide us to those hungry for You. We trust You to give us the words to speak. In Jesus' name, amen.

Day 360

"Beloved, I wish above all things that thou mayest prosper and be in health, even as thy soul prospereth" (III John 2).

The early beginnings of our radio and television ministry demanded hard, hard work. Our budget was stretched in so many different directions that, for the first five years of my ministry, I refused a salary.

My husband Wally used to get very cross with me on this issue. But I felt that I was being very spiritual—after all, Wally had a good salary from the church. We could live on his salary, so why should I take a salary that we couldn't afford?

One night we exchanged some very angry words over this issue. Wally told me that I was just stubborn and rebellious. I rolled over in bed, looked at the wall, and thought, "He's just stingy. He is just after money."

The Lord really dealt with me that night and said, "Your husband is right. You are afraid that there won't be enough money. But a workman is worthy of his hire. Don't you think that I have made you worthy to receive a salary?"

I was the one who had been unscriptural, and my husband had been right. Since that time I have always taken a salary. And God has always provided enough money in our budget to cover my salary.

Dear heavenly Father, help us to know that the Word will work in every area of our lives. OUR worthiness does not hold up, but JESUS' worthiness gives us abundance. In Jesus' name, amen.

Day 361

"Be not rash with thy mouth,...for God is in heaven, and thou upon earth: therefore let thy words be few" (Ecclesiastes 5:2).

Our mouths can be our greatest blessing OR our greatest curse.

When I travel in communist countries to minister in local churches and Bible study groups, the seriousness of the situation is very noticeable. One slip of the lips can be disasterous. There are times, however, when God wants us to open our mouths and speak of His love.

Several years ago we sent 10,000 Bibles into Poland by way of Sweden. As the Swedish missionaries drove their large truck to the Polish border, they prayed in the Spirit continuously. At the border they were stopped by the communist guards, who examined the truck's contents and found the Bibles. Fortunately, the missionaries carried papers that granted permission to bring these Bibles into Poland.

The missionary's wife suddenly heard an inner voice whispering that one of the guards was hungry for the Lord. "Would you like a Bible?" she asked. He began to weep. The guard had been praying for someone to give him a Bible. The Holy Spirit knew and guided the missionary's wife by HIS voice.

Dear heavenly Father, help us to be sensitive to the Holy Spirit. Show us when to speak and when NOT to speak. Teach us sensitivity to Your promptings. In Jesus' name, amen.

Day 362

"He brought me to the banqueting house, and his banner over me was love" (Song of Solomon 2:4).

God sometimes shocks and delights me with His goodness and mercy!

Several years ago Rosie Grier was the featured speaker at a local luncheon. This luncheon was a small one, but God gave me a desire to attend. I felt that my desire was spiritual, but I wasn't sure.

The day of the luncheon, a woman called to ask, "Marilyn, would you like to attend a luncheon with Rosie Grier today? I know that this is 'last minute,' but I felt that the Holy Spirit wanted you to be present."

At the luncheon I was seated by a Christian man from Guatemala. I sensed that God had given me favor, and indeed He had! This man invited me to visit Guatemala to interview their ex-president. This man had also felt that God had placed us together at the luncheon and that the Holy Spirit wanted me to do a work in Guatemala.

Within two months my husband and I were in Guatemala where we received a televised interview with the ex-president. Before the interview we prayed with him, and he, in turn, prayed in the Spirit with us.

Dear heavenly Father, we thank You that Your banner covers us with love. Your hand is always reached out to us in love. As we reach out to You, we will always experience Your love. We thank You in Jesus' name. Amen.

Day 363

"And the man believed the word that Jesus had spoken unto him, and he went his way" (John 4:50b).

From time to time during my radio taping, the Lord will give me a scripture as revelation knowledge. These broadcasts are taped at least two months in advance.

At a crusade a woman once told me a story about a young man who had been injured in a car accident. Since he was unable to walk, he spent many a depressing day in bed. One day he turned on my TV program. That day I gave a scripture that was exactly what the Holy Spirit wanted the young man to hear—but remember, I was led to do it two months before the program even was aired!

Later in the program I invited people to receive Jesus—something that I rarely do on television broadcasts. The young man prayed and was saved. Within two days God sent him a nurse who was also a Rhema Bible school graduate. She witnessed to the young man and advised him to listen to my program. When he heard my name, he exclaimed, "That's the woman whose program I listened to when I was born again."

Dear heavenly Father, we thank You that when we believe Your Word, we have assurance of prosperity in our way. Thank You for those whom You send us to be washed and healed in Your Word. In Jesus' name, amen.

Day 364

"Hope deferred maketh the heart sick, but when the desire cometh, it is a tree of life" (Proverbs 13:12).

I remember a crusade in Detroit, Michigan, where I said, "Name out loud a person whose salvation you are seeking." We each named a person and claimed salvation for them some time in the next six months. That was on a Friday night.

One woman had named her employer, a man with a foul mouth and an immoral life—a very "unlikely prospect" for salvation.

On Monday morning God urged the woman to tell her employer what she had done. She told the man, "I have been to a crusade. I prayed your name aloud and am believing for your salvation. You will have a transformation because Jesus will come into your heart."

The employer began to weep. That Sunday night he had gone to church with a friend and received Christ.

How beautifully God works when we extend our faith and hope in Him! Don't let your hope die—no matter what the outward circumstances may tell you. Dead hope brings sickness to the heart. But hope, alive with faith, is like a tree of life that blooms eternal and gives us sustenance to remain strong.

Dear heavenly Father, don't ever let us look at anyone as being hopeless. Always let us see You with hope in our hearts. Thank You today, Father, that we speak in faith and tell others of Your love. Amen.

Day 365

"And I will pray the Father, and he shall give you another Comforter, that he may abide with you for ever" (John 14:16).

I will never forget when a priest argued vehemently with me about the baptism of the Holy Spirit. He told me, "You CANNOT invite people to receive the baptism of the Holy Spirit. You CANNOT just give scriptures and expect it to happen."

While I talked with the priest, a couple knocked on the door. They had heard about the baptism of the Holy Spirit and wanted to ask me questions. The priest told them, "It is impossible for you to be baptized in the Holy Spirit tonight."

But the young man finally turned to me in frustration and said, "We surely didn't come here in vain! You can give us scriptures and pray with us, can't you?"

I asked the priest for permission to do so, and he said, "Yes." I gave the couple scriptures to encourage their faith. They were beautifully filled with the Holy Spirit that night—right in front of the priest.

Later the priest asked me, "Will you write down what you did? I want to lead my parishioners into this baptism too."

Aren't you glad to have the Holy Spirit? He WILL lead you to truth.

Dear heavenly Father, lead us into Your truth today. Show us by Your Spirit where we walk in the flesh and not in the Spirit. Help us to walk daily in Your Word in the Spirit. In Jesus' name, amen.

For Your Information

Free Monthly Magazine

☐ Please send me your free monthly magazine OUTPOURING (including daily devotionals, timely articles, and ministry updates)!

Tapes and Books

☐ Please send me Marilyn's latest product catalog.

Name ☐ Miss ☐ Mrs. ☐ Mr._____

Please Print

Address_____

City_____

State_____ Zip_____

Phone (_____)_____

Mail to
Marilyn Hickey Ministries
P.O. Box 17340
Denver, CO 80217

Receive Jesus Christ as Lord and Savior of Your Life

The Bible says, "That if thou shalt confess with thy mouth the Lord Jesus, and shalt believe in thine heart that God hath raised him from the dead, thou shalt be saved. For with the heart man believeth unto righteousness; and with the mouth confession is made unto salvation" (Romans 10:9-10).

To receive Jesus Christ as Lord and Savior of your life, sincerely pray this prayer from your heart:

Dear Jesus,

I believe that You died for me and that You rose again on the third day. I confess to You that I am a sinner and that I need Your love and forgiveness. Come into my life, forgive my sins, and give me eternal life. I confess You now as my Lord. Thank You for my salvation!

Signed _____

Date _____

Write to us. We will send you information to help you with your new life in Christ. Marilyn Hickey Ministries • P.O. Box 17340 • Denver, CO 80217.

BOOKS BY MARILYN HICKEY

A CRY FOR MIRACLES ($5.95)
ACTS ($7.95)
ANGELS ALL AROUND ($7.95)
BEAT TENSION ($.75)
BIBLE CAN CHANGE YOU, THE ($12.95)
BOLD MEN WIN ($.75)
BREAK THE GENERATION CURSE ($7.95)
BULLDOG FAITH ($.75)
CHANGE YOUR LIFE ($.75)
CHILDREN WHO HIT THE MARK ($.75)
CONQUERING SETBACKS ($.75)
DAILY DEVOTIONAL ($5.95)
DEAR MARILYN ($5.95)
DIVORCE IS NOT THE ANSWER ($4.95)
ESPECIALLY FOR TODAY'S WOMAN ($14.95)
EXPERIENCE LONG LIFE ($.75)
FASTING & PRAYER ($.75)
FREEDOM FROM BONDAGES ($4.95)
GIFT-WRAPPED FRUIT ($2.00)
GOD'S BENEFIT: HEALING ($.75)
GOD'S COVENANT FOR YOUR FAMILY ($5.95)
GOD'S RX FOR A HURTING HEART ($3.50)
GOD'S SEVEN KEYS TO MAKE YOU RICH ($.75)
HOLD ON TO YOUR DREAM ($.75)
HOW TO BE A MATURE CHRISTIAN ($5.95)
HOW TO BECOME MORE THAN A CONQUEROR ($.75)
HOW TO WIN FRIENDS ($.75)
I CAN BE BORN AGAIN AND SPIRIT FILLED ($.75)
I CAN DARE TO BE AN ACHIEVER ($.75)
KEYS TO HEALING REJECTION ($.75)
KNOW YOUR MINISTRY ($3.50)
MAXIMIZE YOUR DAY . . . GOD'S WAY ($7.95)
NAMES OF GOD ($7.95)
#1 KEY TO SUCCESS—MEDITATION, THE ($3.50)
POWER OF FORGIVENESS, THE ($.75)
POWER OF THE BLOOD, THE ($.75)
RECEIVING RESURRECTION POWER ($.75)
RENEW YOUR MIND ($.75)
SATAN-PROOF YOUR HOME ($7.95)
SAVE THE FAMILY PROMISE BOOK ($14.95)
SIGNS IN THE HEAVENS ($5.95)
SOLVING LIFE'S PROBLEMS ($.75)
SPEAK THE WORD ($.75)
STANDING IN THE GAP ($.75)
STORY OF ESTHER, THE ($.75)
WINNING OVER WEIGHT ($.75)
WOMEN OF THE WORD ($.75)
YOUR MIRACLE SOURCE ($3.50)
YOUR PERSONALITY WORKOUT ($5.95)